"This is an important and comprehensive book covering the links between networks and network governance, two topics often treated separately. The fact that they are integral to the design of this book makes it unique and allows Kapucu and Hu to weave in theory, methods, and examples that make it useful for both student and scholar. The emphasis on network leadership, decision-making, and politics adds human agency to research that largely uses structure to evaluate network performance."
—H. Brinton Milward, University of Arizona, USA

"In a shared-power, no-one-wholly-in-charge world, we have no choice but to make use of networks and network governance to address public challenges that spill beyond organizational and jurisdictional boundaries. Naim Kapucu and Qian Hu have performed an invaluable service in synthesizing and clarifying a great deal of literature on network theory, methods, and governance experience to help all of us better understand how to address these major challenges."
—John M. Bryson, University of Minnesota, USA

"The field of network governance is still evolving and Kapucu and Hu present an excellent base in which they present the state of the art of the field and at the same time make some original contributions to the field. More importantly, they also indicate how and where this field could be developed further."
—Patrick Kenis, Tilburg University, the Netherlands

"Now governance and networks have become the 'new normal', books that elaborate and clarify this are more than welcome. This book offers a very good addition to the literature, covering the emergence and evaluation of networks as well as a number of important topics in the network literature."
—Erik Hans Klijn, Erasmus University Rotterdam, the Netherlands

"This comprehensive guide to network governance across disciplines is a creative and innovative contribution to the literature. It is a 'must read' for anyone learning, doing, or just trying to understand network analysis. Highly recommended."
—Rosemary O'Leary, Edwin O. Stene Distinguished Professor, University of Kansas, USA

Network Governance

Network governance has received much attention within the fields of public administration and policy in recent years, but surprisingly few books are designed specifically to help students, researchers, and practitioners examine key concepts, synthesize the growing body of literature into reliable frameworks, and to bridge the theory–practice gap by exploring network applications. *Network Governance: Concepts, Theories, and Applications* is the first textbook to focus on interorganizational networks and network governance from the perspective of public policy and administration, asking important questions such as: How are networks designed and developed? How are they governed, and what type of leadership do they require? To whom are networks accountable, and when are they effective? How can network governance contribute to effective delivery of public services and policy implementation?

In this timely new book, authors Naim Kapucu and Qian Hu define and examine key concepts, propose exciting new theoretical frameworks to synthetize the fast-growing body of network research in public policy and administration, and provide detailed discussion of applications. *Network Governance* offers not only a much-needed systematic examination of existing knowledge, but it also goes much further than existing books by discussing the applications of networks in a wide range of management practice and policy domains—including natural resource management, environmental protection, public health, emergency and crisis management, law enforcement, transportation, and community and economic development. Chapters include understudied network research topics such as power and decision-making in interorganizational networks, virtual networks, global networks, and network analysis applications. What sets this book apart is the introduction of social network analysis and coverage of applications of social network analysis in the policy and management domains. PowerPoint slides and a sample syllabus are available for adopters on an accompanying website. Drawing on literature from sociology, policy sciences, organizational studies, and economics, this textbook will be required reading for courses on network governance, collaborative public management, cross-sector governance, and collaboration and partnerships in programs of public administration, public affairs, and public policy.

Naim Kapucu is Pegasus Professor of Public Administration and Policy and Director of the School of Public Administration in the College of Community Innovation and Education at the University of Central Florida, USA.

Qian Hu is Associate Professor of Public Administration in the College of Community Innovation and Education at the University of Central Florida, USA.

Network Governance
Concepts, Theories, and Applications

Naim Kapucu and Qian Hu

Routledge
Taylor & Francis Group

NEW YORK AND LONDON

First published 2020
by Routledge
52 Vanderbilt Avenue, New York, NY 10017

and by Routledge
2 Park Square, Milton Park, Abingdon, Oxon OX14 4RN

Routledge is an imprint of the Taylor & Francis Group, an informa business

Library of Congress Cataloging-in-Publication Data
A catalog record for this book has been requested

ISBN: 978-1-138-48285-2 (hbk)
ISBN: 978-1-138-48286-9 (pbk)
ISBN: 978-1-351-05654-0 (ebk)

Typeset in Times New Roman
by Apex CoVantage, LLC

Visit the eResources: www.routledge.com/9781138482869

To Ayşegül Rose Kapucu and Dawei Gong

Contents

Figures

Tables

Preface

I (Naim Kapucu) was introduced to network analysis by Dr. David Krackhardt in his course, "Organizational Design and Implementation," in 1996 at Heinz College of Carnegie Mellon University. I was able to delve deeper into the topic thanks to Dr. Kathleen M. Carley's 2002 and 2003 summer Computational Analysis of Social and Organizational Systems (CASOS) Institutes at Carnegie Mellon University. Dr. Louise K. Comfort provided further recommendations and support on networks and complexity studies as my dissertation chair at the Graduate School of Public and International Affairs of University of Pittsburgh. Ever since, I have applied network theory and network analysis in my research projects. After two decades I am still passionate about applying network theory and analysis to issues of governance. I created a graduate course on network analysis in public policy and management as well as a doctoral seminar on network governance. I teach both classes to this day.

During my PhD study at Arizona State University, I (Qian Hu) conducted experiments to examine the role of immersive information technology in fostering collaborative behaviors. With a continued passion for studying collaborative governance, I decided to focus more on networks after joining the University of Central Florida faculty in 2011. Since then, I have studied dynamic interorganizational interactions and the governance of interorganizational networks in emergency management, human and social service delivery, and economic development. I teach a graduate course on cross-sector governance and always find myself inspired by students to learn more about networks and network governance.

We began to collaborate on a series of network-related projects seven years ago. Our recent articles reviewed the evolution of network research, theoretical foundations, and methodological issues of network scholarship in public administration. Our ongoing research on networks and our teaching of network-related courses encouraged us to embark on a big endeavor—writing this book on network governance.

We believe there is a need for such a book that helps students grasp network governance and analysis, helps academics design and implement network research, and informs policy makers in an increasingly networked world. We feel there is a need to examine key concepts, propose theoretical frameworks that synthesize a growing body of knowledge, and bridge the theory-practice gap by providing detailed applications. Although network governance has become prevalent in recent years, it still lacks conceptual clarity. Network literature in public administration has been largely descriptive, lacked generalizability, and offered limited implications for practitioners. We wrote this book not only to offer a systematic examination of existing knowledge, but also to discuss the applications of networks in a variety of management practice and policy domains.

In this book, we focus primarily on interorganizational networks and network governance in public policy and public administration. The book is divided into three major sections: The first section (Chapters 1–4) focuses on networks and network analysis. We define the key concepts of networks and network governance, provide brief synopsis of network analysis as an analytical technique, discuss network types and characteristics, and examine network structures and function. We further explain the emergence, design, development, sustainability, and resilience of networks. The second section (Chapters 5–9) covers key aspects of network governance. We cover network leadership and management, network performance and evaluation, power and decision-making, and legitimacy and accountability issues in network governance. The third section (Chapters 10–14) provides examples of network governance applications in diverse contexts, ranging from community and economic development to human and social services, virtual environments, and emergency and crisis management. The conclusion chapter provides some observation on advancement in network scholarship and discusses the need for further research.

The following list of research questions is illustrative of the concepts and relationships examined in this book:

- What are the critical roles networks (interorganizational networks) play in public policy and administration?
- How can network governance contribute to effective delivery of public services and policy implementation?
- What are the structures and function of networks?
- How are networks designed and developed?
- How do networks evolve?
- Do networks fail? If so, can we learn from failed networks?
- How are networks governed and what type of leadership do they require?
- Are networks legitimate and to whom are they accountable?
- When are networks effective?
- What is known about networks in virtual environments?
- How are network applied in community and economic development, in human and social services, in emergency and crisis situations, virtual environments, and global scale?

This book is intended for use by students, scholars, public leaders, and practitioners interested in networks and network governance. This book will provide these groups with a theoretical framework to study network governance and synthesized literature of the most recent network research in public policy and administration. The questions raised in this book can inspire scholars to further expand the horizon of network governance research. This book can be used as a textbook for teaching courses on networks, network governance, collaborative public management, cross-sector governance, collaboration, and partnerships in undergraduate and graduate programs of public administration, public affairs, political science, and public policy.

Unlike a traditional textbook, this book also attends to the needs of practitioners by covering a wide range of network governance applications and implications for managing in a networked world. The diverse examples of network applications can be also used as cases studies or as a supplemental text in management or policy courses that highlight the importance of a network approach to address public problems and effective public service delivery.

The two authors equally contributed to the book. Dr. Kapucu conceived of the initial book idea and structure based on the doctoral seminar on network governance and then invited Dr. Hu to further develop the book structure and finalize a detailed book outline. Dr. Kapucu and Dr. Hu cowrote Chapters 1 and 15, the introduction and conclusion. Dr. Hu completed the initial drafts for Chapters 2, 3, 5, 9, 10, 11, and 12. Dr. Kapucu completed the initial drafts for Chapters 4, 6, 7, 8, 13, and 14. The final version of the book manuscript is a result of numerous intensive meetings and lengthy dialogues between the two authors over the past two years.

We would like to express gratitude to many individuals who supported the completion of this book. Doctoral students in the network governance class provided invaluable feedback on the topics covered in the book. Keith G. Provan, Brint Milward, Rosemary O'Leary, Richard Feiock; Christopher Koliba, Kim Isett, Branda Nowell, Kun Huang, Louise K. Comfort, Christopher Hawkins, Erik Johnston, Sana Khosa participated as guest speakers to the network governance class over the years and contributed ideas to the book.

Parker Toro, MPA student and a wonderful graduate assistant in the UCF School of Public Administration, read the entire manuscript and provided substantial editorial suggestions. Tamara Dimitrijevska-Markoski, assistant professor of public administration and public policy at Mississippi State University, and Fatih Demiroz, assistant professor of political science at Sam Houston State University read earlier versions of the chapters and provided constructive feedback. Jungwon Yeo, assistant professor in the UCF school of Public Administration also provided good feedback on Chapter 10.

Earlier versions of some of the chapters were presented at Public Management Research Association (PMRA) conferences; Annual American Society for Public Administration (ASPA) conferences, International Research Society for Public Management (IRSPM) conferences; and the UCF Public Administration Research Conference. We would like to thank colleagues who attended our presentations and raised great questions.

The homeless service network data used in Chapter 12 came from the project Dr. Hu completed with the funding support from the UCF Center for Public and Nonprofit Management. Data for Chapter 14 came from initial exploratory stage of Belmont Forum Collaborative Research Food-Water-Energy Nexus: Enabling adaptive integration of technology to enhance community resilience (NSF Award #1830036). Dr. Kapucu is an investigator in this project. Sean Beaudet, MPA student and a graduate assistant, assisted in data collection. The data used for Figure 13.1 in Chapter 13 came from a project conducted by Dr. Xuesong Guo and Dr. Zhengwei Zhu, with support from the National Social Science Fund of China (No. 16BZZ052).

We would like to give special thanks to our families. The book could not be completed without their tremendous support. I (Naim) am grateful for the support and understanding from my family. I am especially grateful for my children Emre, Selim, and Yusuf for their understanding and support for the time I spend over the weekends and evenings to complete the book manuscript. I (Qian Hu) am so grateful for my parents Dedi Hu and Wanxia Zhou for their unconditional love. They offered generous help to take care of my newborn so that I could have more time for teaching, reading, and writing. Thanks to my husband Dawei Gong for being my biggest supporter of the book. Ryan Gong, my son, thank you for bringing so much joy to my life!

Section I
Networks

1 Introduction

Networks and Network Governance

A collaborative approach to address societal issues is nothing new to the field of public administration and public policy. Intergovernmental and cross-sector collaborations among public, nonprofit, and private sectors have existed for a long time. Some scholars connect the development of collaborative governance, or the engagement of non-state stakeholders in the production and delivery of public service, to increased intergovernmental cooperation in the 1960s (Emerson, Nabatchi, & Balogh, 2012). Other scholars argue that the history of networks can be traced back to the beginning of American federalism and the division of federal, state, and local governments (Kettl, 2006; Koliba, Meek, & Zia, 2010).

Over the past few decades, the scope of cross-sector collaborations has expanded rapidly, demanding attention from researchers and practitioners. Cross-sector collaborations abound in a wide range of policy domains and management areas: emergency management, community and economic development, social services, and environmental protection (Kapucu, Hu, & Khosa, 2014). Between 1998 and 2012, peer reviewed journals of public administration and related disciplines published more than 600 journal articles focused on networks in various forms (Kapucu et al., 2014). In this book, we focus on the rapid growth of interorganizational networks and the use of network governance in public policy and administration in recent decades. This chapter begins by defining networks and network governance, followed by a discussion of the rise of, and the growing demand for, network governance. We then define the key concepts in network governance, propose a theoretical framework to organize the relevant literature, and conclude this chapter with the organization and aims of the book. In particular, we address the following questions:

*   How to define networks and network governance?
*   Why do we need to study networks and network governance?
*   What are the key theories and frameworks in network governance?
*   What is the aim of the book?
*   How is the book structured?

Defining Networks and Network Governance

Definitions of Networks and Network Governance

There is no current consensus on how to define networks. From the perspective of network science, a *network* consists of a set of nodes, or actors, and the ties between these nodes (Borgatti, Everett, & Johnson, 2013). As shown in Figure 1.1, each circle represents a node or actor. These can be persons, teams, organizations, regions, countries, and so on (Borgatti et al., 2013). The ties, represented by lines, connect actors in networks to each other. These ties can be directional or non-directional. These ties can represent relations among the nodes, such as friendship, knowledge exchange, advice seeking, competition, collaboration and so on (Carpenter, Li, & Jiang, 2012). This book focuses on interorganizational networks that comprise organizations as actors and their relations.

In the field of public administration and public policy, there are different streams of research on interorganizational networks (Isett, Mergel, LeRoux, Mischen, & Rethemeyer, 2011; Kapucu et al., 2014). Some scholars examined networks as formal, collaborative arrangements working to achieve management or policy goals that a lone organization could not (Agranoff & McGuire, 2001). Other scholars studied networks as a governance structure that differs from traditional bureaucratic hierarchy, as networks involve non-state stakeholders in policymaking and implementation (Koliba et al., 2010; Rethemeyer & Hatmaker, 2008). This book not only examines networks in public service delivery, policymaking, and implementation, but also discusses the application of network governance in public service.

Some researchers define *network governance* as a form of governing where public, nonprofit, and private sectors are involved in collective action and consensus-oriented decision-making (Ansell & Gash, 2008; Emerson et al., 2012; Kapucu, 2012). Provan and Kenis (2008) describe network governance

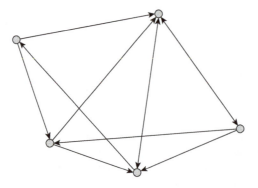

Figure 1.1 An Example of a Random Network With Five Nodes

as "the use of institutions and structures of authority and collaboration
to allocate resources and to coordinate and control joint action across
the network as a whole" (p. 230).
In this book, we build on Provan
and Kenis's definition and define
network governance as the use of

> **Network**
>
> A set of various nodes tied together by various forms of relationships.

formal and informal institutions to allocate resources and coordinate joint
action in a network of organizations (Bryson, Crosby, & Stone, 2006; Isett &
Miranda, 2015; Kapucu, 2012; Provan & Kenis, 2008). We highlight the roles
of horizontal relationships, social norms, social capital, and trust in addressing
issues requiring collective action.

Although some scholars use the terms "governance," "collaborative
governance," and "network governance" interchangeably, there are subtle
differences among these concepts
(Kapucu, Yuldhasev, & Bakiev,
2010). Governance is a broad concept that encompasses both collaborative governance and network
governance. Although the term
"governance" can have many distinct meanings (Rhodes, 1996),
most scholars in public administra-

> **Network Governance**
>
> The use of formal and informal institutions to allocate resources and coordinate joint action in a network of organizations.

tion use it to describe "the development of governing style in which boundaries
between and within public and private actors have become blurred" (Stoker,
1998, p. 17). Governance can also refer to multilevel or intergovernmental
management (Rhodes, 1996). The lack of clarity in defining governance causes
confusion and misunderstanding (Kettl, 2006; Klijn & Koppenjan, 2016). To
avoid this, we adopt Stoker's broad definition of governance and perceive network governance as part of it.

Collaborative governance has both broad and narrow connotations. In a
broad sense, collaborative governance can be defined as inclusive and participatory approaches in dealing with complex issues in public administration,
policymaking, and implementation. In this sense, governance and collaborative governance share the same essence. For instance, Emerson et al. (2012)
defined collaborative governance as

> the processes and structures of public policy decision-making and man-
> agement that engage people constructively across the boundaries of
> public agencies, levels of government, and/or the public, private, and
> civic spheres to carry out a public purpose that could not otherwise be
> accomplished.
>
> (p. 2)

Or, collaborative governance can refer to

> a governing arrangement where one or more public agencies directly engage non-state stakeholders in a collective decision-making process that is formal, consensus oriented, and deliberative and that aims to make or implement public policy or manage public programs or assets.
>
> (Ansell & Gash, 2008, p. 544)

According to this definition, collaborative governance requires the initiation of collaboration by a government entity, the direct involvement of non-state actors in decision-making, and formal engagement structures.

Since both collaborative and network governance are quite similar, and interchangeably used, it is important to list their similarities and differences. The two concepts share many similarities: both concepts differ from a traditionally hierarchical form of government and highlight the engagement of non-state actors in policymaking and public service delivery. Both collaborative and network governance stress the importance of cross-sector collaboration; thereby sharing some common challenges. For example, there are multiple actors involved, each with different backgrounds, missions, organizational culture, operational procedures, stakeholder groups, and levels of power (Bingham & O'Leary, 2008). This can create significant communication and coordination issues between organizations.

Different from Ansell and Gash's definition of collaborative governance, network governance does not require government's initiation and can include both formal and informal networks of collaboration across sectors (Koliba et al., 2010). Formal engagement processes and structures are not required for a network form of arrangements. Connections within and across organizations are the key elements of network governance, whereas collaborative governance focuses on individual groups of actors, such as the role of organizations in cross-sector governance or the role of citizens and communities in citizens-centric governance. The unit of analysis in collaborative governance often includes individuals, groups, and organizations, while the unit of analysis in network governance focuses on the pairs of individuals, groups, and organizations that have relations with each other. Our emphasis is more on interorganizational networks to increase collective performance of service delivery or public policy implementation. Table 1.1 summarizes the similarities and differences between collaborative governance and network governance.

Network governance can advance the understanding of "the internal mechanics of collaborative governance instances" (Kenis, 2016, p. 155). In particular, the network approach to governance addresses how "specific cases of governance develop, function, and perform" by focusing on "how the governance, leadership, and management of relationships between the actors involved

Table 1.1 A Comparison Between Collaborative Governance and Network Governance

Collaborative Governance and Network Governance

Similarities:
- Differs from a traditionally hierarchical form of government.
- The engagement of non-state stakeholders in policy making and service delivery.
- The emphasis on antecedents, processes, and structures of cross-sector collaboration.
- Face common communication and coordination challenges in collaborations.

Differences:
- Network governance does not require the initiation from government, while collaborative governance demands government's initiation.
- Network governance includes both formal and informal governance structures and processes, while collaborative governance focuses more on formal arrangements.
- Network governances focuses on relationships, while collaborative governance focuses more on individual groups of actors such as the role of organizations in cross-sector governance or the role of citizens and communities in citizens-centric governance.
- The unit of analysis in collaborative governance often include individuals, groups, and organizations, while the unit of analysis in network governance focuses on the pairs of individuals, groups, and organizations that have relations with each other.

are structured" (Kenis, 2016, p. 155). These are considered key elements of network governance study, which forms the core of this book.

Network Studies and Examples of Networks

The focus of network studies is the relationships among nodes, their patterns, and their implications (Wasserman & Faust, 1994). Relationships, rather than individual attributes, are used to explain social structures and processes. These relationships are not limited to dyadic, or two-ways ties between two actors, but also include relationships among triads, subgroups, and groups (Wasserman & Faust, 1994). Network studies examine the patterns of relations by visualizing, characterizing, and analyzing the links between nodes, substructures, and structures of networks (Kenis, 2016; Kilduff & Brass, 2010). Furthermore, network research studies how an actor's embeddedness in networks influences their interactions with other network members and other actors outside their network (Kilduff & Brass, 2010).

Network arrangements are utilized in various management and policy areas (Kapucu & Hu, 2016) such as human and social service delivery (Milward & Provan, 2003; Milward, Provan, Fish, Isett, & Huang, 2009; Steen & Duran, 2013), emergency management (Kapucu, 2006), regional economic development (Lee, Feiock, & Lee, 2012), and environmental management (Robins, Bates, & Pattison, 2011). In human and social service delivery, organizations build networks to meeting growing and diverse service needs. Take homeless services as an example. The homeless population often needs a wide range of services, including, but not limited to, housing, transportation, employment, and health and social services, thus demanding coordination among service providers. In community and economic development, consider regional transportation planning as an example. Regional transportation planning often requires the engagement of a diverse group of stakeholders. Local government is responsible for developing and managing local transportation infrastructures and services. State and federal governments are often involved in regional transportation planning through providing funding and implementing regulations. Other organizations such as regional transportation authority, businesses, and community organizations, are also important actors in regional planning. These organizations and the interactions among them form a transportation network. In emergency management, the nature of disasters often demands coordination among governments at all levels and coordination across organizational, sector, and jurisdictional boundaries, thus forming multilevel and cross-sector emergency management networks. In Exhibit 1.1 we include an example to illustrate the key elements of interorganizational networks in response to the Boston Marathon bombings in 2013, including the organizations in the network, the different types of interactions between organizations, such as information sharing, resource sharing, and joint action. Using the terminology of networks, these organizations are the nodes or actors, and these interactions are the ties that connect the nodes. The network lens allows researchers to take a close look at various interactions among organizations, identify the key actors, describe the structural characteristics, and evaluate the effectiveness of disaster response by comparing the actual response networks with the planned networks.

Exhibit 1.1 Interorganizational Networks in Response to the Boston Marathon Bombings

On April 15, 2013, two improvised explosive devices detonated at the finish line of the annual Boston Marathon event, which claimed three lives, wounded 264 people, caused as much as $333 million damage to local economy (Dedman & Schoen, 2013). One hundred thirty-eight government agencies, nonprofit and community-based organizations, and businesses were involved in response and initial recovery efforts during and after the incident (Hu, Knox, & Kapucu, 2014). The 138 organizations are the actors in the interorganizational networks. In the response and immediate recovery efforts, 172 unique interactions occurred among these actors. These interactions are the ties that connect organizations in the network. To understand the coordinated efforts, we can identify, examine, and compare different types of networks. For instance, the formal affiliation network consists of 39 primary and support organizations and 15 local emergency support functions (LESFs) based on the positional role and responsibilities listed in the Boston Emergency Operation Plan. Based on situations reports, after-action reports, and newspaper articles, we can also identify the affiliation networks that were formed in the actual response (Hu et al., 2014).

The Rise of Networks and the Demand for Network Governance

The wide application of networks in public administration has been driven by the practical need to address public problems and to seek effective public service delivery mechanisms. Increasing complexity of public problems makes it challenging for individual government agencies to solve public issue alone. Complex public problems require a productive collaboration across different organizations, professions, and sectors (Geddes, 2012). Moreover, "to bring public administration in sync with the multiorganizational, multisector operating realities of today's government requires a collaborative, network-based approach" (Kettl, 2006, p. 17). Networks can offer solutions to complex, interdependent policy implementation and service delivery problems (Bardach, 1998; Kettl, 2006; Provan & Lemaire, 2012).

In addition to complexity, the search for more effective service delivery mechanisms and rapid technological advancements encourage the use of collaboration (O'Leary & Vij, 2012). The three basic forms of organizing are hierarchies, markets, and networks (Podolny & Page, 1998). Table 1.2 lists

Table 1.2 Three Forms of Organizing

	Hierarchies	*Markets*	*Networks*
Behaviors of actors	Actors follow rules and authoritative inputs to take actions	Independent decision makers utilize pricing information to guide their action	Actors' behaviors will be interdependent of others' behaviors
Relations between actors	Actors have long relations but often rely on an authority in solving conflicts	Episodic relations for transactions of goods and resources	Often involves repeated and enduring relations
Coordination mechanisms	Bureaucratic structure, rules and regulations, authority	Price mechanism, laissez-faire	Formal governance structure or informal self-governance through interdependent relationships

Source: Based on Powell, 1990; Podolny & Page, 1998; Thompson, 2003

the differences across the three forms of organizing with a focus on behaviors of actors, relations among actors, and coordination mechanisms. Compared with formal hierarchies and the pure form of markets, networks have their advantages in promoting learning, enhancing organizational legitimacy, and producing economic benefits (Podolny & Page, 1998). Knowledge can be better channeled in networks through diverse types of nodes and ties, and through the nodes that reach disconnected actors, which leads to organizational learning and innovation (Podolny & Page, 1998). Organizations can achieve and enhance their legitimacy and improve status by connecting with a prominent organization in the network or decentralizing their assets and responsibilities to buffer from external uncertainty (Podolny & Page, 1998). Furthermore, trust built through repeated interactions among organizations often lead to long-term collaborations and produce economic benefits or improve organizational performance (Podolny & Page, 1998). Recently, there has been a growing emphasis on replacing or supplementing strict hierarchical structures with more integrated horizontal networks (Provan & Kenis, 2008; Provan & Lemaire, 2012).

The recent shift in the role of government from direct service provision toward steering, partnering, and contracting out allows collaborative networks to emerge (Agranoff, 2007). This is in line with the view that "the role of the government is to steer, not to man the oars" (Rosenbloom & Gong, 2013, p. 545). As the number of these collaborative arrangements rises, scholars see that "it is no exaggeration that the enduring foundation of [traditional] American public administration—hierarchy—is eroding under the pressures of 21st-century American government" (Kettl, 2006, p. 15). These interagency collaborations include many players, each of whom shape the network by way of their interactions (Bardach, 2001). Now more than ever, collaboration is imperative in public administration to manage boundaries and to utilize social capital in advancing solutions that are effective, efficient, and equitable. Furthermore, the advances in technology allow citizens to engage in governance through different platforms. An example is challenge.gov launched in 2010. This online platform lists a variety of challenges facing government and crowdsourced solutions and ideas from citizens.

The economic and social changes that occurred in the last three to four decades also led to networks' increased significance (Isett et al., 201). The Reagan and Thatcher administrations supported the notion of small government and the adoption of market-based strategies, such as contracting out and privatization to improve efficiency in government, which were reflected in the New Public Management (NPM) movement that started in the late 1980s (Isett et al., 2011). Devolution, privatization, and partnering are social, political, and economic trends that led to an increased use of networks in the United States (Koliba et al., 2010). On one hand, government needs to partner with various stakeholder groups in policy implementation and service delivery; on the other hand, governments use networks, a more flexible form of organizing, to pursue public value and overcome the limitations of the market approach in NPM.

Naisbett even went as far as predicting that networks would become the dominant meta-organization in the future (1982).

In addition, the rapid growth of network research can be attributed to the development of analytical tools and the methodological advancement of network research in other disciplines such as sociology (Berry et al., 2004). A number of software programs, such as UCINET, Organizational Risk Analyzer (ORA), Pajek, GePhi, and StOCENT are available for researchers to visualize and characterize network data as well as conduct both simple and advanced network analysis. An increasing number of researchers use R—an object-oriented programming language—to conduct network analysis due to its flexibility in advanced analysis (Acton & Jasny, 2012; Kapucu et al., 2014). Network research in public administration has abandoned simple descriptive network analysis to depict the characteristics of nodes and network structures. With the recent development in inferential network analysis, such as Quadratic Assignment Procedure (QAP), Exponential Random Graph Model (ERGM), and Stochastic Actor-Oriented Models (SAOMs), researchers can address relationships among networks as well as the influence of endogenous network substructures on tie formation, and network evolution (Kapucu et al., 2014).

Key Theories and Frameworks in Network Governance

There are differences between the theory of networks and network theory: theory of networks focuses on the antecedents of networks such as prior relations, similarities between actors, and resources constraints, while network theory focuses on the outcomes of networks (Borgatti & Lopez-Kidwell, 2011; Keast, 2014). Academics are still searching for an ideal network theory of organizations (Salancik, 1995). Network theory, in general, analyzes the resources embedded within and available through relationships. More work is needed to advance both the theory of networks and network theory (Hu et al., 2016). In this book, we will address the antecedents of networks by discussing network formation and development; furthermore, we cover the outcomes of networks by looking into network performance, network management and leadership, evaluation, legitimacy and accountability issues. The key topics covered in this book are depicted in Table 1.3. Next, we introduce complexity theory and system theory that illustrates the composition, elements, and function of networks. Then, we discuss theories that network researchers draw upon from other disciplines to build the theoretical foundation of network governance research in public policy and administration.

Network governance receives attention from scholars from a variety of disciplines including public policy, public administration, sociology, political science, management, and economics. As Table 1.4 shows, theories from multiple disciplines contribute to the development of the theoretical foundations of network governance research (Berry et al., 2004; Hu et al., 2016). For instance, *social capital theory* (Burt, 1992; Coleman, 1988, 1990; Uzzi, 1997) is used to evaluate the connections and resources embedded

Table 1.3 Key Concepts of the Book

Networks	Network Governance	Applications
• Interorganizational Networks and Social Network Analysis • Network Types, Function, Structures in Public Policy and Administration • Network Formation, Development, Resilience, Sustainability, Demise, and Transformation	• Network Management and Leadership • Knowledge Management and Information Exchange • Power and Decision-making • Legitimacy and Accountability • Performance and Evaluation	• Emergency and Crisis Management • Community and Economic Development • Health and Social Services • Virtual Environments • Global Perspectives

Table 1.4 Theoretical Frameworks for Analysis of Networks and Network Governance

Political Science	Sociology	Economics
• Pluralism • Public Choice Theory • Policy Networks • Group Theory	• Sociometry • Social Capital Theory • Resource Dependency Theory • Organizational Life Cycle	• Principal Agent Theory • Transaction Cost Theory • Game Theory • Collection Action • New-Institutional Economics

in networks, study organizational structures, and evaluate network performance (Agranoff, 2007; Provan & Lemaire, 2012). Scholars apply *resource dependency theory* (Pfeffer & Salancik, 1978) to examine the influence of resource availability and interdependence on network structures (Huang & Provan, 2007; Park & Rethemeyer, 2012) and network formation (Akkerman, Torenvlied, & Schalk, 2012).

The intellectual structure of network research in public administration is informed by many streams of research and theory development (Bingham & O'Leary, 2008; Hu et al., 2016), as illustrated in Table 1.4. Examples include, but are not limited to, complexity theory, system theory, principal-agency theory, transaction cost theory, game theory, group theory, collective action, public choice theory, new institutional economics, advocacy coalition framework, issue networks, and policy networks (Berry et al., 2004; Emerson et al., 2012; Hu et al., 2016). In Table 1.5, we present a few commonly used theories and their applications in network research.

Aims of this Book

In this book, we stress that it is crucial for public, private, and nonprofit organizations to work together across institutional, geographic, economic, and social

Table 1.5 Theories or Frameworks That Informs Network Research in Public Administration

Theories or Frameworks	Definitions or Brief Descriptions	Example of Applications in Network Research
Social capital theory (Burt, 1992; Coleman, 1988, 1990; Uzzi, 1997)	Social capital refers to "connections among individuals—social networks and the norms of reciprocity and trustworthiness that arise from them" (Putnam, 2001, p. 19)	Evaluate resources and connections in networks and network performance (Agranoff, 2007; Provan & Lemaire, 2012)
Resource dependency theory (Pfeffer & Salancik, 1978), and social exchange theory (Cropanzano & Mitchell, 2005)	The external resources such as funding and labor can influence behaviors of organizations.	Examine how resource availability and interdependence influences network structures (Huang & Provan, 2007; Park & Rethemeyer, 2012) and network formation (Akkerman et al., 2012)
Collective action theory, polycentric governance, and institutional development analysis (Ostrom, 1990, 2007)	Individuals' behaviors can lead to fundamental consequences on the collective level. Institutional arrangements can overcome the common problems in collective action with diverse stakeholders and decision makers (Ostrom, 2007; Ostrom, Tiebout, & Warren, 1961)	Investigate collective action issues in interorganizational networks, adaptive governance for environmental policy research, and coordinating municipal services in a metropolitan environment (Berardo & Lubell, 2016; Ostrom et al., 1961; Schneider, Scholz, Lubell, Mindruta, & Edwardsen, 2003; Hawkins, Hu, & Feiock, 2016)
Advocacy coalition framework (Sabatier & Jenkins-Smith, 1993), issue networks (Heclo, 1978)	Issue networks refer to the grouping of various interest groups to influence decision-making for specific policy issues (Heclo, 1978). With a focus on the process of policy change, advocacy coalition framework suggests that key actors build different coalitions based on policy beliefs and hence form policy subsystems for issue-specific policy. Policy learning or change can occur due to the changes of belief systems or the challenge to the beliefs from external factors (Sabatier & Jenkins-Smith, 1993)	Use these frameworks to understand the roles played by diverse group of actors and to examine power distribution in networks (Brass & Burkhardt, 1993; Fung, 2006; Weible, 2018; Weible & Ingold, 2018)

boundaries in many different policy domains. These can include issues related to natural resource management, public health, law enforcement, and economic development. The book brings together the network perspectives of academic researchers, practitioners, and policymakers and its relevance to public policy and administration. It also provides a unique opportunity to explore current thinking on the role of networks and look at the relationship between networks and public management from both a policy and operational viewpoint. The book will examine networks in their various forms along with their effects on behavior within and between organizations. Drawing on literature from sociology, policy sciences, organizational studies, management, and economics, this book will cover the basic theoretical models of networks and investigating different methods that have been used in network research. This book approaches the investigation from multiple levels of analysis and discusses various applications of network theory. The main goals of this book are as follows:

- Identify the fundamental changes in public policy and administration that have led to the increasing use of intergovernmental, interagency, and cross-sector collaboration.
- Evaluate the context and theoretical foundation of network governance.
- Use theories, concepts, and frameworks in understanding network governance.
- Describe network types, characteristics, functions, and structures in public policy and administration.
- Advance the understanding of the design, formation, and development of effective networks in public policy and administration.
- Discuss the key elements of network governance: network management and leadership, network evaluation and performance, power and decision-making, legitimacy and accountability.
- Review theoretical knowledge and practical tools of network governance and their applications to a wide range of public policy and administration domains from local to global levels.
- Improve analytical and practical skills in design and evaluation of network governance for both scholars and practitioners.

Organization of the Book

The book is organized into three sections. In the first section, we define the key concepts of networks and network governance, discuss network types and characteristics, and examine network structures and function. We explain network formation, development, resilience, sustainability, demise, and transformation. The book starts with an introduction of networks and network governance (Chapter 1) and network analysis, with specific focus on interorganizational networks (Chapter 2). The book continues with a discussion of network types, structure, and function in public policy and management (Chapter 3) and moves on to cover the evolution of networks (Chapter 4).

Chapter 1 introduces and defines the concepts of networks and network governance within public policy and administration. It discusses the rise of networks and the demand for network governance from both theoretical and practical perspectives. It then summarizes the key theories and frameworks to inform network governance scholarship and practice and concludes with the aim and organization of this book.

Chapter 2 starts by introducing interorganizational networks and the elements of these networks, and then addresses why we use interorganizational networks in addressing complex public policy and administration issues. It touches upon both the benefits and limitations of interorganizational networks and the conditions for their effectiveness. This chapter provides a synopsis of social network analysis as one of the most appropriate analytical tools in studying interorganizational networks. The chapter also provides a brief overview of software packages available for conducting research with social network analysis.

Chapter 3 focuses on the diverse types of networks and their function in public policy and administration. It covers three streams of network research—collaborative networks, policy networks, and governance networks, in addition to briefly addressing informal and formal networks. This chapter then discusses the concept of network structures as it relates to network types, functions, and effectiveness. It concludes with a discussion of challenges of network governance within interorganizational networks.

Chapter 4 covers the evolution of networks, including formation, development, resilience, sustainability, demise, and transformation. It first addresses the driving factors for network formation and then discusses how networks develop. It further illustrates what network resilience and sustainability means and how networks can collapse and transform by using examples of failed networks. This chapter concludes with management and policy implications.

In the second section, we cover the key elements of network governance. The five chapters examine issues such as management and leadership (Chapter 5), knowledge management and information exchange (Chapter 6), the power distribution and decision-making processes (Chapter 7), legitimacy and accountability issues (Chapter 8), and performance and evaluation (Chapter 9).

Chapter 5 discusses the complexity of network management and leadership. It covers in depth what differentiates network management activities and behaviors from those of general management. It discusses the unique network leadership activities such as trust building and boundary spanning. It proposes a contingency framework and highlights the relationship between network management, leadership, and governance structures. This chapter ends by discussing practical implications and future research in network management and leadership.

Chapter 6 discusses knowledge management and information exchange in networks with a central focus on open-source participatory knowledge tools. This chapter deals with the process of information seeking in networks, mainly in relation to advice seeking and crowdsourced data gathering. It addresses the nature of knowledge management within networks. In addition, it covers the barriers to knowledge sharing in networks and the use of current information and communication technology (ICT) for facilitating knowledge sharing across organizational boundaries.

Chapter 7 analyzes power distribution and decision-making processes and mechanisms in networks. It examines power relations among network members and complexity of decision-making in networks. It further disentangles the relationships among power structure, leadership, decision-making mechanisms, network structures, and network capacity. It concludes by summarizing existing literature and identifying future research needs.

Chapter 8 discusses legitimacy and accountability issues in order to advance high performing democratic network governance. It discusses the characteristics and nature of network accountability systems and proposes a framework that includes both formal and informal accountability systems. In conclusion, it provides recommendations about how to ensure network members assume accountability when pursuing collaborative goals.

Chapter 9 defines network performance and discusses the tools and approaches to evaluate network performance. It conceptualizes network performance at multiple levels and introduces a multilevel approach to evaluate performance at organizational, network, and community levels. It also covers performance measurement tools in general along with network analysis tools. Furthermore, this chapter discusses how governance structures influence network performance and highlights measurement challenges in evaluating network performance.

In the third section, we provide examples of network governance applications in diverse contexts, ranging from community and economic development to human and social services, virtual environments, and emergency and crisis management. The book then continues with more practicality-oriented chapters that explore networks in emergency and crisis management (Chapter 10), community and economic development (Chapter 11), and human and social services (Chapter 12). Lastly, the book discusses virtual networks (Chapter 13), global perspectives on networks (Chapter 14), and emerging research on network governance and its implications (Chapter 15).

Chapter 10 highlights the importance of networks in emergency and crisis management, as the function of emergency management often requires cross-sector collaboration. This chapter introduces different types and structures of emergency and crisis management networks. This chapter also illustrates how interorganizational networks are designed in response to disasters and how to evaluate the performance of emergency and crisis management networks. In addition, it provides application examples of network analysis in emergency and crisis management.

Chapter 11 discusses how organizations, especially local governments, use networks to strengthen communities and develop economy. It emphasizes the necessity of collaboration in promoting regional economic development. It introduces different types of collaborative networks for community and economic development and addresses how these networks influence communities.

In addition, it provides application examples of network analysis in community and economic development.

Chapter 12 covers the application of network governance in human and social services. Delivering human and social services often demands collaboration among public, nonprofit, and private sector organizations, which provides a rich environment for examining performance, structures, and network management and governance. This chapter also provides a homeless service delivery network to illustrate how network analysis can be used to strengthen community partnerships in human and social service delivery.

Emerging ICT foster the development of virtual networks. Chapter 13 defines the key concepts in virtual environments, examines their attributes, and provides key theories and methods for analysis. In addition to addressing this important topic, the chapter highlights how virtual networks can complement regular networks. It also discusses several network analysis applications to exemplify how network analysis is used in understanding virtual networks.

Chapter 14 draws attention to how networks in a global context require flexible and adaptable forms of coordination across national boundaries. It conceptualizes global policy networks and discusses their characteristics. Moreover, it provides a few examples of policy networks in other countries and globally. This chapter also provides network analysis applications to illustrate how network analysis can be used to study complex networks in a global context.

Chapter 15 concludes the book with a discussion of the conceptual, theoretical, and methodological issues for advancing network governance research. It also reiterates the practical implications of network governance research and highlights both opportunities and challenges facing this research field.

In sum, after reading Chapters 1–4, readers can develop a basic understanding of networks and network governance. Before they design and implement network research, they should be able to define networks and network governance, understand different types of networks, describe functions, characteristics, and structures of networks, and grasp the evolution of networks. Chapters 5–9 expose readers to the key elements of network governance, and the intertwined relationships among network management, network structures, network legitimacy and accountability, and performance. Chapters 10–14 introduce the real-world applications of network governance and help readers apply network concepts and theoretical frameworks to analyzing a wide range of public management and policy issues. Chapter 15 concludes the book by reviewing the conceptual, theoretical, and methodological issues in advancing network governance research and discussing both opportunities and challenges facing this research field.

References

Acton, R. M., & Jasny, L. (2012). *An introduction to network analysis with R and statnet*. Retrieved from https://statnet.org/trac/raw-attachment/wiki/Resources/introToSNAinR_sunbelt_2012_tutorial.pdf

Agranoff, R. (2007). *Managing within networks: Adding value to public organizations.* Washington, DC: Georgetown University Press.

Agranoff, R., & McGuire, M. (2001). Big questions in public network management research. *Journal of Public Administration Research and Theory, 11*(3), 295–326.

Akkerman, A., Torenvlied, R., & Schalk, J. (2012). Two-level effects of interorganizational network collaboration on graduate satisfaction: A comparison of five intercollege networks in Dutch higher education. *The American Review of Public Administration, 42*(6), 654–677.

Ansell, C., & Gash, A. (2008). Collaborative governance in theory and practice. *Journal of Public Administration Research and Theory, 18*(4), 543–571.

Bardach, E. (1998). *Getting agencies to work together: The practice and theory of managerial craftmanship.* Washington, DC: Brookings Institution Press.

Bardach, E. (2001). Developmental dynamics: Interagency collaboration as an emergent phenomenon. *Journal of Public Administration Research and Theory, 11*(2), 149–164.

Berardo, R., & Lubell, M. (2016). Understanding what shapes a polycentric governance system. *Public Administration Review, 76*(5), 738–751.

Berry, F. S., Brower, R. S., Choi, S. O., Goa, W. X., Jang, H. S., Kwon, M., & Word, J. (2004). Three traditions of network research: What the public management research agenda can learn from other research communities. *Public Administration Review, 64*(5), 539–552.

Bingham, L. B., & O'Leary, R (Eds.). (2008). *Big ideas in collaborative public management.* New York, NY: M. E. Sharpe.

Borgatti, S. P., Everett, M. G., & Johnson, J. C. (2013). *Analyzing social networks.* Los Angeles, CA: Sage Publications.

Borgatti, S. P., & Lopez-Kidwell, V. (2011). Network theory. In J. Scott & P. J. Carrington (Eds.), *The SAGE handbook of social network analysis* (pp. 40–54). Thousand Oaks, CA: Sage Publications.

Brass, D., & Burkhardt, M. (1993). Potential power and power use: An investigation of structure. *Academy of Management Journal, 36*(3), 441–470.

Bryson, J. M., Crosby, B. C., & Stone, M. M. (2006). The design and implementation of cross sector collaborations: Propositions from the literature. *Public Administration Review, 66*(Suppl. 1), 44–55. doi:10.1111/j.1540-6210.2006.00665.x

Burt, R. S. (1992). *Structural holes: The social structure of competition.* Cambridge, MA: Harvard University Press.

Carpenter, M. A., Li, M., & Jiang, H. (2012). Social network research in organizational context: A systematic review of methodological issues and choices. *Journal of Management, 38*(4), 1328–1361.

Coleman, J. S. (1988). Social capital in the creation of human capital. *American Journal of Sociology, 94*(Suppl.), S95–S120.

Coleman, J. S. (1990). *Foundations of social theory.* Cambridge, MA: The Belknap Press of Harvard University Press.

Cropanzano, R., & Mitchell, M. S. (2005). Social exchange theory: An interdisciplinary review. *Journal of Management, 31*(6), 874–900.

Dedman, B., & Schoen, J. (2013). *Adding up the financial costs of the Boston Bombings.* Retrieved June 26, 2017, from www.cnbc.com/2013/05/01/Adding-Up-the-Financial-Costs-of-the-Boston-Bombings.html

Emerson, K., Nabatchi, T., & Balogh, S. (2012). An integrative framework for collaborative governance. *Journal of Public Administration Research and Theory, 22*(1), 1–29.

Fung, A. (2006). Varieties of participation in complex governance. *Public Administration Review, 66*(Special issue), 66–75.

Geddes, L. (2012). In search of collaborative public management. *Public Management Review, 14*(7), 947–966.

Hawkins, C., Hu, Q., & Feiock, R. (2016). Self-organizing governance of local economic development: Informal policy networks and regional institutions. *Journal of Urban Affairs, 48*(5), 643–660. doi:10.1111/juaf.12280

Heclo, H. A. (1978). Issue networks and the executive establishment. In A. King (Ed.), *The new American political system* (pp. 87–124). Washington, DC: AEI.

Hu, Q., Khosa, S., & Kapucu, N. (2016). The intellectual structure of empirical social network research in public administration. *Journal of Public Administration Research and Theory, 26*(4), 593–612. doi:10.1093/jopart/muv032

Hu, Q., Knox, C. C., & Kapucu, N. (2014). What have we learned since September 11th? A network study of the Boston marathon bombings response. *Public Administration Review, 74*(6), 698–712.

Huang, K., & Provan, K. G. (2007). Resource tangibility and patterns of interaction in a publicly funded health and human services network. *Journal of Public Administration Research and Theory, 17*(3), 435–454.

Isett, K. R., Mergel, I. A., LeRoux, K., Mischen, P. A., & Rethemeyer, R. K. (2011). Networks in public administration scholarship: Understanding where we are and where we need to go. *Journal of Public Administration Research and Theory, 21*(Suppl. 1), i157–i173.

Isett, K. R., & Miranda, J. (2015). Watching sausage being made: Lessons learned from the co-production of governance in a behavioural health system. *Public Management Review, 17*(1), 35–56.

Kapucu, N. (2006). Interagency communication networks during emergencies: Boundary spanners in multi-agency coordination. *The American Review of Public Administration, 36*(2), 207–225.

Kapucu, N. (2012). *The network governance in response to acts of terrorism: Comparative analyses.* New York, NY: Routledge.

Kapucu, N., & Hu, Q. (2016). Understanding multiplexity of collaborative emergency management networks. *The American Review of Public Administration, 46*(4), 399–417.

Kapucu, N., Hu, Q., & Khosa, S. (2014). The state of network research in public administration. *Administration & Society.* doi:10.1177/0095399714555752

Kapucu, N., Yuldhasev, F., & Bakiev, E. (2010). Collaborative public management and collaborative governance: Conceptual similarities and differences. *European Journal of Economic and Political Studies, 2*(1), 39–60.

Keast, R. (2014). Network theory tracks and trajectories: Where from, where to? In K. Robyn, M. Mandell, & R. Agranoff (Eds.), *Network theory in the public sector: Building new theoretical frameworks* (pp. 15–30). New York, NY: Routledge.

Kenis, P. (2016). Network. In C. Ansell & J. Torfing (Eds.), *Handbook on theories of governance* (pp. 149–157). Northampton, MA: Edward Elgar Publishing.

Kettl, D. F. (2006). Managing boundaries in American administration: The collaboration imperative. *Public Administration Review, 66*(1), 10–19.

Kilduff, M., & Brass, D. J. (2010). Organizational social network research: Core ideas and key debates. *The Academy of Management Annals, 4*(1), 317–357.

Klijn, E. H., & Koppenjan, J. (2016). *Governance networks in the public sector.* New York, NY: Routledge.

Koliba, C., Meek, J., & Zia, A. (2010). *Governance networks in public administration and public policy*. New York, NY: CRC Press.

Lee, I. W., Feiock, R. C., & Lee, Y. (2012). Competitors and cooperators: A microlevel analysis of regional economic development collaboration networks. *Public Administration Review, 72*(2), 253–262.

Milward, H. B., & Provan, K. G. (2003). Managing the hollow state: Collaboration and contracting. *Public Management Review, 5*(1), 1–18.

Milward, H. B., Provan, K. G., Fish, A., Isett, K. R., & Huang, K. (2009). Governance and collaboration: An evolutionary study of two mental health networks. *Journal of Public Administration Research and Theory, 20*(Suppl. 1), i125–i141.

Naisbett, J. (1982). *Megatrends*. New York, NY: Warner Books.

O'Leary, R., & Vij, N. (2012). Collaborative public management: Where have we been and where are we going? *American Review of Public Administration, 42*(5), 507–522.

Ostrom, E. (1990). *Governing the commons: The evolution of institutions for collective action*. New York, NY: Cambridge University Press.

Ostrom, E. (2007). A diagnostic approach for going beyond panaceas. *Proceedings of the National Academy of Sciences of the United States of America, 104*(39), 15181–15187.

Ostrom, V., Tiebout, C. M., & Warren, R. (1961). The organization of government in metropolitan areas: A theoretical inquiry. *American Political Science Review, 55*(4), 831–842.

Park, H. H., & Rethemeyer, R. K. (2012). The politics of connections: Assessing the determinants of social structure in policy networks. *Journal of Public Administration Research and Theory, 24*(2), 349–379.

Pfeffer, J., & Salancik, G. R. (1978). *The external control of organizations: A resource dependence perspective*. Stanford, CA: Stanford University Press.

Podolny, J. M., & Page, K. L. (1998). Network forms of organization. *Annual Review of Sociology, 24*, 57–76.

Powell, W. W. (1990). Neither market or hierarchy, network forms of organization. *Research in Organizational Behavior, 12*, 295–336.

Provan, K. G., & Kenis, P. (2008). Modes of network governance: Structure, management, and effectiveness. *Journal of Public Administration Research and Theory, 18*(2), 229–252.

Provan, K. G., & Lemaire, R. H. (2012). Core concepts and key ideas for understanding public sector organizational networks: Using research to inform scholarship and practice. *Public Administration Review, 72*(5), 638–648.

Putnam, R. (2001). *Bowling alone: The collapse and revival of American community*. New York, NY: Simon and Schuster.

Rethemeyer, R. K., & Hatmaker, D. M. (2008). Network management reconsidered: An inquiry into management of network structures in public sector service provision. *Journal of Public Administration Research and Theory, 18*(4), 617–647.

Rhodes, R. A. W. (1996). The new governance: Governing without government. *Political Studies, 44*(4), 652–667.

Robins, G., Bates, L., & Pattison, P. (2011). Network governance and environmental management: Conflict and cooperation. *Public Administration, 89*(4), 1293–1313.

Rosenbloom, D. H., & Gong, T. (2013). Coproducing 'clean' collaborative governance: Examples from the United States and China. *Public Performance and Management Review, 13*(4), 544. doi:10.2753/PMR1530-9576360403

Sabatier, P. A., & Jenkins-Smith, H. C. (Eds.). (1993). *Policy change and learning: An advocacy coalition approach.* Boulder, CO: Westview Press.

Salancik, G. R. (1995). Wanted: A good network theory of organization. *Administrative Science Quarterly, 40*(2), 345–349.

Schneider, M., Scholz, J., Lubell, M., Mindruta, D., & Edwardsen, M. (2003). Building consensual institutions: Networks and the national estuary program. *American Journal of Political Science, 47*(1), 143–158.

Steen, J. A., & Duran, L. (2013). The impact of foster care privatization on multiple placements. *Children and Youth Services Review, 35*(9), 1503–1509.

Stoker, G. (1998). Governance as theory: Five propositions. *International Social Science Journal, 50*(155), 17–28.

Thompson, G. F. (2003). *Between hierarchies and markets: The logic and limits of network forms of organization.* Retrieved from www.oxfordscholarship.com/view/10.1093/acprof:oso/9780198775270.001.0001/acprof-9780198775270-chapter-2

Uzzi, B. (1997). Social structure and competition in interfirm networks: The paradox of embeddedness. *Administrative Science Quarterly, 42*(1), 35–67.

Wasserman, S., & Faust, K. (1994). *Social network analysis: Methods and applications.* New York, NY: Cambridge University Press.

Weible, C. M. (2018). Instrument constituencies and the Advocacy Coalition Framework: An essay on the comparisons, opportunities, and interactions. *Policy and Society, 37*(1), 321–338.

Weible, C. M., & Ingold, K. (2018). What are advocacy coalitions and why they matter? *Policy and Politics, 46*(2), 325–343.

2 Interorganizational Networks and Social Network Analysis

In this chapter, we introduce interorganizational networks, covering key elements of an interorganizational network and why we use interorganizational networks. We discuss the benefits and limitations of interorganizational networks and the conditions for network effectiveness. In addition, this chapter illustrates why social network analysis is one of the most used tools in studying interorganizational networks. The chapter also provides a brief overview of software packages available for conducting network research. This chapter addresses the following questions:

- What is an interorganizational network composed of?
- Why are interorganizational networks important?
- What challenges do interorganizational networks face?
- What conditions are required for interorganizational networks to function?
- What social network analysis means and what are key measures?

Interorganizational Networks

Components of An Interorganizational Network

Interorganizational networks are composed of organizations as actors (nodes) and the relations that connect the organizations. Interorganizational networks can be goal-oriented ones, which are formed to achieve common goals that cannot be achieved by a single organization (Provan, Fish, & Sydow, 2007); or, the networks can be emergent, or lacking specific pre-identified goals (Kilduff & Tsai, 2003). Scholars in public policy and public administration often examine collaborative interorganizational networks to achieve management or policy goals that cannot be achieved effectively by one single organization (Agranoff & McGuire, 2001; Popp, MacKean, Casebeer, Milward, & Lindstrom, 2014). The following are some commonly referenced definitions of interorganizational networks that state their focus on the commitment to shared goals.

"A whole network is viewed here as a group of three or more organizations connected in ways that facilitate achievement of a common goal."

(Provan et al., 2007, p. 482)

"Networks, as the term is used in the literature, typically refers to multiorganizational arrangements to for solving problems that cannot be achieved, or achieved easily, by single organizations."

(Agranoff & McGuire, 2001, p. 296)

"A group of goal-oriented interdependent but autonomous actors that come together to produce a collective output (tangible or intangible) that no one actor could produce on its own."

(Isett, Mergel, LeRoux, & Mischen, 2011, p. 1161)

Actors and Relations

Actors in interorganizational networks can be public, nonprofit, and for-profit organizations. In the domain of public administration and public policy, these actors come mostly from public and nonprofit sectors (Popp et al., 2014). Actors in a network could also be classified by geographic scales, such as localism, regionalism, nationalism, and internationalism (Koliba et al., 2010). Applying the categorizing of ties by Borgatti and his colleagues, we provide examples of different categories of ties that organizations may have in Table 2.1: *"Co-occurrence," "social relations," "interactions," and "flow"* (2013, p. 31). The relations among actors can be information exchange, flow of financial and other resources, client referrals, and joint services; and the relations can also be resource competition or client competition (Provan et al., 2007; Hawkins, Hu, & Feiock, 2016).

Table 2.1 Types of Ties Studied in Interorganizational Networks

Categories	Examples
Co-occurrence	• Similarities in organizational attributes (e.g., size, age, budget, sector affiliation, and geographic location) • Co-membership (e.g., member organizations of an association) • Co-participation (e.g., attending the same events or conferences)
Social relations	• Perceptual relations (e.g., perceived collaborators or competitors)
Interactions	• Activities (e.g., 'consult with,' 'talk to,' 'coordinate with,' and 'coproduce with')
Flows	• Information and resources • Client referrals

Source: Adapted from Borgatti et al., 2013, p. 31

Examples of Interorganizational Networks

Relations or connections can take on different forms. The networks can be informal ones, formed primarily based on trust or personal relationships; or can be formalized through a contract or memorandum of agreements (MOU) (Provan et al., 2007). In Exhibit 2.1, we list two examples of interorganizational networks, in the contexts of emergency management and economic development, to illustrate the varieties of actors and the different forms of connections organizations can have. These examples will be discussed in detail later.

Exhibit 2.1 Interorganizational networks in emergency management and economic development

A collaborative approach is crucial for effective emergency and crisis management (Waugh, 2003; Waugh & Streib, 2006). A total of 1,607 organizations, including public, private, and nonprofit organizations, were involved in the response efforts to the terrorist attacks on September 11th in 2011 in New York City. During the response, Organizations shared information and resources and coordinated activities, which resulted in the formation of interorganizational networks in response to the man-made disaster (Kapucu, 2006).

Economic development is one area where cities compete and cooperate through both formal and informal mechanisms. In the Orlando Metropolitan area, a total of 34 city governments not only reach formal agreements to coordinate land use and infrastructure building, but also have informal interactions on economic development matters, such as sharing information about sustainable economic development (Hawkins et al., 2016).

Benefits of Interorganizational Networks

Interorganizational networks allow member organizations to pool various types of resources, coordinate action, share risks, and achieve goals that cannot be reached individually (Huxham & Vangen, 2005). The benefits of developing interorganizational networks can be manifested at both individual organizational levels as well aggregate (whole) network levels (Provan & Milward, 2001). Individual members can benefit from being part of the network while the whole network can produce other desired outcomes. Through collaboration, organizations can access more information and resources to address complicated issues (Agranoff & McGuire, 2001; Bryson, Crosby, & Stone, 2006).

Networks, having a more flexible organizing structure that function across organizational boundaries and jurisdictions, can enhance organizational learning and foster innovation and knowledge sharing, improve service provisions, and better prepare organizations to respond to emergent situations (Isett et al., 2011; Provan & Lemaire, 2012). Due to these benefits, interorganizational networks have been widely applied to address complex management and policy issues, such as economic development, the delivery of human and social services, and emergency management (Agranoff & McGuire, 1998; Kapucu, Hu, & Khosa, 2014; Lee, Feiock, & Lee, 2012; Provan & Milward, 1995).

Interorganizational networks can also produce network-level outcomes, such as the establishment of an informal accountability system, the development of social capital, the improvement of service quality and integration. At the network level, an informal accountability system may be built to ensure shared accountability among member organizations (Romzek, LeRoux, & Blackmar, 2012; Romzek, LeRoux, Johnston, Kempf, & Piatak, 2014) (see Chapter 8 for details on accountability in networks). Through networks, organizations can strengthen existing relationships or build new relationships with other organizations, which results in the accumulation of social capital and increase members' commitment to collective action or achieving network goals (Berardo & Scholz, 2010). Well-connected, coordinated networks may strengthen service integration and service delivery quality. For example, the regional economic development network presented in Exhibit 2.2 provides channels for organizations to share information and discuss issues pertaining to local economic development, but also produce a tangible outcome that can benefit the community at large.

Exhibit 2.2 Myregion.org

Myregion.org is a regional network created to promote regional economic growth. It connects 86 cities, seven counties, businesses, nonprofits, and citizens. This network functions across political jurisdictions to focus on strategic issues in the region. It provides platforms for government officials, business and nonprofit leaders, and individual residents to sit together and discuss issues pertaining to local economic development, economic competitiveness, education, health, civic health, and regional water management. A tangible output of this network is the Central Florida Scorecard, a tool that can assist leaders in tracking progress in service quality of various domains (details can be found on the website: www. thefloridascorecard.org).

Challenges of Interorganizational Networks

Not all interorganizational networks will achieve desired outcomes. The use of networks can create problems and challenges, and sometimes result in negative consequences or outcomes (Bryson et al., 2006; McGuire & Agranoff, 2011; Provan & Lemaire, 2012). Member organizations join the networks with different missions, divergent cultures, backgrounds, operational procedures, and perspectives (Bryson et al., 2006; Vangen & Huxham, 2012; O'Leary & Vij, 2012; Popp et al., 2014). Coordinating efforts among member organizations costs time and resources, and it takes time to build and maintain trust among organizations (Bryson et al., 2006; Provan & Lemaire, 2012). Member organizations may lose autonomy in order to make joint decisions (Provan & Lemaire, 2012). Managing interorganizational networks and figuring out the most effective governance structure remains a great challenge to scholars and practitioners (Agranoff & McGuire, 2001; Provan & Kenis, 2008).

McGuire and Agranoff (2011) discussed the potential limitations of networks in detail. They asserted that although networks present reasonable solutions to complex public management issues, they often "run into operational, performance, or legal barriers that prevent the next action step" (p. 265). By operational barriers, they refer to imbalanced power distribution, extensive processing costs, and the difficulty of converting network-based solutions into policy. Furthermore, they highlighted the performance limitations of networks by discussing the measurement challenges and the multidimensional nature of network performance. Lastly, they noted that networks do not "render government agencies obsolete" (p. 275), but rather make it more crucial to understand traditional bureaucracy and the role of government in networks.

Table 2.2 Benefits and Challenges of Interorganizational Networks

	Organization Level	*Network Level*
Benefits	• Access to information and resources • Increased capacity to address complex problems • Organizational learning and knowledge sharing • Innovation • Improved service provision • Better response to emergent situations	• Stakeholder engagement • Establishment of informal accountability systems • Member organizations' commitment to collective action and shared network goals • Relationship building and trust building among member organizations • Integrated service and quality service
Challenges	• Loss of autonomy • Different missions, cultures, procedures, and perspectives • Complexity	• Operational barriers such as imbalanced power distribution, extensive processing costs • Ensure network performance • Network management and governance • Increased complexity

Depending on the type of regime, size of economy, and other factors, the size of government might differ from country to country. Yet, the key role of government does not diminish or become obsolete. Through policymaking and implementation, government lays out rules, processes, and procedures that guide the development and function of public interorganizational networks. The complex environment of democratic governance in modern times brings additional challenges (such as accountability issues) to government in coordinating public service delivery or co-production of services with the nonprofit and private sectors (Bryson et al., 2006). Hence, it is crucial to study the role of government in network governance.

Conditions Required for Interorganizational Networks

The situation and initial conditions should be evaluated to determine whether an interorganizational network is the appropriate organizational form (Bryson et al., 2006; Popp et al., 2014). The benefits need to outweigh the costs of using interorganizational networks in addressing complex problems. First, the management problem or policy issue should be assessed to decide whether the problem is too complex to be addressed by one organization and whether it can to be addressed through traditional approaches (Popp et al., 2014). Many management problems (such as emergency management) or policy issues (such as healthcare) are often unstructured, complex, or ill-defined, and lack information about the nature, cause, and consequences of and solution to the problems in question (Klijin & Koppenjan, 2015). Solving these problems often require the joint, well-coordinated efforts from multiple organizations and jurisdictions.

Second, environmental factors—especially the institutional environment— need to be considered before establishing an interorganizational network. A favorable institutional environment will foster the development of the "normative, legal, and regulatory elements" that can set the tone for interorganizational relations and exert influence on the formation, structures, and outcomes of interorganizational networks (Bryson et al., 2006, p. 45).

Third, a series of questions need to be asked about the missions, values, cultures, and backgrounds of potential member organizations and their previous collaboration experience (Bryson et al., 2006; Provan & Lemaire, 2012; Popp et al., 2014). To build interorganizational networks successfully, it is important to understand the diversity of member organizations or stakeholders and recognize the differences among these groups.

Fourth, a common goal or purpose needs to be agreed upon by member organizations. Furthermore, resources are required to build and sustain an interorganizational network (Bryson et al., 2006; Provan & Lemaire, 2012; Popp et al., 2014). Individual organizations should evaluate the compatibility of their missions with the goal of the interorganizational network (O'Leary & Vij, 2012). Despite the divergent organizational missions or goals, organizations need to reach consensus on defining the problem and develop shared network-level goals or purpose (Bryson et al., 2006; O'Leary & Vij, 2012).

Finally, a well-functioning network demands trust building, capacity building, management, and leadership (Bryson et al., 2006; Provan & Lemaire, 2012), which will be further discussed in other chapters of the book. It takes time and resources to build and enhance trust among organizations. Furthermore, individual organizations may lack collaboration experience and need additional resources and training to build capacity (i.e., human resources, technological capacity, and leadership) for engaging in a network (O'Leary & Vij, 2012; Gazley, 2008). Managing interorganizational networks requires the mobilization of resources, coordination of action, and addressing potential conflicts (Agranoff, 2007).

In summary, networks are not panacea to address complex problems. Before investing resources in initiating or building an interorganizational network, public managers should assess the situation, the need, and initial conditions carefully before proposing a network as an alternative as it takes time and energy.

Social Network Analysis: A Brief Overview

Research Design, Unit of Analysis, and Network Boundary Setting

Social network analysis refers to a set of tools and methods for analyzing the relations among actors and for examining the patterns of relational structures, processes, and outcomes (Scott, 2013; Wasserman & Faust, 1994). Actors can be individuals, organizations, things, artifacts, or countries. Different from conventional statistical analysis, social network analysis focuses on the relations among actors rather than attributes. The relations can be similarities or interactions between actors, relational roles, or flows of information or resources (Borgatti et al., 2013). In this section of the chapter, after briefly introducing network research and research designs, we discuss the use of social network analysis in understanding interorganizational networks and cover key measures of social network analysis at the node level, group level, and network level.

> **Social Network Analysis**
>
> The set of analytical tools and methods to analyze relations, structures, processes, and outcomes for networks.

There are two types of network research designs: ego-network research and whole-network research. In ego-network research, a network includes focal nodes (or egos), alters, and the ties between egos and alters (Borgatti et al., 2013). Ego-network research focuses on the ego's direct ties with others and how egos perceive the relationships among others. For instance, an example of an ego-network research is a study of graduate students' advice networks. To understand how advice networks may influence students' academic performance, we ask a sample of graduate students to list up to five people with whom they discuss study-related matters. The purpose of the study is to examine the social support that the students have, not to construct the entire network of ties among all the students. By contrast, a whole network includes the ties among all the nodes in a given setting (Borgatti et al., 2013). An example of a whole network is a study of the human service delivery network in the Orlando metropolitan area. The service delivery network is composed of all the service providers and the ties among these service providers. The aim of this research is to investigate the relational patterns and structures among all the service providers.

The selection of ego-network research designs or whole-network designs depends on the research question. Table 2.3 compares the pros and cons of whole-network designs and ego-network designs (Borgatti et al., 2013). Whole-network designs allow researchers to depict the full picture of the network and investigate the overall structure and pattern, yet the cost of conducting whole-network research is high for a large network study. Ego-network designs enable researchers to collect detailed information about the egos' (actors) connections, yet this type of design does not present a whole picture. Furthermore, ego-network designs make boundary specification easy and allow confidentiality as egos do not need to provide the real names of the alters (Borgatti et al., 2013).

Network variables can be explanatory variables or outcome variables. The unit of analysis in network research is *not* individual actors (organizations) but the relations or ties among actors (Provan, Veazie, Staten, & Teufel-Shone, 2005). The level of analysis in network research can be individual nodes, dyadic, triadic, substructure, and whole-network levels (Wasserman & Faust, 1994; Borgatti et al., 2013).

A network approach allows researchers to examine the problem across different levels of analysis (Kapucu et al., 2014). A *dyad* refers to ties between two actors, and the dyad is "frequently the basic unit for the statistical analysis of social networks" (Wasserman & Faust, 1994, p. 18). A *triad* refers to a set of three actors and ties among them. A *substructure*-level refers to

Table 2.3 Whole-Network Designs Versus Ego-Network Designs

	Whole-network designs	*Ego-network designs*
Pros	• Include all actors in a given setting and their ties • Examine features and structures of an entire network	• Include focal actors and alters and the ties between actors and alters • Detailed information about egos' network
Cons	• Costly for a large network • Requires specific boundary setting	• Allows confidentiality in research • Easy boundary setting

Source: Adapted from Borgatti et al., 2013

subsets or cliques of actors and the ties among them. A *whole network* level examines the patterns or structure of a network in its entirety (Wasserman & Faust, 1994).

Defining the network boundary is important for network research, especially whole-network research (Borgatti et al., 2013). The network boundary has practical implications for network governance and management as well. Laumann, Marsden, and Prensky (1989) proposed two approaches to address network boundary specification: the nominalist approach and the realist approach. Following the nominalist approach, researchers define the network boundary based on theory or other justifications, such as affiliation or formally defined positions. The realist approach asks the actors to define the boundary. Researchers can start with a small group of nodes, expand the network based on the relationship identified by the small group, and repeat the snowballing technique for several waves to reach certain level of redundancy (Borgatti et al., 2013; Laumann et al., 1989; Prell, 2012). Researchers can combine the realist approach or positional approach in one study (Borgatti et al., 2013). For example, researchers may begin with a nominalist approach and develop a list of member organizations in a network based on formal documents and then supplement with a realist approach by asking member organizations to identify any additional organizations they have worked with. In Exhibit 2.3 we provide two examples of boundary setting using these two approaches.

Exhibit 2.3   Two Approaches to Defining Network Boundary

Examples of boundary setting for whole-network designs

A nominalist approach: To identify the formal emergency response network, researchers can examine the emergency operation plans and identify the key actors listed in the plan. For instance, according to positional role and responsibilities listed in the city of Boston Emergency Operation Plan, 39 primary and support organizations are responsible for the 15 local emergency support functions (ESFs). Therefore, the formal affiliation network is composed of the 39 organizations and their affiliation with the 15 ESFs (Hu, Knox, & Kapucu, 2014).

A realist approach: To examine the homeless veteran network in the Orlando, Florida, area, researchers may reach out to a small group of homeless veterans and ask them to provide more names of homeless veterans in this area. Repeat this snowballing step for a few waves until certain level of redundancy occurs.

Use of Social Network Analysis for Interorganizational Collaboration

The focus of this book is on interorganizational networks. Network analysis, with its focus on relations and patterns and structures of relations, is not only useful to study the type, structure, formation, and evolution of interorganizational networks, but also can be used to study the performance, management, and accountability and legitimacy of interorganizational networks (Hu, Khosa, & Kapucu, 2016). The previous section already discussed the two types of network research—ego-network research and whole-network research. In this section, we introduce the frequently used network measures for interorganizational network research.

Interorganizational network research can be grouped into egocentric network research and whole network research based on its focus on individual organizations or networks (Kilduff & Tsai, 2003; Provan et al., 2007). Egocentric or organization-level research typically address how network ties, different types of relations, and network positions influence organizational outcomes or performance (Provan et al., 2007). Whole network research often examines the overall patterns, processes, and structures of a network. The frequently asked questions are: Which organizations are most central in the network? Which organizations serve as brokers that bridge the unconnected organizations? Are organizations well connected in the network? Are there subgroups of member organizations in the network? In Table 2.4 we discuss the commonly used network measures.

Similar to other types of research, both primary and secondary data can be used for social network analysis (Borgatti et al., 2013). In the field of public policy and public administration, researchers frequently use surveys and interviews to collect network data (Kapucu et al., 2014). Researchers also draw network data from secondary sources (e.g., archival data from government documents and newspapers; data from social media). If carefully identified, documents can be invaluable resource for network research as people can forget the events or network related information on the past (Hu, 2015). In the application chapters—Chapters 10 and 11—we will discuss in depth how to use a survey questionnaire and conduct content analysis of documents to collect network data.

Several software platforms, such as UCINET, Organizational Risk Analyzer (ORA), Pajek, GePhi, and StOCENT are available for visualize, describe, and analyze network data. UCINET is the most frequently used software platform used in public administration and policy (Kapucu et al., 2014). In recent years, an increasing number of researchers conduct network analysis using R, an object-oriented programming language, due to its open source nature and great flexibility for advanced analysis (Acton & Jasny, 2012; Kapucu et al., 2014; Yi & Scholz, 2016). This book is not a method book for social network analysis, and it does not provide step-by-step guidance for network analysis. Readers may check additional books and resources on this topic, such as Borgatti

Table 2.4 Frequently Used Network Measures for Interorganizational Network Research

Network Measures		Definition	Examples of Research Questions
Node-Level Measures: "Centrality" measures an actor's position in the network (Borgatti et al., 2013)	Degree centrality Indegree centrality Outdegree centrality	For undirected non-valued networks, degree centrality calculates the number of ties an actor has; For directed non-valued networks, indegree centrality refers to the number of ties that an actor receives from other actors; and outdegree centrality calculates the number of ties that an actor sends to other actors (Borgatti et al., 2013; Prell, 2012)	Which organizations have/receive/the highest number of connections with others? Which organizations send the highest number of connections to others?
	Eigenvector centrality	Commonly used for undirected networks, eigenvector centrality "count the number of nodes adjacent to a given node but weight each adjacent node by its centrality" (Borgatti et al., 2013, p. 168).	Which organizations are popular in terms with having ties with organizations that are well connected?
	Closeness centrality	Commonly used for undirected networks, closeness centrality is an inverse measure and it calculates "the sum of geodesic distance from a node to all others" (Borgatti et al., 2013, p. 173).	Which organizations can influence or reach out to the entire network in a timely manner?
	Betweenness centrality	For undirected networks, betweenness centrality measures the extent to which "the actor falls on the geodesic paths between other pairs of factors in the network" (Hanneman & Riddle, 2011, p. 366).	Which organizations can serve the role of mediator or information broker or boundary spanner?
Node-Level Measure	Multiplexity	The number of different types of ties a node has (Borgatti et al., 2013).	Do organizations have strong connections with others?
Node-level Measure	Structural holes	"A structural hole is the lack of a tie between two alters within an ego network" (Borgatti et al., 2013, p. 275)	To what extent does an organization bridge the gaps in a network?
Network-level measures	Density	"The probability that a tie exists between any pair of randomly chosen nodes" (Borgatti et al., 2013, p. 150)	To what extent are organizations connected in the network?
	Centralization	Centralization measures the extent to which a network is dominated by the connections of one or a few actors (Borgatti et al., 2013).	What structural characteristic does the interorganizational network exhibit?
	Cliques (can be used at node-level)	Cliques refer to the number of subgroups of three or more fully connected nodes (Borgatti et al., 2013).	Are there any fully connected subgroups in an interorganizational network?
	Fragmentation (Connectedness)	Connectedness refers to "the proportion of pairs of nodes that are located in the same component" (Borgatti et al., 2013, p. 153).	To what extent are member organizations connected or disconnected?

and his colleagues' book, *Analyzing Social Networks* (2017), Scott's (2013) book, *Social Network Analysis*, Hanneman and Riddle's free online book, *Introduction to Social Network Methods* (https://faculty.ucr.edu/~hanneman/nettext/) and Robin's book, *Doing Social Network Research: Network-based Research Design for Social Scientists* (2015).

Conclusion

The chapter introduced interorganizational networks in addressing complex public policy and public administration issues. This chapter also addressed both benefits and limitations of interorganizational networks and the conditions for effectiveness. Interorganizational networks allow organizations to get access to information and resources through building direct ties with others or reaching out to resourceful organizations through intermediate organizations. The flexible structure of organizing also encourages organizations to learn and innovate, which will lead to better service provision. At the aggregate level, networks allow member organizations to work on their strengths and integrate services, build trust and social capital in the long run. But networks are not without challenges. Organizations in a network may face loss of autonomy when working with other organizations. Further, conflicts often emerge when organizations with different missions, cultures, procedures, and perspectives come together to address a complex issue. Managing a network gets more complex and costlier as a network grows and becomes more diverse. Therefore, it is worthwhile to evaluate the conditions to assess whether forming a network is a good option for specific scenarios.

This chapter differentiated two types of network designs—ego-network research and whole network research—and discussed the pros and cons of both designs. It also covers how to use the nominalist approach or the realist approach to define network boundary. In addition, the chapter provided a brief overview of social network analysis method as a widely used analytical tool in studying interorganizational networks. The chapter concluded with a brief overview of software packages available for social network analysis research. The analytical guide included in the chapter would be useful to better understand the chapters included in the application part of the book.

References

Acton, R. M., & Jasny, L. (2012). *An introduction to network analysis with R and statnet*. Retrieved from https://statnet.org/trac/raw-attachment/wiki/Resources/introToSNAinR_sunbelt_2012_tutorial.pdf

Agranoff, R. (2007). *Managing within networks: Adding value to public organizations*. Washington, DC: Georgetown University Press.

Agranoff, R., & McGuire, M. (1998). The intergovernmental context of local economic development. *State & Local Government Review, 30*(3), 150–164.

Agranoff, R., & McGuire, M. (2001). Big questions in public network management. *Journal of Public Administration Research and Theory, 11*(3), 295–326.

Berardo, R., & Scholz, J. T. (2010). Self-organizing policy networks: Risk, partner selection, and cooperation in estuaries. *American Journal of Political Science, 54*(3), 632–649.

Borgatti, S. P., Everett, M. G., & Johnson, J. C. (2013). *Analyzing social networks.* Los Angeles, CA: Sage Publications.

Bryson, J. M., Crosby, B. C., & Stone, M. M. (2006). The design and implementation of cross sector collaborations: Propositions from the literature. *Public Administration Review, 66*(Suppl. 1), 44–55. doi:10.1111/j.1540-6210.2006.00665.x

Gazley, B. (2008). Beyond the contract: The scope and nature of informal government-nonprofit partnerships. *Public Administration Review, 68*(1), 141–152.

Hanneman, R. A., & Riddle, M. (2011). A brief introduction to social network data. In J. Scott & P. J. Carrington (Eds.), *The Sage handbook of social network analysis* (pp. 331–339). Thousand Oaks, CA: Sage Publications.

Hawkins, C., Hu, Q., & Feiock, R. (2016). Self-organizing governance of local economic development: Informal policy networks and regional institutions. *Journal of Urban Affairs, 48*(5), 643–660. doi:10.1111/juaf.12280

Hu, Q. (2015). Conducting content analysis of documents in network research: A review of recent scholarship. *Complexity, Governance, & Networks, 2*(1), 83–102. doi:10.7564/14-CGN11

Hu, Q., Khosa, S., & Kapucu, N. (2016). The intellectual structure of empirical social network research in public administration. *Journal of Public Administration Research and Theory, 26*(4), 593–612. doi:10.1093/jopart/muv032

Hu, Q., Knox, C. C., & Kapucu, N. (2014). What have we learned since September 11th? A network study of the Boston marathon bombings response. *Public Administration Review, 74*(6), 698–712.

Huxham, C., & Vangen, S. (2005). *Managing to collaborate: The theory and practice of collaborative advantage.* New York, NY: Routledge.

Isett, K. R., Mergel, I. A., LeRoux, K., & Mischen, P. A. (2011). Networks in public administration scholarship: Understanding where we are and where we need to go. *Journal of Public Administration Research and Theory, 21*(Suppl. 1), i157–i173.

Kapucu, N. (2006). Interagency communication networks during emergencies: Boundary spanners in multi-agency coordination. *The American Review of Public Administration, 36*(2), 207–225.

Kapucu, N., Hu, Q., & Khosa, S. (2014). The state of network research in public administration. *Administration & Society.* doi:10.1177/0095399714555752.

Kilduff, M., & Tsai, W. (2003). *Social networks and organizations.* Thousand Oaks, CA: Sage Publications.

Klijin, E. H., & Koppenjan, J. (2015). *Governance networks in the public sector.* New York, NY: Routledge.

Koliba, C., Meek, J., & Zia, A. (2010). *Governance networks in public administration and public policy.* New York, NY: CRC Press.

Laumann, E. O., Marsden, P. V., & Prensky, D. (1989). The boundary specification problem in network analysis. In L. C. Freeman, D. R. White, & A. K. Romney (Eds.), *Research methods in social network analysis* (pp. 61–87). Fairfax, VA: George Mason University Press.

Lee, I. W., Feiock, R. C., & Lee, Y. (2012). Competitors and cooperators: A micro-level analysis of regional economic development networks. *Public Administration Review, 72*(2), 253–262.

McGuire, M., & Agranoff, R. (2011). The limitations of public management networks. *Public Administration, 89*(2), 265–284.

O'Leary, R., & Vij, N. (2012). Collaborative public management: Where have we been and where are we going? *American Review of Public Administration, 42*(5), 507–522.

Popp, J., MacKean, G., Casebeer, A., Milward, H. B., & Lindstrom, R. (2014). *Interorganizational networks: A review of the literature to inform practice.* Washington, DC: IBM Center for The Business of Government.

Prell, C. (2012). *Social network analysis: History, theory, and methodology.* Washington, DC: Sage Publications.

Provan, K. G., Fish, A., & Sydow, J. (2007). Interorganizational networks at the network level: A review of the empirical literature on whole networks. *Journal of Management, 33*(3), 479–516.

Provan, K. G., & Kenis, P. (2008). Modes of network governance: Structure, management, and effectiveness. *Journal of Public Administration Research and Theory, 18*(2), 229–252.

Provan, K. G., & Lemaire, R. H. (2012). Core concepts and key ideas for understanding public sector organizational networks: Using research to inform scholarship and practice. *Public Administration Review, 72*(5), 638–648.

Provan, K. G., & Milward, H. B. (1995). A preliminary theory of network effectiveness: A comparative study of four mental health systems. *Administrative Science Quarterly, 40*(1), 1–33.

Provan, K. G., & Milward, H. B. (2001). Do networks really work? A framework for evaluating public sector organizational networks. *Public Administration Review, 61*(4), 414–431.

Provan, K. G., Veazie, M. A., Staten, L. K., & Teufel-Shone, N. I. (2005). The use of social network analysis to strengthen community partnerships. *Public Administration Review, 65*(5), 603–613.

Robin, G. (2015). *Doing social network research: Network-based design for social scientists.* Thousand Oaks, CA: Sage Publications.

Romzek, B. S., LeRoux, K., & Blackmar, J. M. (2012). A preliminary theory of informal accountability among network organizational actors. *Public Administration Review, 72*(3), 442–453. doi:10.1111/j.1540-6210.2011.02547.x

Romzek, B. S., LeRoux, K., Johnston, J., Kempf, R. J., & Piatak, J. C. (2014). Informal accountability in multisector service delivery collaborations. *Journal of Public Administration Research and Theory, 24*(4), 813–842.

Scott, J. (2013). *Social network analysis.* Los Angeles, CA: Sage Publications.

Vangen, S., & Huxham, C. (2012). The tangled web: Unraveling the principle of common goals in collaborations. *Journal of Public Administration Research and Theory, 22*(4), 731–760.

Waugh, W. L. (2003). Terrorism, homeland security and the National Emergency Management Network. *Public Organization Review, 3*(4), 373–385.

Waugh Jr., W. L., & Streib, G. (2006). Collaboration and leadership for effective emergency management. *Public Administration Review, 66* (s1), 131–140.

Wasserman, S., & Faust, K. (1994). *Social network analysis: Methods and applications.* New York, NY: Cambridge University Press.

Yi, H., & Scholz, J. T. (2016). Policy networks in complex governance subsystems: Observing and comparing hyperlink, media, and partnership networks. *Policy Studies Journal, 44*(3), 248–279.

Additional Bibliographical Resources

Networks & Network Theory Bibliography (compiled by Kapucu). Retrieved from https://www.academia.edu/6159124/Network_bibliography_for_researchers

PARCC, Collaborative Governance Annotated Bibliography. Retrieved from www.maxwell.syr.edu/uploadedFiles/parcc/Research/Collaborative/2011%20PARC%20Collaboration-Annotated%20Bibliography.pdf

Schneider, V., et al. (2007). *Political networks- A structured bibliography.* Retrieved from www.uni-konstanz.de/FuF/Verwiss/Schneider/ePapers/PolNetw_StructBibliography.pdf

3 Network Types, Function, and Structures

Network research has gained momentum and network applications cover an increasingly wide array of policy domains and management issues, ranging from social services to environmental protection, to emergency management, and to regional economic and community development (Berry et al., 2004; Kapucu, Hu, & Khosa, 2014; Provan & Lemaire, 2012). Notwithstanding these advancements, it remains a relatively new field of inquiry that continues to face many challenges (Isett, Mergel, LeRoux, Mischen, & Rethemeyer, 2011). This chapter introduces the diverse types of networks and their function in public policy and public administration. This chapter addresses also informal and formal networks. Furthermore, it covers three types of networks—collaborative networks, policy networks, and governance networks, which are based on the foci of network research. This chapter then discusses the concept of network structures as it relates to network types, functions, and effectiveness. It concludes with a discussion of the challenges of network governance within an interorganizational context. In this chapter, we examine the following questions:

- How do we group networks into different categories?
- How do networks function in public policy and administration?
- How are formal networks different from informal networks?
- What are collaborative networks, policy networks, and governance networks?
- What are common network structures?
- What challenges does network governance face?

Types of Networks and Their Function in Public Policy and Administration

Interorganizational networks can be categorized into a variety of types based on different dimensions: purpose, function, formality, and domain.

Different Types of Interorganizational Networks

Networks can be grouped into four types based on their purpose: informational networks, developmental networks, outreach networks, and action networks (Agranoff, 2007). Within informational networks, organizations exchange information about policy issues, technologies, and potential solutions. Developmental networks go beyond information exchange and provide opportunities for member organizations to develop capacities to solve the issue. Outreach networks allow organizations to strategically make interorganizational adjustments, program activities, and design new programming solutions. Action networks involve joint action or service delivery.

Network Function

What a network can accomplish to fulfill its purpose.

Although the terms "network type" and "network function" are often used interchangeably, *network function* refers to what networks can accomplish, and network type refers to the form of networks (Popp, MacKean, Casebeer, Milward, & Lindstrom, 2014). Networks allow organizations share information, leverage and exchange resources, learn and distribute new knowledge, build capacity, facilitate collective action, solve problems, and provide services (Bingham & O'Leary, 2008; Koliba, Meek, & Zia, 2010; McGuire, 2006; Milward & Provan, 2006; Popp et al., 2014). Therefore, networks can function as information sharing networks, knowledge sharing networks, resource exchange networks, capacity building networks, and service provision networks (Milward & Provan, 2006; Popp et al., 2014). These types are discussed in the following paragraphs.

Information Sharing Networks

Information sharing is a crucial function that interorganizational networks can serve. Organizations utilize existing ties or build new connections to have access to useful information or distribute information in networks. For instance, an organization can reach out to central actors that are the source of key information or may contact an intermediate organization to get information from a disconnected organization. From a network perspective, a well-connected network fosters smooth communication processes and allows timely information exchange (Milward & Provan, 2006; Koliba et al., 2010).

Knowledge Sharing Networks

Knowledge sharing, distinct from information sharing, is another important function that networks serve. Knowledge is different from information as knowledge is informed by evidence and experience and applied in solving problems. Ties among organizations, whether at the interpersonal or interorganizational level, provide channels for organizations to exchange both tangible and tacit knowledge with one other (Huang, 2014). Knowledge sharing is a social process that requires the source's willingness to share, the knowledge recipient's willingness to learn, and the trust between the two parties (Huang, 2014; Rogers, 2003). Trust and strong ties encourage organizations to exchange knowledge. Furthermore, the relational context can also contribute to or accelerate the diffusion of knowledge in a network through different types of connections (Binz-Scharf, Lazer, & Mergel, 2012; Popp et al., 2014).

Resource Exchange Networks

Members in a network may leverage and exchange resources, such as human capital and financial resources. Organizations join the network with different assets and cultures. Resources are rarely shared or contributed equally among member organizations. Those organizations offering sufficient financial resources and staffing usually take on lead roles (Gazley, 2008; Koliba et al., 2010). Individual organizations may partner with others or make best use of resources through connections. Furthermore, interorganizational networks may mobilize different kinds of resources from individual organizations to accomplish network goals (Koliba et al., 2010).

Capacity Building Networks

Capacity building networks, both emergent or designed, focus on the development of social capital among member organizations and within communities (Milward & Provan, 2006). Mapping the relations among member organizations in a network can help communities to identify untapped or underused assets in the community. More importantly, the interactions among organizations promotes trust-building, strengthens community partnerships, and increases capacity to address community needs (Milward & Provan, 2006).

Service Provision Networks

Member organizations may form networks to act and solve specific management or policy problems. Service provision is one of the primary reasons that many networks are built (Huang, 2014). Interorganizational networks exist in a wide range of service domains, such as human and social services (Milward & Provan, 2003) and emergency management (Kapucu, 2006), to produce or deliver services.

Table 3.1 lists different types of networks. The ensuing sections will discuss other types of networks based on formality and research foci. The application chapters of the book will discuss different sets of networks based on their application domains.

Table 3.1 Types of Networks

Dimensions	Network types
Network purpose: What is the network's mission?	Informational networks, developmental networks, outreach networks, and action networks (Agranoff, 2007).
Network function: How does a network fulfill its purpose?	Information diffusion networks, resource exchange networks, capacity building networks, and service provision networks (Milward & Provan, 2006; Popp et al., 2014).
Network formality: How much structure does a network have built in?	Informal and formal networks (Isett et al., 2011;)
Network research foci: what is the central theme of the network research?	Public management networks/collaborative networks, policy networks, and governance networks (Berry et al., 2004; Isett et al., 2011; Kapucu et al., 2014; Lecy, Mergel, & Schmitz, 2014; Lewis, 2005)
Network application domains: In what domains are these networks applied?	Emergency management networks, economic development networks, social service networks, and so on (Kapucu et al., 2014)

Formal and Informal Networks

Definition and Importance of Formal and Informal networks

Network formality refers to how arrangements within networks can be formal or informal, depending on how networks are formed (Isett et al., 2011). *Formal networks* are built according to binding documents such as contracts or joint agreements, while *informal networks* emerge naturally when multiple players come together to solve problems or exchange information (Isett et al., 2011). Informal interorganizational networks are often built upon interpersonal interactions and do not have legally binding governance structure or formal authority (Isett et al., 2011; Lee, Feiock, & Lee, 2012; Siciliano, 2015). Despite the different origins of network formation, both formal networks and informal networks play important roles in public policy and administration. Most of existing service implementation networks are formally

Formal Network

Clearly defined network arrangements created by formal documents such as agreements and contracts. Also referred to as "designed" networks.

Informal Network

Naturally occurring groupings of actors, which are often built upon interpersonal interactions.

created, and these networks have established roles, rules, and structures that can enhance actors' commitment and contribute to networks' functional stability and effectiveness (Isett et al., 2011). For instance, a formal coordination network in emergency management is composed of organizations and their coordination ties. These organizations are defined by the emergency operation plans as either primary or support organizations for different emergency support functions (ESFs) (Hu, Knox, & Kapucu, 2014). These primary or support organizations are expected to coordinate with one another to implement ESFs. As shown in Figure 3.1, according to the National Response Framework (US Department of Homeland Security, 2016), the ESF coordinators for firefighting include the US forest service, the US Department of Agriculture (USDA), the US Department of Homeland Security (DHS), the Federal Emergency Management Agency (FEMA), and US Fire Administration. There are formal coordination ties among these organizations.

As Isett and her colleagues noted (2011), formal networks have been intensively examined, yet informal networks deserve more attention. Informal networks, compared with formal networks, have fewer clear structures and defined actor roles. Still, informal networks may encourage the growth of social capital and trust among member organizations. Furthermore, informal networks can serve as channels for organizations to share and exchange information, solve problems, and build capacity. In the long run, informal networks can foster the development of formal network ties among member organizations (Berardo & Scholz, 2010; Isett & Provan, 2005; Isett et al., 2011; LeRoux, Brandenburger, & Pandy, 2010).

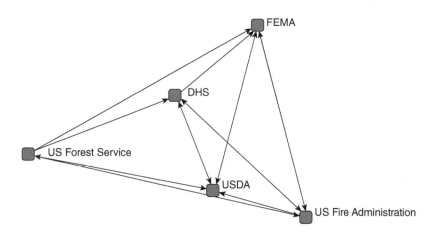

Figure 3.1 An Example of a Formal Affiliation Network Based on the National Response Framework

Informal network ties were found to contribute to the establishment of formal agreements on economic development among city governments (Hawkins, Hu, & Feiock, 2016). An example of informal networks is the network built among city officials in the Orlando Metropolitan area that discussed or shared information about economic development matters (e.g., Hawkins et al., 2016). Another example is "the network of practice"—the interpersonal knowledge sharing network among scientists working in public forensics laboratories, which promotes interorganizational knowledge diffusion (Binz-Scharf et al., 2012, p. 202). A study of the interpersonal advice networks among school teachers (Siciliano, 2015), also suggests that it is important for public mangers to understand the dynamics of informal networks in order to promote organizational learning and improve performance.

As there little systematic categorizing of informal networks in public administration literature, we borrowed literature from business management to illustrate the varieties of informal networks. Krackhardt and Hanson's (1993) seminal article "Informal networks: The company behind the chart" suggested that there are three types of informal networks: advice networks, trust networks, and communication networks. Advice networks identify key players within an organization on whom others rely to provide information and solve problems. The trust network exhibits trusting and reliable relationships between employees and helps to delineate which employees back each other in difficult situations. The communication network maps the regular work-related, two-way communications that take place between employees. To make best use of informal networks, managers should examine whether informal networks contribute to organizational goals and can adapt the formal organizational structure to complement the informal organizational structure (Krackhardt & Hanson, 1993).

Social Capital and Trust

The concepts of social capital and trust are important for understanding the value of informal and formal networks (Rethemeyer & Hatmaker, 2008; Edelenbos & Klijn, 2007; Willem & Lucidarme, 2014). Social capital is viewed as "attributes of individuals and of their relationships that enhance their ability to solve collective-action problems" (Ahn & Ostrom, 2008, p. 70); or, social capital can be defined as features of networks, and as "trust and norms of reciprocity which helps cement cooperative relationships" (Henry, Lubell, & McCoy, 2010, p. 420). Despite the caution against the dark side of social capital, scholars generally agree that "investments" in social relations produce benefits for both individual member organizations and networks (Provan & Lemaire, 2012).

Two forms of social capital have been intensively examined in organizational network research: bridging social capital and bonding social capital

(Burt, 1992, 2005; Halpern, 2005; Putnam, 2002). Bonding social capital refers to connections and resources within homogenous groups, and bridging social capital refers to ties that connect heterogeneous groups (Putnam, 2002). Bridging social capital is characterized by "weak ties" (Granovetter, 1973) while bonding social capital is characterized with intensive "strong ties" (Berardo & Scholz, 2010). Another type of social capital—linking social capital—refers to connections to individuals or organizations that have institutional power or authority (Woolcock, 1998). Scholars have examined social capital by studying the strengths of ties or describing the types of connections in a network (Shrestha, 2013). Other scholars have investigated how social capital reduces transaction costs, minimize collaboration risks, increases trust and commitment, and encourages coordination (Hawkins et al., 2016; Provan & Lemaire, 2012; Siegel, 2009).

Trust is a key factor in ensuring effective and successful collaboration, as member organizations face power differentials and resource imbalances (Edelenbos & Klijn, 2007). The concept of trust still lacks a comprehensive definition; yet, it is agreed upon that trust involves the trustee's willingness to accept vulnerability to someone in situations of risks and uncertainty (Luhmann, 1988). Trust is a multidimensional concept. There are multiple types of trust: companion trust, competence trust, and commitment trust (Newell & Swan, 2000). Companion trust is based on judgments of others' goodwill; competence trust is based on perceptions of others' skills and competencies to perform the tasks; and institutional trust is based on contractual agreements or institutional basis (Newell & Swan, 2000).

On the one hand, trust can grow from network relationships; on the other hand, trust can benefit network formation and development in multiple aspects. Trust can be developed through stable and frequent interactions within networks, and the use of network management strategies (Rethemeyer & Hatmaker, 2008; Edelenbos & Klijn, 2007; Klijn, Edelenbos, & Steijn, 2010). Through their relations based on trust, managers and boundary-spanners within networks keep networks stable and sustainable (Rethemeyer & Hatmaker, 2008). Existing trust among actors can foster information sharing, resource exchange, and interorganizational collaboration.

Collaborative Networks, Policy Networks, and Governance Networks

In a series of literature review articles (e.g., Berry et al., 2004; Isett et al., 2011; Kapucu et al., 2014; Lecy et al., 2014), scholars have highlighted that network research can be grouped into different research streams, depending on its foci and network application domains. For instance, Policy networks differ from public management networks or collaborative networks. Policy networks focus on ties among actors in specific policy arenas and their influence on policy outcomes, whereas public management networks or collaborative networks focus on network applications in public service delivery (Berry et al., 2004; Rethemeyer & Hatmaker, 2008). Later on, researchers added a third research stream—governance networks, which focus on coordination processes and structures to achieve common goals (Isett et al., 2011; Koliba et al., 2010). In what follows, we introduce three major streams and research topics published in public administration journals.

Collaborative Networks

Collaborative networks, also known as service implementation or public management networks, focus on the collaborative production and provision of public services (Berry et al., 2004; Isett et al., 2011; Kapucu et al., 2014). Actors in collaborative networks can be public agencies, nonprofit organizations, and businesses. The ties among organizations can range from information sharing to resource exchange, client referral, and joint services (Milward, Provan, Fish, Isett, & Huang, 2009). The goal of collaborative networks is to build or strengthen connections among service providers, improve service quality, and integrate service to better serve the public (Kapucu et al., 2014).

A community mental health network is an example of a collaborative network. In Arizona, the Division of Behavioral Health Services under the Department of Health Services contracted with either community-based organizations or private firms to deliver mental health services (Milward et al., 2009). Another example of collaborative network comes from the field of emergency management. Formal government documents, such as the National Response Frameworks, along with state and local comprehensive emergency management plans (CEMPs), establish the boundary of the collaborative emergency management network and define the formal emergency response network (Kapucu & Hu, 2016). Organizations in the network communicate and coordinate with one another to respond to emergency situations.

Policy Networks

Policy networks should be distinguished from other types of interorganizational networks because of their focus on policies, such as policy agenda, policy change and innovation, and policy making in resource allocation (Berry et al., 2004; Koliba et al., 2010; Isett et al., 2011). A policy network often includes government agencies, legislative offices, nonprofit advocacy organizations, private firms, and other stakeholder with interests in decision-making in a particular policy area (Isett et al., 2011). Policy theories and frameworks have been used to understand the formation and development of policy networks (Lubell, Scholz, Bernardo, & Robins, 2012), including but not limited to Institutional Analysis and Development framework (Ostrom, 1990; Lee, Feiock, & Lee, 2012), the ecology of games framework (Lubell, 2013), the

Advocacy Coalition Framework (Sabatier & Jenkins-Smith, 1993), and policy diffusion theory (Berry & Berry, 1990).

Policy networks can be examined at several levels: individual behaviors of citizens, politicians, and organizations the micro level, network structures at the meso level, and institutional arrangements at the macro level (Lubell et al., 2002, 2012). For instance, scholars have studied how actors seek their partners to protect regional estuaries (Robins, Bates, & Pattison, 2011), how local governments work with other governments and actors in the region to develop local economies (Hawkins et al., 2016); and how the structures of policy networks in the Swiss telecommunication industry evolved over two decades (Fischer, Ingold, Sciarini, & Varone, 2012).

Governance Networks

Organizations come together because they realize that working individually could not give them the best solution. Therefore, the essential aim of networking is to let all the actors coordinate and work for a common mission (Koliba et al., 2010; Mintzberg, 1979; Raab, Mannak, & Cambré, 2013). The foci in governance networks research are no longer on policies or services, but on the coordination processes and structures to achieve goals (Isett et al., 2011). For instance, studies on network effectiveness and governance structures have examined different forms of governance structures. Provan and Kenis (2008) suggested three types of network governance structures: participant-governed or shared governance (members of the network collectively govern the networks), governance by a lead organization (a lead organization in the network coordinate network-level decision-making and major activities), and governance by a network administrative organization (NAO). The proper form of governance structure depends on many factors such as the size and diversity of the network, and existing trust level in the network (Provan & Kenis, 2008). Compared with many studies on collaborative networks and policy networks, research on governance processes and structures remained limited (Kapucu et al., 2014).

Network Structure

Network structures refer to the characteristics and patterns of ties among network actors or nodes. Network structures should be distinguished from networks and networking (Keast, Mandell, Brown, & Woolcock, 2004), although these concepts are related. Networking often involves activities taken by nodes to make connections with other nodes. Networks consist of nodes and their connections. Network structures highlight the positioning of nodes in the network and the patterns of ties between nodes (Borgatti, Everett, & Johnson, 2013; Keast et al., 2004).

Network structures are influenced by key elements of a network, such as the number of nodes, the content and strengths of ties, and the positioning

Network Structures

The characteristics of ties and their patterns. It can depict individuals' position in a network in an ego-network, or describe the overall network structure and substructures in a whole network

of nodes, and the patterns of connections among nodes (Ahuja, Soda, & Zaheer, 2012). The number of nodes will influence the size of the network and possibility of tie formation. A node's location within a network matters because it determines the node' access to information and resources and power. Different roles that the actors play within the network can also relate to the type of capital that they draw upon or which capital that they contribute to the network. Ties are important components in the network structure because their content and strengths shape the overall structure of the network. Both actors and ties will influence the size and scope of the network structure (Hanneman & Riddle, 2005).

The Importance of Network Structures

Network structures differ from traditional organizational structures in that network structures rely more on the informal power (based on relations) rather than formal power, and the typical form of hierarchical power structure is no longer preeminent in network settings (Keast et al., 2004). Network structure is considered less hierarchical and more flexible (Keast et al., 2004). To form a network structure, member organizations need to realize the interdependency of their action and recognize the necessity of building a network structure to work together (Keast et al., 2004).

From an ego-network perspective, network structure can depict nodes' centrality and constraint (structural holes) (Ahuja et al., 2012). From a whole network perspective, network structure can describe the density, centralization, connectedness, and clustering of a network (Borgatti et al., 2013; Provan, Fish, & Sydow, 2007; Scott, 2013). In Chapter 2, we discussed the key network measures at both node, dyad, and network levels. Here, we illustrate network structures in the context of public administration and policy, focusing on a few key structural measures.

Key Measures of Network Structures

Network structures matters to public policy and administration because structural patterns influence network effectiveness, especially service provision and integration (Milward & Provan, 1998; Nowell, Steelman, Velez, & Yang, 2018; Provan & Milward, 1995; Raab et al., 2013; Shrestha, 2018; Yi, 2018). Network centralization and density have been used to describe network structures and examine their relationship with service integration (Milward & Provan, 1998; Provan & Milward, 1995). Compared with simply

counting the number of ties, the calculation of network density presents information about the proportion of ties that exists among all possible pairs of ties
(Borgatti et al., 2013). Figures 3.2a and b show two networks with different
levels of density. Compared with the network in Figure 3.2a, the network in
Figure 3.2b is denser, with more connections among nodes. Yet it should be
noted that it is relatively easy to build a dense network for a small network
than a larger one. Therefore, "average degree of the network" is often used
instead to measure "the average number of ties that each node has" (Borgatti
et al., 2013, p. 152).

Network centralization measures the extent to which a network is dominated by the connections of one or a few actors (Borgatti et al., 2013) or
the extent to which the network ties center around one or a few focal points
(Provan & Milward, 1995). Figures 3.3a and b show a centralized network
and a decentralized network. The centralized network in Figure 3.3a has
the center node dominating the network, while the decentralized network
(Figure 3.3b) does not center around one or a few key nodes. Interorganizational networks may have a centralized structure in which one or a few
organizations have many ties with others (Figure 3.3a), or a decentralized network structure in which connections are dispersed in the network

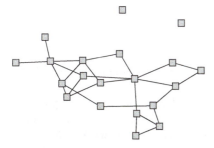
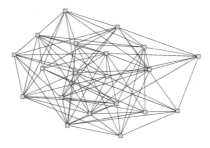

Figure 3.2a A Network With Low Density   *Figure 3.2b* A Network With High Density

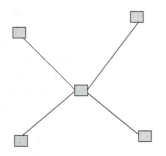
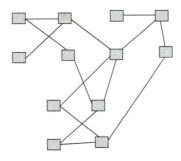

Figure 3.3a A Centralized Network   *Figure 3.3b* A Decentralized Network

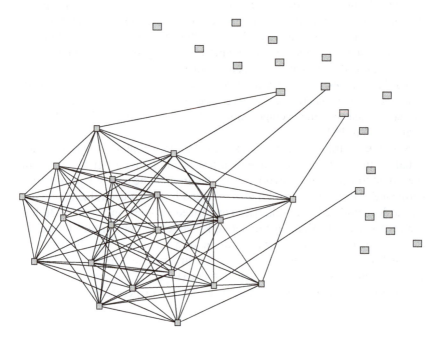

Figure 3.4 A Core-Periphery Network

(Figure 3.3b), or some type of structure in between such as the core-periphery structure (Figure 3.4).

The measures of network centralization and network density complement each other (Provan & Milward, 1995). Network density measures how network organizations are connected or how cohesive the network is. Network centralization measures whether network ties are organized around one or a particular group of organizations and reflects the power structure of the network (Provan & Milward, 1995). Network density itself might not enough to explain network effectiveness, as it might be difficult to coordinate agencies in a highly decentralized network even with dense connections (Provan & Milward, 1995). In a comparative study of four mental health systems, Provan and Milward suggested that a centralized system and a dense network may contribute to better service integration. In other words, a core agency can effectively coordinate a dense service network. A centralized structure allows the central agency to facilitate and coordinate the activities of member organizations in a service implementation network (Provan & Milward, 1995).

The relationship between network structures and network effectiveness is complex and contingent upon many other factors, such as the application domain (Provan & Milward, 1995; Raab et al., 2013). A central structure may facilitate coordination in a service implementation network; whereas in a disaster management context, a core-periphery structure might work more effectively (Nowell et al., 2018; Robinson, Eller, Gall, & Gerber, 2013). A network with a core-periphery structure has two types of nodes as shown in Figure 3.4: core nodes (represented by grey squares) and periphery nodes (denoted by rectangles) (Borgatti et al., 2013). Core nodes are well connected with each other and the other nodes in the network; whereas periphery nodes only have connections to core nodes. The nature of emergency situations requires that the response network needs to be able to quickly adapt to the environmental changes. On one hand, the incident command system requires a centralized command and control structure. On the other, emergency response organizations need to coordinate efforts with many government agencies at all levels and other organizations from all sectors. An adaptive core-periphery structure allows for both centralized coordination and flexibility for emergent coordination (Nowell et al., 2018)

Network closure and brokerage (Burt, 2005) are concepts used to describe network connectedness. "Weak ties," "brokerage," and "structural holes" are measures that are often used to measure network closure and brokerage. Structural holes refer to "the lack of a tie between two alters within an ego network" (Borgatti et al., 2013, p. 275). Having a closed network can encourage trust building and information sharing, whereas structural holes are important for organizations to access new ideas and innovate (Provan & Lemaire, 2012).

Researchers also used cliques to study the structure of networks (e.g., Milward & Provan, 1998; Kapucu & Demiroz, 2011). Cliques refer to the number of subgroups of three or more fully connected nodes (Borgatti et al., 2013). Clique analysis identifies the number of groups that are fully connected within a network. The organizations within the group are closely connected with one another, but the group is weakly connected with organizations outside the group (Provan, Veazie, Staten, & Teufel-Shone, 2005).

There are other measures to assess network structures, such as the fragmentation score, calculating "the proportion of pairs of nodes that are located in the same component" (Borgatti et al., 2013, p. 152); and clustering coefficient (a measure of bridging capital), measuring "the extent to which a network had areas of high and low density" (Borgatti et al., 2013). The structural characteristics also influence network performance, though studies on these network structures remain limited in public policy and administration.

Conclusion

In this chapter, we address different types of networks. Networks can be categorized into different types based on their purpose, function, formality, domain, and foci. Networks can serve a wide range of function, such as information sharing and resource sharing, knowledge sharing, capacity building, and service provision. Based on formality, there are formal and informal networks. Although most service implementation or collaborative networks are formal networks, informal networks are important for trust-building and the development of formal networks in the long run.

We discuss the importance of network structures. In addition, we introduce a few frequently used measures of network structures—density, centralization, closure—and discuss their relationship with network effectiveness. The chapter provides important information for the following chapters on power, accountability, performance, and network leadership. The following chapter discusses the design, formation, development, and sustainability of networks.

References

Agranoff, R. (2007). *Managing within networks: Adding value to public organizations.* Washington, DC: Georgetown University Press.

Agranoff, R., & McGuire, M. (2001). Big question in public management research. *Journal of Public Administration Research and Theory, 11*(3), 295–326.

Ahn, T. K., & Ostrom, E. (2008). Social capital and collective action. In D. Castiglione, J. van Deth, & G. Wolleb (Eds.), *The handbook of social capital* (pp. 70–100). Oxford, UK: Oxford University Press.

Ahuja, G., Soda, G., & Zaheer, A. (2012). The genesis and dynamics of organizational networks. *Organization Science, 23*(2), 434–448.

Berardo, R., & Scholz, J. T. (2010). Self-organizing policy networks: Risk, partner selection, and cooperation in estuaries. *American Journal of Political Science, 54*(3), 632–649.

Berry, F. S., & Berry, W. D. (1990). State lottery adoptions as policy innovations: An event history analysis. *American Political Science Review, 84*(2), 395–415.

Berry, F. S., Brower, R. S., Choi, S. O., Goa, W. X., Jang, H. S., Kwon, M., & Word, J. (2004). Three traditions of network research: What the public management research agenda can learn from other research communities. *Public Administration Review, 64*(5), 539–552.

Bingham, L. B., & O'Leary, R. (2008). *Big ideas in collaborative public management.* New York, NY: M. E. Sharpe.

Binz-Scharf, M. C., Lazer, D., & Mergel, I. (2012). Searching for answers networks of practice among public administrators. *The American Review of Public Administration, 42*(2), 202–225.

Borgatti, S. P., Everett, M. G., & Johnson, J. C. (2013). *Analyzing social networks.* Los Angeles, CA: Sage Publications.

Burt, R. S. (1992). *Structural holes: The social structure of competition.* Cambridge, MA: Harvard University Press.

Burt, R. S. (2005). *Brokerage and closure: An introduction to social capital.* New York, NY: Oxford University Press.

Edelenbos, J., & Klijn E-H. (2007). Trust in complex decision-making networks: A theoretical and empirical explanation. *Administration and Society, 39*(1), 25–50.

Fischer, M., Ingold, K., Sciarini, P., & Varone, F. (2012). Impacts of market liberalization on regulatory network: A longitudinal analysis of the Swiss telecommunications sector. *Policy Studies Journal, 40*(3), 435–457.

Gazley, B. (2008). Beyond the contract: The scope and nature of informal government—Nonprofit partnerships. *Public Administration Review, 68*(1), 141–154.

Granovetter, M. S. (1973). The strength of weak ties. *American Journal of Sociology, 78*(6), 1360–1380.

Halpern, D. (2005). *Social capital.* Malden, MA: Polity Press.

Hanneman, R. A., & Riddle, M. (2005). *Introduction to social network methods.* Riverside, CA: University of California, Riverside. Retrieved from http://faculty.ucr.edu/~hanneman

Hawkins, C., Hu, Q., & Feiock, R. (2016). Self-organizing governance of local economic development: Informal policy networks and regional institutions. *Journal of Urban Affairs, 48*(5), 643–660. doi:10.1111/juaf.12280

Henry, A. D., Lubell, M., & McCoy, M. (2010). Belief systems and social capital as drivers of policy network structure: The case of California regional planning. *Journal of Public Administration Research and Theory, 21*(3), 419–444.

Hu, Q., Knox, C. C., & Kapucu, N. (2014). What have we learned since September 11th? A network study of the Boston marathon bombings response. *Public Administration Review, 74*(6), 698–712.

Huang, K. (2014). Knowledge sharing in a third-party-governed health and human services network. *Public Administration Review, 74*(5), 587–598.

Isett, K. R., Mergel, I. A., LeRoux, K., Mischen, P. A., & Rethemeyer, R. K. (2011). Networks in public administration scholarship: Understanding where we are and where we need to go. *Journal of Public Administration Research and Theory, 21*(Suppl. 1), i157–i173.

Isett, K. R., & Provan, K. G. (2005). The evolution of dyadic interorganizational relationships in a network of publicly funded nonprofit agencies. *Journal of Public Administration Research and Theory, 15*(1), 149–165.

Kapucu, N. (2006). Interagency communication networks during emergencies boundary spanners in multiagency coordination. *The American Review of Public Administration, 36*(2), 207–225.

Kapucu, N., & Demiroz, F. (2011). Measuring performance for collaborative public management using network analysis methods and tools. *Public Performance and Management Review, 34*(4), 551–581.

Kapucu, N., & Hu, Q. (2016). Understanding multiplexity of collaborative emergency management networks. *The American Review of Public Administration, 46*(4), 399–417.

Kapucu, N., Hu, Q., & Khosa, S. (2014). The state of network research in public administration. *Administration & Society.* doi:10.1177/0095399714555752

Keast, R., Mandell, M. P., Brown, K., & Woolcock, G. (2004). Network structures: Working differently and changing expectations. *Public Administration Review, 64*(3), 363–371.

Klijn, E-H., Edelenbos, J., & Steijn, B. (2010). Trust in governance networks: Its impact on outcomes. *Administration & Society, 42*(2), 193–221.

Koliba, C., Meek, J. W., & Zia, A. (2010). *Governance networks in public administration and public policy*. Boca Raton, FL: CRC Press, Inc.

Krackhardt, D., & Hanson, J. R. (1993). Informal networks: The company behind the chart. *Harvard Business Review, 71*(4), 104–111.

Lecy, J. D., Mergel, J. A., & Schmitz, H. P. (2014). Networks in public administration: Current scholarship in review. *Pubic Management Review, 16*(5), 643–665.

Lee, I. W., Feiock, R. C., & Lee, Y. (2012). Competitors and cooperators: A micro-level analysis of regional economic development networks. *Public Administration Review, 72*(2), 253–262.

LeRoux, K., Brandenburger, P. W., & Pandy, S. K. (2010). Interlocal service cooperation in U.S. cities: A social network perspective. *Public Administration Review, 70*(2), 268–278.

Lewis, J. M. (2005). *Health policy and politics: Networks, ideas and power*. IP Communications. East Hawthorn, Victoria.

Lubell, M. (2013). Governing institutional complexity: The ecology of games framework. *Policy Studies Journal, 41*(3), 537–559.

Lubell, M., Schneider, M., Scholz, J. T., & Mete, M. (2002). Watershed partnerships and the emergence of collective action institutions. *American Journal of Political Science, 46*(1), 148–163.

Lubell, M., Scholz, J., Berardo, R., & Robins, G. (2012). Testing policy theory with statistical models of networks. *The Policy Studies Journal, 40*(3), 351–374.

Luhmann, N. (1988). Familiarity, confidence, trust: Problems and alternatives. In D. Gambetta (Ed.), *Trust: Making and breaking cooperative relations* (pp. 94–107). New York, NY: Blackwell.

McGuire, M. (2006). Collaborative public management: Assessing what we know and how we know it. *Public Administration Review, 66*(Suppl. 1), 33–43.

Milward, H. B., & Provan, K. G. (1998). Measuring network structure. *Public Administration, 76*(2), 387–407.

Milward, H. B., & Provan, K. G. (2003). Managing the hollow state: Collaboration and contracting. *Public Management Review, 5*(1), 1–18.

Milward, H. B., & Provan, K. G. (2006). *A manager's guide to choosing and using collaborative networks*. Retrieved from www.businessofgovernment.org/sites/default/files/CollaborativeNetworks.pdf

Milward, H. B., Provan, K. G., Fish, A., Isett, K. R., & Huang, K. (2009). Governance and collaboration: An evolutionary study of two mental health networks. *Journal of Public Administration Research and Theory, 20*(Suppl. 1), i125–i141.

Mintzberg, H. (1979). *The structuring of organizations: A synthesis of the research*. University of Illinois at Urbana-Champaign's Academy for Entrepreneurial Leadership Historical Research Reference in Entrepreneurship.

Newell, S., & Swan, J. (2000). Trust and inter-organizational networking. *Human Relations, 53*(10), 1287–1328.

Nowell, B., Steelman, T., Velez, A., & Yang, Z. (2018). The structure of effective governance of disaster response networks: Insights from the field. *American Review of Public Administration, 48*(7), 699–715.

Ostrom, E. (1990). *Governing the commons: The evolution of institutions for collective action*. New York, NY: Cambridge University Press.

Popp, J., MacKean, G., Casebeer, A., Milward, H. B., & Lindstrom, R. (2014). *Interorganizational networks: A review of the literature to inform practice*. Washington, DC: IBM Center for The Business of Government.

Provan, K. G., Fish, A., & Sydow, J. (2007). Interorganizational networks at the network level: A review of the empirical literature on whole networks. *Journal of Management, 33*(3), 479–516.

Provan, K. G., & Kenis, P. (2008). Modes of network governance: Structure, management, and effectiveness. *Journal of Public Administration Research and Theory, 18*(2), 229–252.

Provan, K. G., & Lemaire, R. H. (2012). Core concepts and key ideas for understanding public sector organizational networks: Using research to inform scholarship and practice. *Public Administration Review, 72*(5), 638–648.

Provan, K. G., & Milward, H. B. (1995). A preliminary theory of interorganizational network effectiveness: A comparative study of four community mental health systems. *Administrative Science Quarterly*, 1–33.

Provan, K. G., Veazie, M. A., Staten, L. K., & Teufel-Shone, N. I. (2005). The use of social network analysis to strengthen community partnerships. *Public Administration Review, 65*(5), 603–613.

Putnam, R. D. (2002). *Democracies in flux: The evolution of social capital in contemporary society*. New York, NY: Oxford University Press.

Raab, J., Mannak, R. S., & Cambré, B. (2013). Combining structure, governance, and context: A configurational approach to network effectiveness. *Journal of Public Administration Research and Theory*. doi:10.1093/jopart/mut039

Rethemeyer, R. K., & Hatmaker, D. M. (2008). Network management reconsidered: An inquiry into management of network structures in public sector service provision. *Journal of Public Administration Research and Theory, 18*(4), 617–647.

Robins, G., Bates, L., & Pattison, P. (2011). Network governance and environmental management: Conflict and cooperation. *Public Administration, 89*(4), 1293–1313.

Robinson, S. E., Eller, W. S., Gall, M., & Gerber, B. J. (2013). The core and periphery of emergency management networks: A multi-modal assessment of two evacuation-hosting networks from 2000 to 2009. *Public Management Review, 15*(3), 344–362.

Rogers, E. M. (2003). *Diffusion of innovations* (5th ed.). New York, NY: Free Press.

Sabatier, P. A., & Jenkins-Smith, H. C. (Eds.). (1993). *Policy change and learning: An advocacy coalition approach*. Boulder, CO: Westview Press.

Scott, J. (2013). *Social network analysis*. Los Angeles, CA: Sage Publications.

Shrestha, M. K. (2013). Internal versus external social capital and the success of community initiatives: A case of self-organizing collaborative governance in Nepal. *Public Administration Review, 73*(1), 154–164.

Shrestha, M. K. (2018). Network structure, strength of relationships, and communities' success in project implementation. *Public Administration Review, 78*(2), 284–294.

Siciliano, M. D. (2015). Advice networks in public organizations: The role of structure, internal competition, and individual attributes. *Public Administration Review*. doi:10.1111/puar.12362

Siegel, D. A. (2009). Social networks and collective action. *American Journal of Political Science, 53*(1), 122–138.

US Department of Homeland Security. (2016). National response framework. Retrieved from https://www.hsdl.org/?view&did=793551

Willem, A., & Lucidarme, S. (2014). Pitfalls and challenges for trust and effectiveness in collaborative networks. *Public Management Review, 16*(5), 733–760. doi:10.1080/14719037.2012.744426

Woolcock, M. (1998). Social capital and economic development: Toward a theoretical synthesis and policy framework. *Theory and Society, 27*(2), 151–208.

Yi, H. (2018). Network structure and governance performance: What makes a difference? *Public Administration Review, 78*(2), 195–205.

4 Network Formation, Development, Resilience and Sustainability, Demise, and Transformation

This chapter covers the evolution of networks, including formation, development, resilience, sustainability, demise, and transformation. It first addresses the driving factors in the success of network formation and then discusses how networks develop. It further illustrates what network resilience and sustainability mean and how networks may dissolve or transform into a different organizational format using learning opportunities from failed networks. The chapter provides information about the network evolution process and concludes with management and policy implications.

As highlighted in the earlier chapters of the book, networks are increasingly used to address complex social and policy problems. We do not know much about the life cycle of networks. Still, forming, designing, developing, and sustaining network arrangements remain a salient task for public managers. We live in a world of shared power and many groups and organizations are either involved in or affected by public problems.

In this chapter, we examine the following research questions:

- What are the key drivers, as well as success factors, of network formation and development?
- What are the core elements of network resilience and sustainability?
- What are some of the design principles in networks? What is(are) the appropriate role(s) for state actors and other participants (communities, nonprofits, and private sector)?
- Are the network relationships kept solely informal or formalized so that they are sustainable over time?

Factors of Success for Network Design and Formation

Networks can be designed or can emerge without any deliberate planning. We will first introduce the elements of designing an interorganizational network, then we discuss other drivers for *network formation* and success factors for effectiveness. Upon establishing the need to engage in a network arrangement, public managers must determine how to best design the network (Agranoff & McGuire, 2003; Goldsmith & Eggers, 2004; Popp,

Network Formation

The creation of the network. In this phase of the network's life-cycle, the mission and level of formality is decided.

MacKean, Casebeer, Milward, & Lindstrom, 2014). One of the tasks associated with designing a network is identifying what organizations and groups should join the network. Johnston, Hicks, Nan, & Auer (2011) argued that identifying which groups to include and the timing of their inclusion in the collaboration process pose a major challenge. Including too many stakeholders too quickly can cause difficulty in building trust and developing shared goals. On the other hand, if the inclusion process occurs too slowly, resources can become stretched thin and momentum may decline (Johnston et al., 2011).

Table 4.1 highlights the core elements of network design and formation. Based on a real need or agreed upon problem, identifying core actors for the network is crucial. Engaging in a deliberative planning process minimizes the chances of new participants destabilizing the collaborative process. Thoughtful inclusion of stakeholders and a deliberative planning process are important steps in designing collaborations, and if managed effectively, can reinforce trust, relationship building, commitment, and communication (Johnston et al., 2011). Once network participants are identified, public managers must work with them to develop shared purpose; consider tasks; identify "boundary spanning leaders" (i.e., the individuals that can help the collaboration; and establish collaborative structures and processes (Bryson, Crosby, & Stone, 2015).

Table 4.1 Key Elements of Network Design and Formation

Identifying core network participants	***Institutional and environmental factors***
• Thoughtful stakeholder inclusion	• Resource constraints
• Deliberative planning process	• Decision-making frameworks
• Deliberative needs assessment	• Sectoral failures
• Collective resources identification	• Formal mandates
	• High costs, high risks
Develop shared purpose	***Drivers and Motives***
• Network strategic planning	• General agreement on the problem
• Determine goals, activities, and tasks	• Interdependency
• Task-oriented design, core tasks and responsible organizations	• Prior network experience
	• Power dynamics among stakeholders
	• Vested interest in the issue or social problem
Identify "boundary spanning leaders"	***Approaches for partners selection***
Relational analytics	• Bottom-up or top-down
• Who knows what	• Informal or formal
• Who knows whom	• Ego-driven, alter-driven, non-extant
• Who has what resources	networks, failed networking

Deliberate design is not the only option for network formation. Networks sometime originate from failures and turbulent environments such as disasters, crises, and economic hardship (Bryson & Crosby, 2008; Bryson, Crosby, & Stone, 2006; Kapucu & Garayev, 2012). Collaboration often emerges when one sector fails to deliver public value to specific communities due to the weaknesses of that sector. This failure then triggers the need to seek other sectors or organizations that have special strengths and that can better address societal issues and problems. Moreover, for collaborations to be effective, they must minimize one another's weaknesses while drawing on one another's strengths (Bryson & Crosby, 2008).

There are a variety of institutional and environmental factors that result in organizations pursuing a collaboration. Such factors include, but are not limited to, resource constraints, legal mandates and decision-making frameworks, and sector failure (Bryson et al., 2015). Organizations may have different motives for building networks such as obtaining additional resources, generating better outcomes, or contributing to public value (Donahue & Zeckhauser, 2011). When organizations are faced with complex problems that can threaten their viability, the best alternative solution is to form networks with other organizations to create public value (Bryson et al., 2006).

For a network to form, potential collaborative partners must recognize their interdependence and perceive that they play a strategic role in addressing the problem at hand (Bryson et al., 2015; Powell, 1992). Another salient driver is prior relationships, or past collaborative experience, as it is through these previous engagements that network partners judge the trustworthiness and legitimacy of other partners. Both former and existing relationships are some of the most frequently identified factors influencing the formation of networks (Evans, Rosen, Kesten, & Moore, 2014). Similarly, Gulati and Gargiulo's (1999) analysis of interorganizational alliances in a sample of American, European, and Japanese businesses revealed that the likelihood of joining new alliances between organizations increases with their interdependence, prior mutual alliances, common third parties, and joint centrality.

Most of the successful network collaborations are bottom-up rather than top-down (Ingraham & Getha-Taylor, 2008). This perspective agrees with Bryson and Crosby (2008) as well as Vangen and Huxham (2003) that successful collaborations take time, require trust and relationship building, and must consider environmental factors. Motivation for partners, especially nonprofit organizations with limited resources and specific missions, comes from a desire to secure whatever resources are most scarce. This leaves nonprofit managers motivated by financial resources to a much greater extent than public managers, who in turn are more interested in accessing private sector skills and expertise (Gazley, 2008).

Selection and mobilization of members of a network are critical success factors. Ryu (2014) developed four scenarios of network partner selection:

ego-driven networking, alter-driven networking, failed networking, and non-extant networking. These four scenarios are developed on the bases of intention to network design and formation (Ryu, 2014). During ego-driven networking, the ego, which is the core partner, "assess itself as attractive networking partner for that candidate and attempts to activate networking with that candidate" (p. 637). Conversely, the alter-driven networking the ego does not perceive itself as attractive and does not attempt to activate networking with the other candidate (called alter), but the alter finds benefits and activate the network by contacting the ego. Failed networking occurs when the "candidate does not find any benefit in networking with the ego" (Ryu, 2014, p. 638) and in a lack of mutual agreement the network is not activated (Ryu, 2014). Lastly in the non-extant networking the networking is also not activated the ego is not perceived as attractive by itself and the candidate and therefore, there is no exchange. Alter driven networking and ego driven networking have the greatest success in forming networks (Ryu, 2014). The network design and formation phase can be considered as creation of the network phase. As the network's lifecycle, the mission and level of formality is decided in this phase, some opportunities can be discovered for network development as well.

Network Development

Network development centers on building necessary components to begin addressing shared problems with partner organizations and building relationships (Keast, Mandell, Brown, & Woolcock, 2004; Popp et al., 2014). This step is somehow similar to an organizational process in completing a project (Strauss, 1988). Several factors are relevant to the development and growth of networks, including but are not limited to, trust (Popp et al., 2014; Vangen & Huxham, 2003), power relations (Popp et al., 2014), readiness and skills of employees (Shaw, 2003), and the capacity of the lead organization (Evans et al., 2014).

> **Network Development**
>
> The phase of a network's lifecycle in which it undergoes active change. This can include adding new members, building trust among existing ones, deciding leadership roles, and more.

Literature consistently notes that the success of networks hinges upon the degree of trust among network participants. Another key factor that influences the development of a network or any interorganizational arrangement is the issue of power differences (Popp et al., 2014; Vangen & Huxham, 2003) (see Chapter 7 for power imbalance issues related to network governance). Efforts need to be made to ensure that the lead organization in the network is not dominant and includes smaller actors in the decision-making process to avoid co-option by more powerful actors (Table 4.2). Researchers

Table 4.2 Key Elements of Network Development

Addressing shared issues and concerns
- Building consensus, shared goals, and expectations
- Continuously articulate the values, purpose, and goals of the network

Network governance and structure
- Formal and informal governance mechanism
- Decentralized focused or centralization focused decision-making structure

Network Process
- Building and sustaining trust
- Conflict management strategies
- Mitigating potential risk
- Building legitimacy and accountability

Collaboration Model
- Collaborative contracts
- Capacity building
- Community building

Address power imbalances
- Avoid co-option by more powerful actors
- Shared, inclusive decision-making

Building network capacity
- Lead (administrative) organization
- Collaborators
- Formal and informal leadership

---

underscored the need for the lead organization to develop the interorganizational arrangement: "unless the lead organization leaders can articulate the values, purpose, and goals of the effort in terms understandable and compelling to their staff and the broader community, people may view the effort with confusion, cynicism or even suspicion" (Evans et al., 2014, p. 10).

In developing networks, informal horizontal networks may institutionalize and begin to resemble a hierarchical structured network. In the network development phase, building and sustaining trust, dealing with power differentiation, building consensus, mitigating potential risks, and building legitimacy and accountability are critical elements. These are discussed in the following chapters in detail, but their role and importance are discussed briefly in the following.

Networks are developed to address shared concerns about societal and policy problems. As part of network development, building consensus, collectively identifying shared goals and expectations among participant network members or stakeholders are central. One of the most critical elements at this stage is trust. Trust is imperative and there are numerous ways to build that trust within collaborations. Trust is both an antecedent to and a result of successful collective action. Furthermore, trust can also be utilized to reduce risk, but trust also requires risk. Trust is the key to build resilience and sustainability in relationships between actors (Vangen & Huxham, 2003). To build trust, practitioners can ensure they have clarity of purpose and objectives, deal with power differences, maintain leadership without allowing for takeovers, allow time to build understanding, share a fair workload, resolve different levels of commitment, equal ownership and no point scoring, and accept the fact that partnerships evolve over time.

Network governance structure, such as formal and informal mechanisms and centralized or decentralized decision-making models, need to be addressed by the network participants as well. The structure of a network "is influenced by environmental factors such as system stability and the collaboration's strategic purpose" (Bryson et al., 2006, p. 49). It is important to understand that the structure is likely to change over time because of uncertainty of membership and complexity in the environment. The structure within the collaboration will influence the overall effectiveness of the network as will both formal and informal governing structure and mechanism (see Chapter 3 for detailed discussion on network types and structures). Whether or not agencies can work together can be approached from the perspective of the network structure itself, or from the process to accomplish the network goals. The design of the decision-making network structure suggests two approaches: one would require an examination of the role of the individual facilitator (lead organization or network administrative organization) to help create a sense of community and shared commitment across the organizations.

Different elements of network process can play important role in developing networks. Careful process discussion needs to be linked to the broader goals of the network. If the process is disconnected from the shared network goals, it will be difficult to develop an effective network arrangement. The process might include building and sustaining trust, identifying conflict management strategies, mitigating potential risk, building legitimacy and accountability mechanism. By focusing on the individual organizations, one can look at every partner agency in the network and find ways to build commitment and ownership to reduce anxiety and ensure and build consensus. The second approach emphasizes centralization, in that key collaborative members, that everyone trusts, would be the ones who make the decisions. Benefits of this include efficiency and effectiveness. Flexibility and openness to trial and error are key when designing the structure. This can only happen with the requisite level of trust, but obstacles can still occur. It is necessary to join resources and systems of responsibility, with an understanding of the core cultural elements of the organization (Grubbs, 2000; Kapucu & Garayev, 2012). The structure of network governance is dependent upon the types of the network. Therefore, it is useful to distinguish between homogeneous and heterogeneous networks (Coffé & Geys, 2007). Homogenous networks are closed networks with a bonding social capital and heterogeneous networks are crosscutting or overlapping network with bridging social capital. An example of bridging association is the Red Cross which connects organizations and communities in serving others while hobby associations and retired people groups are more of bonding associations established based on strong level of social capital and friendship (Coffé & Geys, 2007).

Different collaboration models can be included in network development discussions. The model can highlight contracts, capacity, and community building. When discussing models of collaborations based on the "financial resources, nonfinancial resources (knowledge exchange), sharing of staff, organizational-based rewards, and service community rewards" (Sowa, 2008, p. 308), Sowa developed three models of collaboration. Namely, shallow- collaborative contracts, medium- capacity building collaboration and deep- community building collaborations. An example of shallow collaboration is cooperation between two organizations that is a function of a contract and does not include ongoing interaction. In this shallow collaboration, the financial resources are shared and there is a little interaction in producing the services. With capacity building collaborations, or medium collaboration, in addition to financial resources, there is "exchange of human resources, including staff and professional development resources that build the capacity of the organization" (Sowa, 2008, p. 311). The community-building collaborations, or deep collaborations, are similar to capacity-building collaborations where the lead organization receives additional benefits (Sowa, 2008). As collaborations "can have differential impacts on the organizations involved in the delivery of services and on the broader community in which the services are being provided" (Sowa, 2008, p. 320), the modes of networks and structure become crucial.

As discussed in detail in chapter seven, members of a network do not bring same level of power and resources to the table. Addressing power imbalances to avoid co-option by more powerful actors in the network and developing a shared and inclusive decision-making model will facilitate effective network development. Accountability in hierarchical settings aims to control and constrain behaviors, however, if implemented in networks it can hamper efficient exchanges (Wachhaus, 2011). Accountability systems allow the collaborators to track inputs, processes, and outcomes by utilizing various methods for gathering, interpreting, and using data. In turn, these results will allow the managers to build strong relationships with key political and professional constituencies (Bryson et al., 2006). The benefits of these organizational outcomes include commitment justification, work flexibility, collective organization, and intellectual capital. Costs include maintenance costs, foregone innovation, and institutionalized power within interorganizational network (Leana & Van Buren, 1999). In order to provide a holistic framework to understand network structures and relationships social network analysis can be used, as described in Chapter 3 (Cross, Borgatti, & Parker, 2002).

Building network capacity needs to be addressed as part of network development. This might include identification or working with a lead or network administrative organization, collaboration for increased network capacity and collective impact, and formal and informal leadership opportunities. Cross-sector collaborations are more likely to succeed if they utilize committed sponsors at many levels within the network to provide both formal and informal leadership. Furthermore, both internal and external stakeholders need to be included to legitimize the collaboration and organize it in such a way that it fosters trusted interaction among members (Bryson et al., 2006, 2015). It is important to utilize resources and tactics to equalize power and manage conflict, as conflict is common in all types of partnerships and collaborations. It is crucial to the success of collaborations to be forward thinking and employ deliberate planning. This is stressed in mandated partnerships. Non-mandated partnerships go a step further and focus on emergent planning. It is also important to utilize the process to foster trust and allows collaboration to grow by building on the specializations of the collaborators in the network (Bryson et al., 2006).

Network Resilience and Sustainability

Network resilience and sustainability are closely aligned with network effectiveness, network learning and adaptation (Popp et al., 2014; Provan, Beagles, & Leischow, 2011; Provan & Kenis, 2007). The concept of resilience has become a key term in many disciplines without a clear definition or identified core elements. There is substantial literature on resilience related to environmental sustainability, health, and disaster management. Based on the classic definition of resilience, "the capacity to cope with unanticipated dangers after they have become manifest, learning to bounce back" (Wildavsky, 1988, p. 77), we define *network resilience* as the capacity of a network to retain and adjust its form, structure, and functionality despite disruptions. Scholarship on

Network Resilience

The capacity of a network arrangement to resist system shocks and external factors.

Network Sustainability

The ability of an arrangement to function in the face of external and internal challenges until a goal is met.

network resilience is only beginning to emerge. From a network perspective, well connectedness refers to resilience. Removing one or some organizational nodes will not (and should not) lead to a network collapse. This will be especially the case if network administrative organization or lead organization is well connected with other members of the network. *Network sustainability* refers to ability of a network arrangement to function, mobilizing resources and building capacity to achieve a network goal, in the face of external and internal challenges. Key elements of network development discussed earlier are important for network resilience and sustainability as well. In this section of the chapter we highlight some elements of network resilience and sustainability. Elements of network resilience and sustainability are listed in Table 4.3.

Table 4.3 Elements of Network Resilience and Sustainability

Legitimacy and Accountability
- High level of trust
- Internal legitimacy
- External legitimacy

Mitigating potential conflicts and tensions
- Power imbalance
- Competing logics
- Autonomy versus interdependency
- Disagreement on problem severity, strategies, and tactics

Network manager/leader capacity
- Embrace substantive and strategic complexity
- Understand diversity
- Monitor and understand existing relationships
- Evaluate and motivate participants

Flexibility in thinking
- Abductive thinking
- Encourage imagination
- Openness to innovation
- Creativity

Developing a collaborative platform
- Cohesion
- Inclusiveness
- Network learning and adaptation

Evaluating networks
- Formal and informal
- Micro and macro

Key Elements of Network Resilience and Sustainability

Research, relatively new and limited, highlights the importance of legitimacy for both network resilience and sustainability. When cross-sector collaborations build on individuals' and organizations' self-interests and strengths, as well as finding ways to minimize, overcome, or compensate for weaknesses, they are more likely to create public value (Bryson et al., 2006). In addition, by maintaining resilience and engaging in regular reassessments, these collaborations can continue to add public value. Ties in the network affect the network outcomes as well. Findings from product development projects indicate that weak inter-unit ties are beneficial for searching for knowledge in other subunits; however, these weak ties negatively affect the transfer of complex knowledge across networks (Hansen, 1999, p. 829).

Internal and external legitimacy and appropriate accountability mechanisms of a network will help build a high level of trust. Legitimacy plays a crucial role, especially during crisis (Popp et al., 2014). Network leaders should place equal importance for internal legitimacy (relationship and trust building within the network) and external legitimacy (relationship and trust building with external stakeholders and perception of the value of the network). Both are critical for resilience and sustainability. This will be especially critical for emergent networks that lack clear guidance, policy, or mandate.

To build network resilience and sustainability, it is critical for leaders and all stakeholders to mitigate potential conflicts and tensions related to power imbalance, competing logics, culture, autonomy versus interdependency in the network, and disagreement on problem severity, strategies, and tactics.

Network resilience and sustainability requires leadership and managerial capacity to embrace substantive and strategic complexity, understanding diversity, monitoring and understand existing relationships, and evaluating and motivating participants. Gazley (2008) explained the nuances of collaboration hinging on leadership and managerial choices with embedded organizational and environmental characteristics. The resilience of a collaboration depends on the motivation of the individuals included. In cross-sector collaborations, it is important for managerial staff to understand the diverse motivations within a group, as that affects the outcome (Bryson et al., 2006).

Cohesion and inclusiveness in a network are required for resilience (Grubbs, 2000). The potential for a network to be sustainable and resilient depends on its inception and ability to create cohesion as "[c]ohesiveness amplifies trust and diminishes the uncertainty associated with future partnerships" (Gulati & Gargiulo, 1999, p. 1446). In addition to cohesion and shared goal creation, all "stakeholders must feel secure that all involved in the process have equal opportunity to influence the decisions made" (Johnston et al., 2011, p. 2). The process of building trust and creating cohesiveness and understanding adds to the ability for a collaboration to be more resilient during difficult situations. To assist in persevering through struggles, groups must engage conflict in a positive way. It is imperative for network resilience, "[a]s groups try to agree on the nature of the problem that concerns them, issues are likely to revolve around convening and inclusion; as they debate the direction they should take . . . collaborators [should] use their resources to put all participants on a more equal footing" (Bryson et al., 2006, p. 48).

Flexibility in thinking, including abductive thinking (also called sense making), imagination, openness to innovation, creativity, and ongoing learning are useful for network resilience and sustainability. Bryson et al. (2015) noted that ongoing learning, along with developing accountability mechanisms, can result in more sustainable and resilient cross-sector collaborations. They also suggested that in order to sustain a network, public managers must be able to address the endemic conflicts and tensions that are likely to occur at some point during a cross-sector collaboration. Conflicts and tensions usually involve power imbalances, competing logics, struggles between autonomy and interdependence, disagreement on problem severity, as well as the strategies and tactics used to address the shared problem (Bryson et al., 2015). Klijn and Koppenjan (2015) suggested that the sustainability of networks is related to public managers capacity to manage both substantive (e.g., differences in perceptions of the nature of the problem) and strategic complexity (e.g., the differences in perceptions, objectives, and strategies of interdependent actors).

Developing a collaborative platform with cohesion, inclusiveness, and network learning and adaptation is another critical element of network resilience and sustainability. Public managers must understand that collaborative partners will have distinct interpretations based on their personal experiences, culture, and influences. If collaborative leaders neglect this diversity, they may lose a valuable opportunity to extend the interorganizational arrangement and reach the shared goal (Grubbs, 2000). Partners in the network must be flexible in their thinking and allow themselves to view public issues in new ways to identify innovative collective solutions.

Collaborations can be better sustained when they are a part of an intentionally created collaborative platform, according to Ansell and Gash (2018). A collaborative platform is defined as "an organization or program dedicated with competencies, institutions, and resources for facilitating the creation, adaptation and success of multiple or ongoing collaborative projects of networks" (Ansell & Gash, 2018, p. 20). The reason collaboration might be better sustained when they are part of a collaborative platform is that they can learn, adapt, and create synergy among participant organizations. The collaborative platform is expected to contribute cohesion among participant actors, inclusive opportunities, and potentially a network learning for a better outcome. The platform can be in person as well as virtual as discussed in Chapter 13.

Ongoing evaluation of networks, in terms of formal and informal elements, as well as micro (ego-network) and macro (whole-network) perspectives, is critical for resilience and sustainability. Although using theories and concepts and diagnostic tools can lead to greater understanding of network dynamics, there is no perfect avenue for knowing how a network will react to difficult situations or external forces. To understand resilience of a network we need to have a comprehensive understanding of the complex relationships which exist within a network and its environment. This is a challenging endeavor. However, understanding network dynamics allows for public administrators to obtain more beneficial outcomes from network arrangements.

In addition to understanding conceptual importance of cohesion and inclusive structure for resilience, social network analysis can provide a better understanding of the strengths and power relationships within the network. The formation of relationships and the choices leading to organization within a network can deepen the understanding of relationships and how the network will be influenced by those relationships and the structure (Morel & Ramanujam, 1999). Social network analysis has been shown to be effective in "promoting effective collaboration within a strategically important group; supporting critical junctures in networks that cross-functional, hierarchical, or geographic boundaries; and ensuring integration within groups following strategic restructuring initiatives" (Cross et al., 2002, p. 28). Later chapters include specific use of social network analysis in studying networks.

How Networks Are Sustained?

Examining the micro aspect of networks is as important as the macro aspect for network resilience and sustainability. It is important to pay attention to those actors that are part of the network and dynamics involved in keeping them motivated to make the network successful (Leana & Van Buren, 1999). A high level of social capital relates actors to each other, generating value in the network. We do discuss the importance of institutionalizing these informal networks for sustainable network arrangements. Trust, probably more than any other factor, has been repeatedly discussed in the literature because of its importance in network development, resilience, and sustainability. It is also critical for its potential role in addressing power differentiation in networks (Johnston et al., 2011; Leana & Van Buren, 1999; Vangen & Huxham, 2003).

The decision-making process for selecting members of a network is important to reduce risk exposure and to increase trust and commitment (Johnston et al., 2011). Evaluating and motivating the participating actors when cross-sector collaboration is involved is necessary. Clear rules should be in place to clarify expectations and measures of progress should be take place within and across boundaries for sustained network relations as well (Ingraham & Getha-Taylor, 2008). Staff-related issues need to be discussed for the sake of network sustainability. Employees may only select the behaviors and actions that will lead them to higher pay. Instead, behaviors connected to the outcomes of the collaboration are a better way to evaluate performance. To recognize and reward employees' successful performance is important in motivating them to continue the success they contributed to the collaboration process (Ingraham & Getha-Taylor, 2008). Flexible working schedules are an example of such a reward. However, the focus on managing networks for results will undermine that network's potential for sustainability since there is no reason to continue the network arrangements once the collaboration goals are met (Page, 2008).

Creation of public value is often associated with sustainable collaboration linked to external legitimacy. "The more value created through collaboration, the greater the likelihood of its sustainability because with value comes commitment and with commitment, continued existence" (Thomson, Perry, & Miller, 2008, p. 103). Network managers should monitor the external environment and internal relationships to maintain network resilience and sustainability. Balancing the proper relationships at the beginning of the network formation help sustain the networks over time.

Figure 4.1 encompasses what the key aspects of design, formation, resilience, and sustaining networks are. The core elements included in the figure are discussed in detail in the earlier sections of the chapter. Efforts might differ from context to context, but there is substantial planning and work that goes into ensuring that any collaboration efforts become successful ones over

Formulation Why networks arise	Development How networks evolve	Sustainability and Resilience How networks survive
• Naturally emergent or deliberately designed • Previous failure by sector • Resource dependency • Preexisting relationships between organizations • Sudden change in external circumstances • Old networks are transformed to suit new purpose	• Power imbalance and tensions • Level of formality • Institutionalizing processes • Building legitimacy and public value • Social capital and trust • Unique solutions • Adding and losing members • Formation of informal and formal leadership roles	• Committed leaders using consensus-based decision-making • Continuous building of legitimacy and trust • Stakeholder analysis and use of specializations • Build in resources to adapt to shock • Evaluations based on quality planning, purge weak links

Network managers build relationships and trust, maintain expectations and open minds, and remain aware that competing logics are likely

Figure 4.1 Network Design, Formation, Resilience, and Sustainability

time. The forming of collaborations involves grasping a correct understanding of the initial conditions that preface a network of organizations. The process within networks requires forward thinking, inclusion, and willingness to collaborate and the structure needs to be built for network to succeed. It is imperative that any constraints and possible issues that could arise from the collaboration are analyzed, with possible solutions in place. All of these factors affect the outcomes of the networks. Thus, it is crucial that appropriate accountability systems and evaluation are in place. All aforementioned issues and viewpoints such as trust, development, and motivation impact the way networks and collaborations function and how likely they are to succeed and sustained over time.

Networks' Demise and Transformation

Networks demise and transformation are not widely addressed in the literature. Networks are usually formed in response to a complex public policy or social problems. If the nature of the problem changes or the needs of the network change, what is the next step? A network's life cycle might be different and probably shorter than that of the members of the organization in the network. If there is no need, the network can be dissolved or transformed to something different. The demise of a network and/or transformation of it is different from network failure. Unfortunately, there is no substantial research in addressing both network demise and failure. We believe that we can learn substantially from failed or transformed networks as we learn from the successful ones.

Many reasons can lead to the demise or transformation of a network: The network may have produced its maximum value, solved the issue that caused the network to form, the network might need to reconsider its added value or external legitimacy, or may not be resilience to external pressures, or the network's vision may become invalided (Popp et al., 2014). There are different types of networks. If network administrative organization successfully completed its function, the structure might be changed, and the network administrative organization can leave the network. This is considered one of the examples of network transformation. In response to Hurricane Maria, for example, a one-stop shop was established at Orlando International Airport in partnership with government agencies, the private sector, nonprofit organizations, and other community organizations. After the need was fulfilled and service coordination was accomplished, the network was dissolved, and the organizations continued performing their own functions after successfully serving to the people impacted from the hurricane. Of course, this was deliberate decision to dissolve the network, as it was not needed any longer is not considered a failure.

Why Do Networks Fail?

As with planning or organizing anything, it is always important to prepare for worse case scenarios. In the instance of collaborations, one must be aware of any contingencies or possible constraints. For example, collaborations that involve system-level planning are likely to consist of negotiation, followed by collaborations focused on administrative-level partnerships and service delivery partnerships. Additionally, it is important to plan for issues that would arise due to power imbalances and shocks. Lastly, because of competing institutional logics, the process, structure, governance, and desired outcomes of a collaboration can be significantly influenced (Bryson et al., 2006).

In addition to constraints from organizational and network logistical standpoints, there are three P's of discretion to be aware of. The three P's are production, payoff, and preference discretion. This essentially involves ensuring that the partners in the collaborative network benefit from the collaboration in certain ways. While collaboration may not be 100 percent effective, it can prove to be much better than stand-alone government, simple contracting, or conventional philanthropy (Donahue & Zeckhauser, 2011). Networks often are innovative and flexible. However, innovation in networks is threatened by uncertainty and lack of institutionalization (O'Toole, 1997). Weak institutionalization can also negatively affect the trust, which is crucial for networks' success and effectiveness (O'Toole, 1997). Therefore, uncertainty and lack of institutionalization are other potential constraints for networks or potential reasons for collapse (Weick, 2005).

No one likes to see a formed network to fail. However, network functions will cease if there is no need for it or it cannot meet the vision laid out at the formation and development phase. It is hard to predict exactly, but when the managers and leaders dissolve the network, it can continue its impact in an informal form to wield knowledge and expertise. It can also be annihilated or transformed into a different form. Regardless of the outcome, we can learn from the failed networks as highlighted briefly in the next section.

Lessons Learned From Failed Networks

Looking at failed networks, we see that organizations join networks for a variety of reasons. Oftentimes, organizations can engage in them without realizing the possible risks involved. It is imperative that invested parties understand where certain boundary tensions lie. The main boundary tensions include differing mission, resources, capacity, responsibility, and accountability (Kettl, 2006). Additionally, collaborations can be limiting if they fail to understand the motivation behind the collaboration for all parties involved, as well as the internal and external factors within the organizations themselves. It is important to establish common ground with set boundaries to provide a proper balance of both a vertical and horizontal structure. One of the major lessons learned in terms of failing networks or a failure to "connect the dots" was a lack of coordination among intelligence agencies before the September 11, 2001, terrorist attacks in New York City and Washington, DC (Weick, 2005). The failure in coordination led to the creation of the Department of Homeland Security (DHS). DHS is one of the largest federal department created after creation of Department of Defense. The DHS aims to facilitate core homeland security initiatives in the United States.

Network Evolution and Implications for Practice

Research on evolution of networks in the public sector is limited. Case-based follow up research in network evolution, or theoretical and empirical research on evolving structure on network performance would be useful to have in greater quantity. Ahuja, Soda, and Zaheer (2012) pointed out that understanding of network outcomes from practical and scholarly perspectives is "incomplete and potentially flawed without an appreciation of the genesis and evolution of the underlying network structures" (p. 434). Some of the factors we discussed earlier in terms of network formation and development might impact the structure of a network and potentially outcomes of a network arrangements.

In order to avoid breakdowns in cross-sector collaborations, four main suggestions are made: require consensus regarding goals and processes, cut weak links out of the network, have group consensus in voting out weak links, and evaluate based on quality of the planning, rather than milestones (Johnston et al., 2011). The inclusion of the aforementioned propositions and the exclusion of elements that will bring about breakdowns are essential to successful collaborative networks. Maintaining trust and keeping an open mind throughout the conflicts that are likely to arise are key to a good collaboration. Staying the course, keeping goals in mind and working through conflict are the way successful collaborations materialize. It is important to note that each of components involved in creating a network build on each other. If the organizations involved do not understand the reason for engaging into collaboration, it will be very difficult to create an effective process and structure. Furthermore, open and transparent communication will influence motives, conflict, and responsibilities. This is imperative in order to establish trust. While trust can reduce the risk involved, it also requires risk. Therefore, it can be concluded that by engaging in open communication throughout the process the likelihood of creating a successful collaboration increases.

The following practices may be beneficial in promoting network evolution, and hopefully a network transformation: successful, visionary, flexible leadership; proactive and situational awareness; strong committeemen to network value creation or co-creation; strong relationship building and maintenance; systematic network strategic planning; identifying the key transition plan and communicating effectively; actor involvement for internal legitimacy and stakeholder engagement for external legitimacy; respect to partnership and expertise; vision for new opportunities for the network and stakeholder engagement at every stages; and finally management and leadership support from lead agency or network administrative organization (Popp et al., 2014). More research needs to be conducted on understanding network transformation and demise and their impact on both organizational members and the broader network.

Conclusion

This chapter suggests that there are several considerations public managers must take into account when forming, designing, developing, and sustaining interorganizational arrangements. The chapter provided the elements and tasks public managers must consider when forming, developing, designing, and sustaining a network arrangement. Network managers aim for some stability at the core of the networks but also maintain some flexibility to learn from others for network resilience, adaptation, and sustainability.

Network governance is not the solution to all the problems that societies and organizations face. The decision to be involved in a collaborative process should be carefully studied considering the positive and negative aspects mentioned in the chapter. If carefully analyzed and planned, network governance can create public value for the community, network, and organizations involved. Network governance requires balancing critical needs and goals of the organizations and the network. The formation, development, and sustainability of networks require careful facilitation by (public) network managers and leaders. Network management and leadership require continued fostering of relationships from the design, formation, and development of networks, which is the topic of the following chapter.

References

Agranoff, R., & McGuire, M. (2003). *Collaborative public management: New strategies for local governments*. Washington, DC: Georgetown University Press.

Ahuja, G., Soda, G., & Zaheer, A. (2012). The genesis and dynamics of organizational networks. *Organization Science, 23*(2), 434–448.

Ansell, C., & Gash, A. (2018). Collaborative platforms as a governance strategy. *Journal of Public Administration Research and Theory, 28*(1), 16–32.

Bryson, J. M., & Crosby, B. C. (2008). Failing into cross-sector collaboration successfully. In L. B. Bingham & R. O'Leary (Eds.), *Big ideas in collaborative public management* (pp. 36–54). Armonk, NY: M. E. Sharpe.

Bryson, J. M., Crosby, B. C., & Stone, M. M. (2006). The design and implementation of cross-sector collaborations: Propositions from the literature. *Public Administration Review, 66*(1), 44–55.

Bryson, J. M., Crosby, B. C., & Stone, M. M. (2015). Designing and implementing cross-sector collaborations: Needed and challenging. *Public Administration Review, 75*(5), 647–663.

Coffé, H., & Geys, B. (2007). Toward an empirical characterization of bridging and bonding social capital. *Nonprofit and Voluntary Sector Quarterly, 36*(1), 121–139.

Cross, R., Borgatti, S. P., & Parker, A. (2002). Making invisible work visible: Using social network analysis to support strategic collaboration. *California Management Review, 44*(2), 25–46.

Donahue, J. D., & Zeckhauser, R. J. (2011). *Collaborative governance: Private roles for public goals in turbulent times*. Princeton, NJ: Princeton University Press.

Evans, S. D., Rosen, A., Kesten, S. M., & Moore, W. (2014). Miami thrives: Weaving a poverty reduction network. *American Journal of Community Psychology, 53*(3), 357–368.

Gazley, B. (2008). Intersectoral collaboration and the motivation to collaborate toward an integrated theory. In L. B. Bingham & R. O'Leary (Eds.), *Big ideas in collaborative public management* (pp. 36–54). Armonk, NY: M. E. Sharpe.

Goldsmith, S., & Eggers, W. D. (2004). *Governing by network: The new shape of the public sector*. Washington, DC: Brookings.

Grubbs, J. W. (2000). Can agencies work together? Collaboration in public and nonprofit organizations. *Public Administration Review, 60*(3), 275–280.

Gulati, R., & Gargiulo, M. (1999). Where do interorganizational networks come from? *American Journal of Sociology, 104*(5), 1439–1493.

Hansen, M. T. (1999). The search-transfer problem: The role of weak ties in sharing knowledge across organization subunits. *Administrative Science Quarterly, 44*(1), 82–111.

Ingraham, P. W., & Getha-Taylor, H. (2008). Incentivizing collaborative performance aligning policy intent, design, and impact. In L. B. Bingham & R. O'Leary (Eds.), *Big ideas in collaborative public management* (pp. 79–96). Armonk, NY: M. E. Sharpe.

Johnston, E. W., Hicks, D., Nan, N., & Auer, J. C. (2011). Managing the inclusion process in collaborative governance. *Journal of Public Administration Research and Theory, 21*(4), 699–721.

Kapucu, N., & Garayev, V. (2012). Designing, managing, and sustaining functionally collaborative emergency management networks. *American Review of Public Administration, 43*(3), 312–330.

Keast, R., Mandell, M. P., Brown, K., & Woolcock, G. (2004). Network structures: Working differently and changing expectations. *Public Administration Review, 64*(3), 363–371.

Kettl, D. F. (2006). Managing boundaries in American administration: The collaboration imperative. *Public Administration Review, 66*(1), 10–19.

Klijn, E. H., & Koppenjan, J. (2015). *Governance networks in the public sector.* New York, NY: Routledge.

Leana, C. R., & van Buren, III, H. J. (1999). Organizational social capital and employment practices. *Academy of Management Review, 24*(3), 538–555.

Morel, B., & Ramanujam, R. (1999). Through the looking glass of complexity: The dynamics of organizations as adaptive and evolving systems. *Organization Science, 10*(3), 278–293.

O'Toole, L. J. Jr. (1997). Implementing public innovations in network settings. *Administration & Society, 29*(2), 115–134.

Page, S. (2008). Managing for results across agencies: Building collaborative capacity in the human services. In L. B. Bingham & R. O'Leary (Eds.), *Big ideas in collaborative public management* (pp. 138–161). Armonk, NY: M. E. Sharpe.

Popp, J., MacKean, G., Casebeer, A., Milward, H. B., & Lindstrom, R. (2014). *Interorganizational networks: A review of the literature to inform practice.* Washington, DC: IBM Center for The Business of Government.

Powell, T. (1992). Organizational alignment as competitive advantage. *Strategic Management Journal,* 119–134.

Provan, K. G., Beagles, J. E., & Leischow, S. J. (2011). Network formation, governance, and evolution in public health: The North American Quitline consortium case. *Health Care Management Review, 36*(4), 315–326.

Provan, K. G., & Kenis, P. (2007). Modes of network governance: Structure, management, and effectiveness. *Journal of Public Administration Research and Theory, 18*(2), 229–252.

Ryu, S. (2014). Networking partner selection and its impact on the perceived success of collaboration. *Public Performance and Management Review, 37*(4), 632–657.

Shaw, M. M. (2003). Successful collaboration between the nonprofit and public sectors. *Nonprofit Management & Leadership, 14*(1), 107–120.

Sowa, J. E. (2008). Implementing interagency collaborations: Exploring variation in collaborative ventures in human service organizations. *Administration & Society, 40*(3), 298–323.

Strauss, A. (1988). The articulation of project work: An organization process. *The Sociological Quarterly,* 163–178.

Thomson, M. A., Perry, J. L., & Miller, T. K. (2008). Linking collaboration processes and outcomes: Foundations for advancing empirical theory. In L. B. Bingham & R. O'Leary (Eds.), *Big ideas in collaborative public management* (pp. 97–120). New York, NY: ME Sharpe.

Vangen, S., & Huxham, C. (2003). Nurturing collaborative relations: Building trust in interorganizational collaboration. *Journal of Applied Behavioral Science, 39*(1), 5–31.

Wachhaus, T. A. (2011). Anarchy as a model for network governance. *Public Administration Review, 71*(1), 33–42.

Weick, K. E. (2005). Organizing and failures of imagination. *International Public Management Journal, 8*(3), 425–438.

Wildavsky, A. B. (1988). *Searching for safety.* Berkeley, CA: University of California Press.

Section II
Network Governance

5 Network Management and Leadership

This chapter discusses the complex environment that managers and leaders face in interorganizational networks. While previous chapters have focused on the design, function, and structure of networks, this chapter discusses management and leadership in networks. It covers what differentiates network management from general management activities and behaviors and what makes network leadership unique. It also highlights how a multitude of factors can influence the behaviors of network management and leadership, including contextual factors, collaborative processes and structures, and network characteristics and governance structures. The chapter ends by discussing practical implications and introducing potential research questions for future study in network management and leadership. This chapter addresses the following questions:

- Why is it complicated to manage and lead in interorganizational networks?
- What does network management involve?
- What does network leadership mean?
- What factors influence the behaviors of network management and leadership?
- What are the practical suggestions to better manage and lead interorganizational networks?

Complexity of Network Management and Leadership

Networks do not replace hierarchy (Agranoff, 2006); yet, compared with a single-organization environment, managers in a networked environment face different challenges. First, mangers need to work across organizational boundaries and have frequent interactions with outside stakeholders. Mangers not only need to understand the command and control system and work within existing hierarchical structures, but more importantly, they need to work with a diverse range of stakeholders from other organizations. For instance, in the setting of public education, in addition to schools' students, faculty, and staff, school superintendents need to interact with school board members, local business leaders, other school superintendents, state legislators (Meier & O'Toole, 2001). In the context of regional economic development, directors of the city department of economic development not only interact with city leaders, but with leaders from local chambers of commerce, business communities, and regional planning organizations as well (Agranoff & McGuire, 2003).

Second, member organizations may have different goals, missions, processes of operation, communication and information sharing protocols, and organizational cultures (O'Leary & Bingham, 2007; Yi, Berry, & Chen, 2018). It becomes crucial for managers to build and manage relationships with all the members to help integrate individual organizational goals with network-level goals. For instance, a homeless service network is composed of organizations from different sectors that serve different segments of the homeless population. Some organizations focus on helping homeless women and children, and others may focus on serving homeless veterans. Some organizations may focus on housing services, and others are dedicated to proving mental health services. Although the network aims to serve the needs of the homeless population, due to different organizational missions, human service organizations may compete for financial resources, volunteers, and reputation (Bunger et al., 2014).

Third, different from a top-down approach, decision-making in networks involves multiple member organizations and demands a deliberative process in which members establish rules, develop trust, and build consensus on problem-solving (Agranoff, 2006). Therefore, managing in and across networks requires a variety of managerial tools and skill sets. The networked environment demands some level of power sharing, flexibility and adaptability, capacity to work with all kinds of interorganizational dynamics, such as competition and potential conflicts (Goldsmith & Eggers, 2004; Huxham & Vangen, 2000; Koliba, Meek, & Zia, 2010).

Lastly, traditional assumptions of hierarchical leadership may not be upheld in a network setting (Huxham & Vangen, 2000). Traditional leadership theories suggest that a formal leader can influence members of a group or organization to achieve specified goals (Huxham & Vangen, 2000). Yet, in a network setting, there might not be a formal leader with managerial responsibility, designated power, or a hierarchical relationship with followers. In addition, the process of reaching collaborative goals can be extremely difficult in networks, as individual different members can bring to the table a variety of goals and priorities (Huxham & Vangen, 2000; O'Leary & Bingham, 2007). In sum, mangers and leaders face a different set of opportunities and challenges when working in a network setting.

Management of Networks

What differentiates network management from general management activities and behaviors within a single-organizational environment? Although a few researchers highlighted the commonalities between the two (e.g., Kelman, Hong, & Turbitt, 2013), more researchers noted the differences (e.g., Edelenbos, Klijn, & Steijn, 2011; Milward & Provan, 2006; McGuire, 2002; Milward &

Provan, 2006). The challenge lies in how to measure and describe management in networks, as management can vary from time to time and from one context to another. One approach is to use a behavioral perspective to examine network management activities (McGuire, 2002), focusing on what mangers do in a network setting.

Although traditional managerial tasks such as "Planning, Organizing, Staffing, Directing, Coordinating, Reporting and Budgeting" ("POSDCORB") remain important (Gulick, 1936), four types of activities become important elements of management in a networked environment: "activation," "framing," "mobilizing," and "synthesizing" (Agranoff & McGuire, 2001, pp. 298–300).

- Acting: Network managers need to know who the member organizations are, who the stakeholders are, what information, skills, and resources exist within the network, and how to activate resources from the network participants.
- Framing: To manage a network, network managers need to establish network rules to coordinate efforts, develop processes to introduce and build collaborative goals or vision.
- Mobilizing: To ensure the effective function of a network, network managers need to gain both internal and external support, motivate member organizations, and build commitment to collaborative goals and missions.
- Synthesizing: Network managers have a responsibility to create and maintain a favorable environment for network members to interact with one another. Furthermore, they need to build and strengthen relationships and address differences and conflicts among network members (Agranoff & McGuire, 2001).

Similarly, Edelenbos et al. (2011) argued that "the role of the manager in a network is different and more equivalent to that of a mediator, a process manager, or a facilitator" (p. 422). They categorized network management activities into four groups: "connecting," "exploring," "arranging," and developing "process agreements" (p. 423). Connecting activities involve the "activation of actors and resources" (p. 423). Exploring activities focus on clarifying collaborative goals and mission for the network. Arranging activities refer to building structures for interactions, whereas developing process agreements involves establishing interactions rules for network participants.

Milward and Provan (2006) summarized five key activities for network managers, including the management of "accountability," "legitimacy," "conflicts," "design (governance structure)," and "commitment" (pp. 6–7). What made their study unique is that they differentiated "management of networks" from "management in networks" (p. 19). On one hand, they noted that managers need to ensure their own organization's involvement with the network, legitimizing their role, solve problems or conflicts with other organizations, work with other members and within network governance structure, and build commitment to network-level goals; on the other hand, they highlighted management tasks related to management of networks.

- Accountability: Define responsibilities, reward and monitor rule compliance.
- Legitimacy: Attract members and resources, build legitimacy through achieving tangible successes.
- Conflict: Build processes and mechanisms for solving or managing conflicts and serve as brokers.
- Design (governance structure): Select and manage appropriate governance structure, develop effective decision-making processes.
- Commitment: Gain trust and commitment from network members, keep members informed of network activities, and help members understand the allocation of resources and the alignment of network goals with organizational goals (Milward & Provan, 2006).

Although scholars have categorized different management activities of networks, *network management* shares some commonalities: it is important for managers to identify members, develop trust and support mobilize resources, establish rules, align organizational and network-level goals, address differences, and manage potential conflicts. Many of these elements will be further discussed in the following chapters, such as accountability and legitimacy and governance structures.

> ### Network Management
>
> Managers in networks, in order to ensure effective collaboration, focus on process: identifying members, developing trust, mobilizing resources, establishing rules, manage conflicts, etc.

Managing conflicts is often neglected or understated in existing literature. As member organizations have their own organizational priorities or goals, operational rules and processes, and diverse cultures, network managers first need to acknowledge the differences among organizations and further address any tension or conflict in the network. Furthermore, network managers represent their organizations in the network while needing to balance their organizational needs with network-level goals (Saz-Carranza & Ospina, 2010). To manage "unity-diversity tension" in networks, managers need to play a mediating role by "creating spaces for dialogue and interaction, recognizing member involvement, mediating among members, and disseminating information across member organizations" (Saz-Carranza & Ospina, 2010, p. 350). Network managers also need to prevent conflicts from further escalating by utilizing discussion or negotiation between their own organization and others. Managers can also serve as negotiators to break stalemates by linking their own organization with their stakeholders or to other organizations in the network (Milward & Provan, 2006).

Leadership in Networks

Research on network leadership has expanded in recent years. Network leadership takes a different approach than other leadership theories. Network leadership is distributed "more broadly than in hierarchical forms of vertical leadership" (Van Wart, 2015, p. 123). Rather than focusing on individual leaders, network leadership acknowledges that leadership is a process that includes not only leaders, but followers too. Network leadership focuses on power sharing across organizational boundaries, where a leader invests time to build relationships and rust, shares control,

> ### Network Leadership
>
> Leaders in networks focus on relationship building and facilitative decision-making to achieve network goals in a collaborative manner.

and encourages stakeholders to work collaboratively (Ansell & Gash, 2012). Leadership and power issues in networks are addressed in Chapter 7 in details. In this section, we take a behavioral approach and examine leadership activities to disentangle the complexity of leadership in networks. Furthermore, we will introduce a social network perspective to network leadership.

A Behavioral Perspective

Leaders are expected to be flexible and adaptable to the changes in their environments. They are also expected to be boundary-spanners in networks of organizations and communities (Van Wart & Kapucu, 2011). The behavioral approach of leadership examines the way the leaders act in response to changes in the environment. Most of the focus was on transformational leadership (Vogel & Masal, 2015). The examination of network leadership from the behavioral perspective within the cross-sector and interorganizational network environment is a recent development (e.g., Crosby & Bryson, 2018, 2010; Edelenbos et al., 2011; Silvia & McGuire, 2010). Systematic empirical studies of network leadership remain limited, with a handful of exceptions. Silvia and McGuire (2010) investigated what behaviors characterize network leadership in the context of emergency management. They surveyed 2,486 emergency managers using Van Wart's (2012) 35 leadership behavior items. They found that leaders in networks demonstrated more people-oriented behaviors and less task-oriented behaviors than those leading individual agencies (p. 264). However, they noted that it remains questionable whether the findings can apply to other contexts such as social services, economic development, or natural resources (p. 275).

Similarly, Edelenbos et al. (2011) developed a 16-item list of leadership behaviors to study network managers and examined the impact of engaging in network management activities on collaborative environmental projects. They suggested that engagement in these network management activities can help achieve better outcomes. Yet, this 16-item network management activity list was tested mainly in an environmental management context. In short, more empirical studies on network leadership within different contexts are needed to better conceptualize and measure this concept.

Another way to examine network leadership is to describe leadership styles or leadership roles. Leaders play an important role in the success and failure of networks. Leaders must adapt to the tasks and demands placed on them and rely on different kinds of leadership skills to fulfill the needs of the collective effort. Several conditions have been identified as influencing the efficacy of network leadership, most important of which are access to resources, strength of relationships with current and potential partners, infrastructure, and historical context (Ansell & Gash, 2012). For instance, scholars have highlighted the importance of collaborative leadership in networks and argued that collaborative leadership takes more of a facilitative, rather than directive, role (Ansell & Gash, 2012). In that vein, the leaders' facilitative role may be further categorized into three roles: steward, mediator and catalyst (Ansell & Gash, 2012).

- Steward: Exercise authority when needed to "convene collaboration and maintain its integrity" (p. 2).
- Mediators: Manage and address conflict, mediate disputes, build and nurtures relationships (p. 8).
- Catalyst: Identify "value-creating opportunities," encourage and engage stakeholders in pursuing collaboration (p. 8).

Collaborative leaders may play multiple roles, depending on the situation (Ansell & Gash, 2012). When there is low trust and high level of conflict, collaborative leaders engage in stewardship and mediation to exercise authority and to manage conflicts. While in a problem solving situation, collaborative leaders play more of a catalyst role to engage stakeholders in joint efforts (Ansell & Gash, 2012).

Holley (2012) described four roles of network leadership: "network catalyst" (connect people and build the network), "project coordinator" (help members manage the execution of collaborative projects), "network facilitator" (developing governance structures and relationships), and "network guardian" (introduce and manage processes, systems, and mechanisms to enable the function of networks). Holley's four roles are similar to Ansell and Gash' depiction of leadership's facilitative roles, except for the addition of project coordinator.

To further understand the behaviors of network leaders, we will introduce Burke et al.'s classification of leadership behavior and discuss its applicability and implication for studying network leadership. In an interorganizational network, organizations are interdependent but not equally empowered. Certain leadership behaviors may be more pronounced than others (Klijn, Steijn, & Edelenbos, 2010). Burke et al. (2006) categorized leadership behaviors into two groups: task-focused and person-focused. Task-focused leadership behaviors consist of transactional, initiating structure, and boundary-spanning activity. Person-focused leadership behaviors are categorized as transformational, consideration, and empowerment (Burke et al., 2006).

Task-focused leadership behaviors emphasize task accomplishment. Under the category of task-focused behavior, transactional behaviors are more pronounced in a formal hierarchical structure than in a network setting as transactional behaviors refer to reward or punishment behaviors (Burke et al., 2006; McGuire & Silvia, 2009). Within an interorganizational network structure, organizations are not in a formally hierarchical arrangement. Leaders may not have formal power structure to execute their rewards or punishment.

The second type of task-focused leadership behaviors are initiating structure behaviors, with two subtypes: directive leadership and autocratic leadership (Burke et al., 2006). Directive leadership includes activities such as initiating, organizing, and assigning task activities, specifying work paths to accomplish goals, and building communication channels. Autocratic leadership refers to decision-making without team consultation (Burke et al., 2006). Directive leadership activities remain relevant in a network environment, whereas autocratic leadership might be less effective in a network structure. This is because tasks are often not formerly delegated, and most tasks in a network setting demand a more consensus-based approach (Agranoff, 2006).

The last set of task-related leadership behaviors are boundary-spanning behaviors (Burke et al., 2006). These behaviors increase the exchange of resources and information (Burke et al., 2006). The boundary-spanning behaviors are similar to the synthesizing behaviors discussed earlier, which increase and strengthen network relationships and thereby increase network effectiveness (McGuire & Silvia, 2009). In their study of integrative leadership, Crosby and Bryson (2005, 2010) called special attention to the importance of *boundary spanners* at the initiation of cross-sector collaboration. They further differentiated boundary spanners into two types: champions and sponsors. By champions, they refer to individuals that are advocates for the collaboration. By sponsors, they mean individuals that use their resources and connections to carry cross-sector collaboration forward.

> **Boundary Spanners**
>
> Members of a network that connect separate actors. These actors play a significant role in facilitating cross-sector collaboration.

Boundary-spanning leadership is needed in multi-organizational arrangements to exchange information, facilitate and solve problems (Kapucu, 2006). For instance, in response to the September 11, 2001, terrorist attacks, existing communication infrastructure and channels were damaged, the New York City Office of Emergency Management (NYCOEM) coordinated efforts among more than 150 public, private, and nonprofit organizations, and bridged disconnected organizations due to the disruption to existing communication systems (Kapucu, 2006).

Person-focused leadership behaviors are categorized as transformational, consideration, and empowerment (Burke et al., 2006). Transformational leaders create a compelling direction and provide expert coaching to followers. In a network structure, transformational leadership may be helpful in creating a compelling direction. The direction and problem solving of the network are part of the network creation and inherent to its continued existence and effective operation. The function of expert coaching in a network setting may require the leader to understand and respect the uniqueness and diversity of member organization. Coaching can be challenging when all member organizations are of similar backgrounds and resource status.

Consideration leadership behaviors refer to activities that "maintaining close social relationships and group cohesion" (Burke et al., 2006, p. 293). To be successful in a network setting, network leaders must communicate effectively with a variety of stakeholders and participants (Eglene, Dawes, & Schneider, 2007). As consideration leadership is a behavior that may be manifested between every dyadic relationship, making it more valuable in a network setting.

The last type of leadership behaviors is empowerment, characterized by emphasizing followers' self-development (Burke et al., 2006). Empowerment is key to the process of facilitating and enabling member organizations to work across organizational boundaries, which are activities inherently important in networks (Agranoff & McGuire, 2003; Klijn et al., 2010).

As Table 5.1 shows, all the people-focused behaviors are pronounced in an interorganizational network. Under the categories of task-focused behaviors, certain leadership activities such as initiating structure behaviors and boundary-spanning behaviors are more relevant to a network setting, although a certain level of adaption is needed. Although many task-focused behaviors remain relevant in a network setting, the person-focused behaviors are more closely related to network effectiveness (McGuire & Silvia, 2009). Relations matter to the success of interorganizational networks, no matter the relations, exchange of information or resources, joint actions, or even competition.

A Social Network Perspective

A network approach to understand leadership has received greater attention in recent years (Balkundi & Kilduff, 2006; Carter, DeChurch, Braun, & Contractor, 2015). As previously discussed, network leadership requires more

Table 5.1 Task and Person-Focused Behaviors in Single Versus Interorganizational Settings

		Single- organization setting	*Interorganizational network setting*
Task-Focused Behaviors	Transactional behaviors	✓	May not have a formal hierarchical structure to support reward or punishment.
	Initiating structure behaviors	✓	Directive leadership, with adaption, may still apply to a network setting
	Boundary spanning behaviors	✓	✓
Person-Focused Behaviors	Transformational behaviors	✓	✓
	Consideration behaviors	✓	✓
	Empowerment behaviors	✓	✓

people-oriented behaviors and demands more attention to relations among people and organizations. A social network approach allows researchers to focus on the relational nature of leadership, its situated context, and to study both formal and informal leadership in networks (Balkundi & Kilduff, 2006; Carter et al., 2015).

A network perspective calls attention to organizational relations with others. These dynamic relations carry different meanings contingent upon the context, time, and situation. Organizations may exchange information and knowledge and share resources or compete for funding and reputation. Organizations are embedded in networks of relations with other organizations and their stakeholders. Depending upon the situation and time, leadership roles may be played by different organizations. For instance, during regular local emergency preparedness, a county office of emergency management may take a lead role in inviting organizations to participate in a tabletop exercise. In response to an actual disaster such as the Boston Marathon bombing in 2013, other organizations, such as police, may take leadership roles in responding quickly to the incident (Hu et al., 2014).

Furthermore, both formal and informal network leadership emerge from intertwined relations. Network leaders may emerge from formal interorganizational networks. As discussed in Chapters 2 and 3, in a lead organization-governed network, an organization, often the one with more power or resources, serves as the leader (Provan & Kenis, 2008). However, organizations may assume leadership roles without formal position or responsibilities.

For instance, organizations may take on a leadership role in communication networks by serving as the source of information; or they may become a leader in the network because of its good reputation.

Within an interorganizational network, one organization's position and relations with other organizations can influence the behaviors of other organizations. We will discuss the central connectors, brokers, and boundary spanners. A central connector, often measured by degree centrality, refers to the organization that has many direct connections in a network, which gives the organization easy access to valuable information and resources, enabling the organization for a leadership role (Balkundi & Kilduff, 2006). A central connector is influential in information flow and important for the function of an interorganizational network. As shown in Figure 5.1, the central position that organization A has allows it to have access to more information and resources than organization C and D. Organization A can facilitate information flow among the member organizations. The caveat is that heavy reliance on a central connector for information dissemination can be catastrophic when the central connector leaves the network or creates bottleneck for information communication.

Organizations with high betweenness centrality can serve as brokers or boundary spanners in an interorganizational network (Balkundi & Kilduff, 2006). Betweenness centrality measures the extent to which "the actor falls on the geodesic paths between other pairs of factors in the network" (Hanneman & Riddle, 2011, p. 366). The high-betweenness organization takes an intermediary position on the shortest paths connecting other pairs of organizations (Balkundi & Kilduff, 2006). A broker bridges unconnected organizations or communities, which gives the organization leveraging power to take on leadership roles. The boundary spanning organization work with organizations of different groups or sector affiliations. The caveat with a broker or boundary spanner is that networks can be left fragmented when the broker or boundary spanner leaves the network or create bottlenecks. As shown in Figure 5.1, actor (organization) B serves as a broker that bridges the two disconnected communities. Actor (organization) B can not only serve as the channel for information sharing and exchange between the two communities, but it can serve as a mediator that facilitates the communication between the two

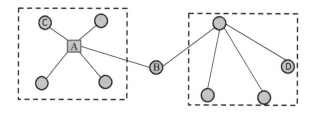

Figure 5.1 Network Position and Leadership

communities. An example of a broker is local community foundations that connect donors with the wide range of small nonprofit organizations that need financial support. An example of a boundary spanner is the NYCOEM that work with other organizations across organizational boundaries, jurisdictions, and sectors (Kapucu, 2006).

A Contingency Model to Understand the Behaviors of Network Management and Leadership

This section proposes a contingency model to understanding network management and leadership. Contingency factors include contextual factors of a network, collaboration processes and structures, network characteristics, and governance structures (Figure 5.2). The relationships among these factors are intertwined and can influence the effectiveness of network management and leadership, which in turn impacts effectiveness.

Contextual Factors

Many factors influence the effectiveness of network management and leadership, including, but not limited to, contextual factors, collaboration processes and structures, network characteristics, and structures (Huxham & Vangen, 2000). McGuire (2002) offers "contingency logic" to examine "when, why,

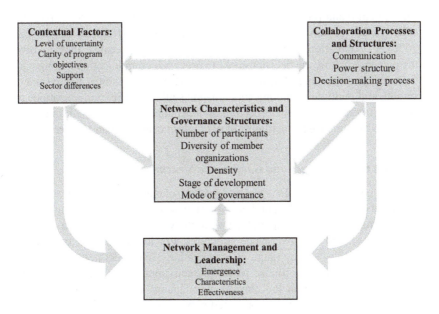

Figure 5.2 A Contingency Model to Understand the Behaviors of Network Management Leadership

and how" network managers undertake certain behaviors (p. 599). He noted that the use of network strategies depends on the contextual factors. A network leader needs to use a "linear strategy," starting with activation, and then moving to mobilizing, framing and synthesizing when he or she is faced with a stable environment, clear program objectives, and enough support. A network manager may need to use a "recursive strategy" to have more emphasis on certain activities such as gaining more support or establishing clear rules when there is lack of support or the institutional environment is not supportive (McGuire, 2002).

Similarly, Herranz (2008) proposed a "passive-to-active continuum of managerial behavior encompassing reactive facilitation, contingent coordination, active coordination, and hierarchical-based directed administration" (p. 4). As networks evolve from a voluntary, consensual, and self-governing type to exchange-based, formally goal-oriented, and a contractual and regulatory one, managers adapt their behaviors from a passive, facilitative style to more active coordination and directed administration (Herranz, 2008). Herranz also called attention to the influence of "sector-based differences in networks" and proposed that the three types of networks—"community-based networks," "entrepreneurial-based networks," and "bureaucratic-based network"— can influence network managers' adoption of different strategic orientation (pp. 26–27).

Collaboration Process and Structures

The structure and processes of a collaboration are central in determining the effectiveness of network leadership and management (Huxham & Vangen, 2000). Collaboration structures and processes matter because they involve the power structure, the decision-making process, communication among participants, and resource allocation (Huxham & Vangen, 2000). For instance, smooth and multiple communication channels allow member organizations to share information and develop common understanding of issues. All of these factors will influence the activities of network management and leadership.

Network Characteristics and Governance Structures

It is crucial for network managers and leaders to understand the interorganizational network, such as the number of participants, the density of communication among members, the central actors in the work, the stage of the network development, and the governance structures. For instance, if the network is large and includes a wide range of organizations, managers need to dedicate more time and energy to the activities of "activating" and "framing" to seek buy-in and support from the network participants. Boundary spanning will be more crucial for a loosely connected network compared with a dense network in which organizations are well connected with one another. As a network evolves from early formation to further development, network managers need to adapt the behaviors and shift their attention from certain dimensions to others.

Network governance structures can influence how leadership emerges and functions at the network level. Within a lead organization governed network, a formal lead organization coordinates network-level activity and facilitates decision-making processes. Within a "network administrative organization (NAO) model" (Provan & Kenis, 2008), an external administrative organization takes on leadership role. In a network with a "shared governance" model, leadership is dispersed among member organizations through a deliberative decision-making process. Informal leadership plays a crucial role due to a lack of formal leadership structure.

Conclusion

In addition to managing within their own organizations, network managers need to build relationships and trust among member organizations, align organizational goals with network-level goals, mobilize resources, build coalitions, and solve potential conflicts. Conflicts are often inevitable in a network setting. Therefore, it is how one manages conflicts that differentiates an effective network manager from others. Boundary spanning activities are crucial part of leadership behaviors, as leaders in a network setting often need to connect organizations with different backgrounds and cultures, leverage resources from different subgroups of the network, and coordinate efforts to accomplish network goals. Network managers and leaders need to pay attention to both the network composition and structure of the interorganizational network that their organization is a part of. Network managers and leaders can utilize network visualization or other tools to understand the intertwined and dynamic relations between their organization and others.

There are formal and informal leaders in a network setting. The leader can be the formal lead organization or the NAO. In a voluntary, loosely connected network, an informal leader can be any organization that has access to information, resources, or has a good reputation. From a social network perspective, organizations that take central position, or serve as "go-between" mediators, often take on leadership roles.

To further examine the effectiveness of network management and leadership, a contingency approach was proposed in this chapter to disentangle the complexity of a network setting. The emergence, characteristics, and effectiveness of network leadership can be influenced by a range of factors, such as collaborative structures, processes, contextual factors, and network characteristics and governance structures (Huxham & Vangen, 2000). Adding to this complexity is that different organizational cultures, history, and goals make management and leadership difficult in networks. Proper leadership styles, behaviors and strategies are crucial to overcome these challenges. Depending on the situation, certain dimensions of leadership and management behaviors are more prominent than others.

There is still a lack of systematic empirical studies of network management and leadership, especially in an interorganizational setting. Existing research has focused on the behavioral dimension of network management and leadership. More research is needed to further explore the network approach to studying management and leadership. We suggest a few research questions for future research: How does informal leadership emerge in a network setting? In addition to high degree centrality and high betweenness centrality, what other network position is advantageous for a leadership role? How does network structural characteristics influence the behaviors of network leadership and management? How can we better test the relationships among the contingency factors and network management and leadership?

References

Agranoff, R. (2006). Inside collaborative networks: Ten lessons for public managers. *Public Administration Review*, *66*(Suppl. 1), 56–65.

Agranoff, R., & McGuire, M. (2001). Big questions in public network management research. *Journal of Public Administration Research and Theory*, *11*(3), 295–326.

Agranoff, R., & McGuire, M. (2003). *Collaborative public management: New strategies for local governments*. Washington, DC: Georgetown University Press.

Ansell, C., & Gash, A. (2012). Stewards, mediators, and catalysts: Toward a model of collaborative leadership. *The Innovation Journal: The Public Sector Innovation Journal*, *17*(1), article 7.

Balkundi, P., & Kilduff, M. (2006). The ties that lead: A social network approach to leadership. *The Leadership Quarterly*, *17*, 419–439.

Bunger, A. C., Collins-Camargo, C., McBeath, B., Chuang, E., Pérez-Jolles, M., & Wells, R. (2014). Collaboration, competition, and co-opetition: Interorganizational dynamics between private child welfare agencies and child serving sectors. *Children and Youth Services Review*, *38*, 113–122. doi:10.1016/j.childyouth.2014.01.017

Burke, C. S., Stagl, K. C., Klein, C., Goodwin, G. F., Salas, E., & Halpin, S. M. (2006). What type of leadership behaviors are functional in teams? A meta-analysis. *The Leadership Quarterly*, *17*(3), 288–307.

Carter, D. R., DeChurch, L. A., Braun, M. T., & Contractor, N. S. (2015). Social network approaches to leadership: An integrative conceptual review. *Journal of Applied Psychology*, *100*(3), 597–622.

Crosby, B. C., & Bryson, J. M. (2005). *Leadership for the common good: Tackling public problems in a shared-power world*. San Francisco, CA: Jossey-Bass.

Crosby, B. C., & Bryson, J. M. (2010). Integrative leadership and the creation and maintenance of cross-sector collaborations. *The Leadership Quarterly*, *21*, 211–230.

Crosby, B. C., & Bryson, J. M. (2018). Why leadership of public leadership research matters: And what to do about it. *Public Management Review*, *20*(9), 1265–1286.

Edelenbos, J., Klijn, E., & Steijn, A. B. (2011). Managers in governance networks: How to reach good outcomes. *International Public Management Journal*, *14*(4), 420–444.

Eglene, O., Dawes, S. S., & Schneider, C. A. (2007). Authority and leadership patterns in public sector knowledge networks. *The American Review of Public Administration*, *37*(1), 91–113.

Goldsmith, S., & Eggers, W. D. (2004). Ties that bind. In *Governing by network: The new shape of the public sector* (Chapter 5, pp. 93–119). Washington, DC: Brookings.

Gulick, L. H. (1936). Notes on the theory of organization. In L. Gulick & L. Urwick (Eds.), *Papers on the science of administration* (pp. 3–35). New York, NY: Institute of Public Administration.

Hanneman, R. A., & Riddle, M. (2011). A brief introduction to social network data. In J. Scott & P. J. Carrington (Eds.), *The Sage handbook of social network analysis* (pp. 331–339). Thousand Oaks, CA: Sage Publications.

Herranz, J. Jr. (2008). The multisectoral trilemma of network management. *Journal of Public Administration Research and Theory, 18*(1), 1–31.

Holley, J. (2012). *Network weaver handbook: A guide to transformational networks.* Athens, Ontario: Network Weaver Publishing.

Hu, Q., Knox, C. C., & Kapucu, N. (2014). What have we learned since September 11th? A network study of the Boston marathon bombings response. *Public Administration Review, 74*(6), 698–712.

Huxham, C., & Vangen, S. (2000). Leadership in the shaping and implementation of collaboration agendas: How things happen in a (not quite) joined-up world. *Academy of Management Journal, 43*(6), 1159–1175.

Kapucu, N. (2006). Interagency communication networks during emergencies: Boundary spanners in multi-agency coordination. *The American Review of Public Administration, 36*(2), 207–225.

Kelman, S., Hong, S., & Turbitt, I. (2013). Are there managerial practices associated with the outcomes of an interagency service delivery collaboration? Evidence from British crime and disorder reduction partnerships. *Journal of Public Administration Research and Theory, 23*, 609–630.

Klijn, E-H., Steijn, B., & Edelenbos, J. (2010). The impact of network management on outcomes in governance networks. *Public Administration, 88*(4), 1063–1082.

Koliba, C., Meek, J. C., & Zia, A. (2010). *Governance networks in public administration and public policy.* New York, NY: CRC Press.

Linden, R. M. (2010). *Leading across boundaries: Creating collaborative agencies in a networked world.* San Francisco, CA: Jossey-Bass.

McGuire, M. (2002). Managing networks: Propositions on what managers do and why they do it. *Public Administration Review, 62*(5), 599–609.

McGuire, M., & Silvia, C. (2009). Does leadership in networks matter? *Public Performance & Management Review, 33*(1), 34–62.

Meier, K. J., & O'Toole, L. J. (2001). Managerial strategies and behavior in networks: A model with evidence from U.S. public education. *Journal of Public Administration Research and Theory, 11*(3), 271–294.

Milward, H. B., & Provan, K. G. (2006). *A manager's guide to choosing and using collaborative Networks.* Washington, DC: IBM Center for the Business of Government.

O'Leary, R., & Bingham, L. B. (2007). *A manager's guide to resolving conflicts in collaborative networks.* Washington, DC: IBM Center for the Business of Government.

Provan, K. G., & Kenis, P. (2008). Modes of network governance: Structure, management, and effectiveness. *Journal of Public Administration Research and Theory, 18*(2), 229–252.

Saz-Carranza, A., & Ospina, S. M. (2011). Is this 2011? In text this is 2010. The behavioral dimensions of governing interorganizational Goal-directed networks- managing the unity-diversity tension. *Journal of Public Administration Research and Theory, 21*(2), 327–365.

Silvia, C., & McGuire, M. (2010). Leading public sector networks: An empirical examination of integrative leadership behaviors. *The Leadership Quarterly, 21*(2), 264–277.

Van Wart, M. (2012). *Leadership in public organizations.* New York, NY: Routledge.

Van Wart, M. (2015). *Dynamics of leadership in public service: Theory and practice* (2nd ed.). New York, NY: Routledge.

Van Wart, M., & Kapucu, N. (2011). Crisis management competencies. *Public Management Review, 13*(4), 489–511.

Vogel, R., & Masal, D. (2015). Public Leadership: A review of the literature and framework for future research preview the document. *Public Management Review, 17*(8), 1165–1189.

Yi, H., Berry, F., & Chen, W. (2018). Management innovation and policy diffusion through leadership transfer networks: An agent network diffusion model. *Journal of Public Administration Research and Theory, 28*(4), 457–474.

6   Knowledge Management and Information Exchange in Networks

Chapter 6 discusses knowledge management and information exchange in networks. It addresses the nature of knowledge and knowledge management within networks and addresses its core issues. It covers the barriers to knowledge sharing in networks and the use of current information and communication technology (ICT) for facilitating knowledge sharing across organizational boundaries. In addition, the chapter addresses the relatively new topic of network learning through knowledge sharing in interorganizational settings. We present characteristics of information exchange and knowledge management for effective network governance by addressing the following questions:

- How can knowledge management be defined? Why should knowledge management be considered an essential element of network governance?
- Why is knowledge sharing and information exchange important for network governance?
- What is the role of informal relationships and trust in the search for information and utilization in networks?
- What is the role of network structure (informal and formal) in knowledge management and information sharing in networks?
- How do networks learn and generate "usable knowledge"?

Nature and Importance of Information and Knowledge for Networks

Knowledge sharing and information exchange are critical elements of effective network governance. On one hand, knowledge management and information exchange are essential components for establishing and maintaining networks in public policy and administration. On the other hand, networks provide a means for the diffusion of innovation and best practices. Organizations seek information from others when there is a need for innovation or lack of readily available information internally (Powell, 1998). Effective exchange of information and knowledge management are indicators of high performing networks (Popp, Milward, MacKean, Casebeer, & Lindstorm, 2014).

Collective knowledge generation and sharing is vital in addressing a problem via networks.

Knowledge is information, but information is knowledge only when actors have the ability to use it to accomplish tasks or improve organizational performance (Brown & Duguid, 2001). To effectively execute knowledge management, the process of moving from data to information to knowledge seamlessly is crucial (Agranoff, 2007). Knowledge, for public sector networks, is defined as "a fluid mix of framed experience, values, contextual information, and expert insight that provides a framework for evaluating and incorporating new experiences and information" (Agranoff, 2008, p. 162). The purpose of *knowledge management* is to identify, extract, and capture knowledge-based assets in order to best utilize them to achieve goals (Agranoff, 2008). While sharing knowledge is a fairly concrete and easily understood topic, there are challenges to address with this within the context of networks.

We usually relate information and knowledge to data sources such as the internet, file cabinets, and instruction manuals. However, these ideas and concepts are changing in the information age. Knowledge has evolved beyond simply knowing information. Now, it is knowing where to seek help for various information-based needs (Agranoff, 2007; Popp et al., 2014). Lack of access to critical knowledge or information might lead to network development in the form of identifying organizations with needed knowledge and information. In the case of the public sector, "[w]hen government lacks information essential to the accomplishment of a public mission—and private actors possess it—collaboration is an imperative, not an option" (Donahue & Zeckhauser, 2011, p. 104). Thus, one of the primary reasons public management networks are created is because certain knowledge gaps and uncertainties regarding problems are present.

Knowledge generally takes on two different forms: explicit or tacit. Explicit, or formal, knowledge can be directly observed, captured, transformed, or/and expressed by formal techniques. Explicit knowledge can be taught in the classroom, shown in a presentation, taught at a training, and easily documented and shared (Pardo, Cresswell, Thompson, & Zhang, 2006; Dawes, Cresswell, & Pardo, 2009). Tacit knowledge, on the other hand, is harder to capture. Tacit, or informal, knowledge is complex, context dependent, non-verbal, culture specific, system-dependent, and has low codifiability and translation and transferability (Nebus, 2006). Obtaining tacit knowledge requires practice, familiarity and often represents informal personal gained experience impacted by context and/or culture (Agranoff, 2007; Huang, 2014; Flyvbjerg, 2001; Mergel, 2016; Weber & Khademian, 2008).

Knowledge sharing strategies differ for explicit and tacit knowledge types. Hartley and Benington (2006) highlighted that tacit knowledge is generally considered "harder to share because it consists both of mental models and metaphors, intuitions and 'know-how'" (p. 103). Since networks promote collective action and knowledge creation via relations, it is expected that tacit knowledge sharing would be easier in a network. Huang (2014) found in his research studying health and human services networks that strong ties and dense networks can enhance knowledge sharing. He suggested that network administrative organizations (NAO) need to develop trust and good working relationships with the member organizations for effective knowledge sharing. This is critical if third party actors are involved in the interorganizational network. Huang (2014) suggested developing a "chief learning officer" and/or "dedicated knowledge diffusion organization" for effective interorganizational learning and knowledge sharing (p. 596).

Networks, as highlighted in Chapter 4, are built on trust and are sustained through the sharing of knowledge. Networks, working toward a common goal, require the sharing of information to reach their collective purpose (Borgatti & Cross, 2003; Popp et al., 2014). The trust in reciprocity between organizations implies that each organization pulls its weight and supports others in the network and can involve the exchange of knowledge (Binz-Scharf, Lazer & Mergel, 2012; Huang, 2014). Where there is trust, there is also risk. Written as the inevitable "what if?" question, risk relates to the failure of organizations to reciprocate, work together, and adhere to shared norms. In knowledge sharing, risk takes on the role of demonstrating a sense of uncertainty or ignorance at a personal level and can threaten information security, privacy, and autonomy on a network level (Binz-Scharf et al., 2012; Dawes et al., 2009; Nonino, 2013).

While all networks exchange information, Public Sector Knowledge Networks (PSKNs), as an example, are created purposefully to give participants access to each other's information and knowledge when needed (Dawes et al., 2009). Dawes et al. (2009) defined PSKNs as "sociotechnical systems in which human, organizational, and institutional considerations exist in a mutually influential relationship with processes, practices, software, and other information technologies" (p. 392). These networks aim to utilize knowledge as their primary resource for solving complex social and policy problems, and must be able to work together to gather, share, and manage said knowledge. Since knowledge gaps and uncertainty are a major catalyst for the organizations of PSKN's, the management of knowledge becomes an increasingly important function in governance (Agranoff, 2007). Thus, these sociotechnical systems increase the value of information held in multiple agencies or actors within the network (Pardo et al., 2006). PSKNs work best when they are deliberately woven into the fabric of the individual members' organizational culture and the processes housed therein (Dawes et al., 2009).

Cognitive consensus among members are significant for effective tacit knowledge management. Nowell (2009) and Augier and Vendelo (1999) highlighted the significance of tacit knowledge and cognitive problem framing in network settings, for achieving higher performance. They also highlighted that extreme cognitive consensus may lead to groupthink (i.e., low innovation and inflow knowledge to organizations). Facilitative network leadership is significant for building relationships, creating collective dialogues and shared cognitive frame for enhancing network legitimacy and effective network performance (Nowell, 2009).

Nowell (2009) tested how the perceptual misalignment of "the problem frame," or differences in worldview between member organizations, affects network effectiveness in community collaboratives of domestic violence prevention organizations. Each organization may bring a different cognitive worldview, resulting in differences in perceiving and understanding problems and how to achieve goals (e.g., social worker's humanitarian worldview.). Differences in this collective perception of an issue and its solution will affect network cohesion and therefore, effectiveness. Worldviews affect how actors determine what needs to be identified, negotiated, and integrated into collective consensus among members to solve complex problems that the network needs to address. This collective consensus can act as the glue to hold all actors together. The results indicated the negative relationships between frame discordance and network effectiveness, and also highlighted that the perceptual misalignment of key network actors also impact network effectiveness more than other type of members.

Similarly, Augier and Vendelo (1999) identified the importance of informal relational ties on tacit knowledge management. Shared cognitive frames among members are needed for the transfer of tacit knowledge, as it is difficult to articulate and manage as such intangible knowledge is found in practices and "routines and cultures" (p. 254). This means that social skills and relationship building among network members are important in managing tacit knowledge in network setting. However, strong ties, although good for tacit knowledge transfer, may hamper innovation development and the inflow of new knowledge. Thus, managers need to assess this trade-off when building or joining knowledge networks in relation to organizational goals. In addition, the cognitive frame among members is also important for constructing knowledge network, as it determines the assumption of underpinned effectiveness of a network.

Table 6.1 highlights the role of informal and formal networks in tacit and explicit knowledge sharing. Informal networks have high potential in sharing tacit knowledge compared to formal ones. Explicit knowledge has higher transferability through formal networks than in informal ones. Formal networks provide structure for knowledge sharing and management. They might act as a barrier for larger-scale dissemination of information, however.

Table 6.1 Sharing Tacit and Explicit Knowledge in Networks

	Informal Networks	*Formal Networks*
Tacit Knowledge	High competitive advantage	Low competitive advantage
Explicit Knowledge	Low transferability	High transferability

Informal networks provide opportunities for wide dissemination of knowledge (Powell, 1998). It is a substantial challenge to institutionalize or build routine based on informal arrangements for regular knowledge sharing. More empirical research is needed for the use of formal or informal venues regarding both knowledge generation and sharing.

Knowledge Management in Networks

Knowledge management in networks is creating, capturing, retrieving, integrating, distributing and translating knowledge into practice to enhance network learning Huang, 2014; Soltani & Lavafan, 2014). This process begins with the creation and/or integrating existing sources of information and databases from external sources. Some of the tools for knowledge management include building data bases, measuring intellectual capital, building intranets, sharing best practices, installing groupware, leading training programs, leading cultural change, fostering collaboration, and creating virtual organizations (Agranoff, 2007). Knowledge sharing and management provide participants access to others' information and knowledge and can help public organizations react to uncertainty and complexity in the environment (Dawes et al., 2009). Knowledge sharing will occur if the reward is sufficient and the risk is sufficiently low, service integration is possible, data collection is streamlined, integrated functions are facilitated, technology infrastructure and data quality improved, and professional networks and communities of practice are reinforced (Dawes et al., 2009; Pardo et al., 2006).

> ### Knowledge Management
>
> Creating, capturing, retrieving, integrating, and distributing knowledge to enhance network learning.

Figure 6.1 is a brief overview of the important factors relating to knowledge sharing and management and its effectiveness in networks discussed in the chapter. The process involves tacit and explicit knowledge being shared in an innovative and open-minded organizational culture, formal and informal structure, and the modification of institutional rules and arrangements. All these categories and elements are both informative and useful in creating successful knowledge management in networks.

There are different ways to search for knowledge in networks. Community and cultural factors consist of certain boundaries and shared norms in network environments. The organizational level factors consist of size, jurisdiction, and location. Some of the relational factors include trust, reciprocity, position in the network, and history. The individual factors consist of personality, expertise, social capital, and reputation. These decisions of how one chooses to acquire knowledge depend on the knowledge they aim to seek. Furthermore, individual strategies for seeking, gathering, and sharing

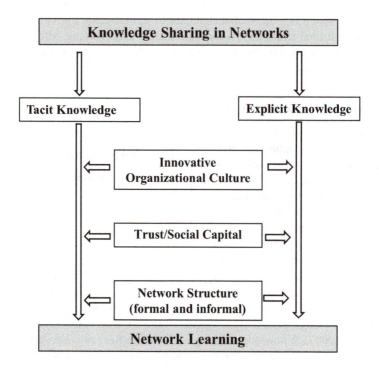

Figure 6.1 Knowledge Sharing and Management in Networks

knowledge are influenced by certain resource characteristics, such as availability, access, and expertise (Binz-Scharf et al., 2012; Díez-Vial & Montoro-Sánchez, 2014).

Agranoff (2007) highlighted informational, developmental, outreach, and action networks in his book, *Managing within Networks*. The informational and developmental networks focus primarily on creating opportunities to handle knowledge interactively. On the other hand, the outreach and action networks focus on ensuring that knowledge management programs are organized and operated effectively and efficiently. He also identifies six different modes of knowledge regarding strategies that help with the management. These include group discussion, political negotiation, application of solutions to issues, formulaic procedures, data-driven decision-making, and pre-decision simulation (Agranoff, 2007).

Successful knowledge management is driven by the members of the network, the types of problems they address, and the severity of the situation. This creates a culture of mutual learning, shared cognitive frames, inclusive culture, and knowledge development. It is necessary for the knowledge managers to be a cornerstone of any strategy, where knowledge-seeking culture and promotion of communities of practice will ease the distinction between explicit and tacit knowledge. In addition, public managers need to understand and develop knowledge programs as part of the collaborative enterprise and network governance (Agranoff, 2008). Deliberately designed knowledge management systems will help network participant willingness to share knowledge and contribution to network success (Mergel, Lazer, & Binz-Scharf, 2008).

Knowledge Sharing and Information Exchange in Formal and Informal Networks

Networks can be formal or informal, with each type of structure influencing the exchange of knowledge differently (see Chapter 3 for the types of networks). Formal and informal networks play a substantial role in learning, diffusion of innovation, and new discoveries. Formal networks are often formed through contracts or other legally binding documents and are easy to locate due to their official status. Formal networks are also viewed as more reliable information sources. When there are formal networks consisting of hierarchal structures, questions may be presented to predetermined individuals in the network (Binz-Scharf et al., 2012; Powell, 1998; Yi, Berry, & Chen, 2018). Contacting the IT department at your institution to solve technical issues is an example of reaching out to a predetermined group within a network. This stance, however, should not lead to neglecting informal networks in knowledge sharing and learning. Informal networks are harder to find in a formal report but represent the interpersonal relationships between individuals, serving as an advice or friendship network. When presented with a problem, Nebus (2006) argued that an individual may turn instead to their friendship or advice network—as there is a strong sense of trust there and the contact is accessible—and willing to share. Interpersonal relationships exist without a formal structure. It is harder to document and measure effectiveness of informal networks. Asking the person in the nearest office to help solve computer or technical issues is an example of information sharing in an informal arrangement.

Informal networks play a key role in information sharing. Communities of practice are one example of an informal network. *Communities of practice* include professionals who work in similar fields, both independently and as part of a collective effort (Kapucu, 2012; Wenger, 2005). Similar to an apprenticeship, individuals who are less familiar with the practices of the group may solicit advice but are usually not fully involved (Binz-Scharf et al., 2012). Communities of practice may include individuals in different geographic locations who are working toward solutions

---

Communities of Practice

Communities formed by professionals of a shared expertise in order to facilitate the sharing of knowledge to solve a common problem.

to common problems as well (Binz-Scharf et al., 2012). The social intranet used in several government organizations is a good example of a "network of practice" related to communities of practice (Brown & Duguid, 2000). "Corridor," a program used in the United States Department of State, is considered a "workaround for tasks that are too bureaucratic or obsolete to add value" as it is a forum for adding to the collective tacit knowledge base (Mergel, 2016, p. 15). Corridor is similar to a wiki page, allowing for real time edits, communities based on specific knowledge areas, internal and external knowledge sharing, and a comprehensive search function, places the advice and knowledge of thousands in a single location (Mergel, 2016). In this way, the intranet provides a trustworthy and low risk solution to knowledge sharing in a network setting.

Network outcomes for knowledge sharing and knowledge management can be observable, content-based or process-based (Klijn, Steijn, & Edelenbos, 2010), performance-based, structural, or relational (Provan & Milward, 2001), and achieved at the individual, network, or organizational level (Eglene, Dawes, & Schneider, 2007). Formal or informal power as well as different leadership styles can influence knowledge sharing and management success for networks. Leaders can help build a team culture as well as trust, which is critical for information sharing in networks. Results often initiate a new set of practices across organizational boundaries, requiring substantial process, behavioral, and structural changes from participating individuals, organizations, and the network as a whole (Pardo et al., 2006).

Both formal and informal network ties are important in understanding how information is exchanged within networks. For instance, Binz-Scharf et al. (2012) claimed that people tend to go through formal structures first when accessing needed information especially in centralized systems or networks. However, this is not to discount the important role that interpersonal networks play in providing access to vital information. Even within formal networks, individuals tend to favor personal sources over impersonal ones. In describing how academics most often turn to personal sources first for information, "[t]oday of course, one would have to add interpersonal contacts facilitated through e-mail or 'blogs' between scientific and technical people" (Agranoff, 2008, p. 163).

Figure 6.2 presents a hypothetical network with two densely connected groups with two boundary spanners. Even though the two groups in the network are deeply connected, only two people connect the two groups. Peter and Mark play a substantial role informally connecting the two groups. If the two are not connected, the information flow or knowledge sharing will not be possible between the two groups or subgroups. Mark and Peter are connected to other individuals in the network besides their own. They are in a good position to bring innovative ideas to their groups because of low constraint (not limited to a small network of individuals). Sarah, on the other hand, can be a creative and innovative individual but her position in the network prevents her from getting different ideas from outside her network (unless shared by Peter).

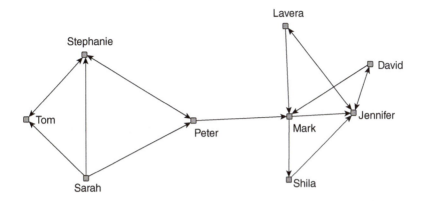

Figure 6.2 Knowledge Sharing in a Network

Knowledge exchange via informal networks is not only reserved for intranets embedded in an organization. Informal networks can be source of knowledge an information, especially in decentralized networks, systems, or communities. Crowdsourced information gathering, through websites like the Participedia project, allows individuals to become producers and user of data and knowledge (Fung & Warren, 2011). Participedia project is an "open-source, participatory knowledge tool that responds to a new global phenomenon: the rapid development of experiments in new forms of participatory politics and governance around the world" (Fung & Warren, 2011, p. 341). It functions much like Wikipedia, in that it invites and encourages open source participation and peer editing and prides itself on containing real-time data. However, Participedia's scope and participants are much more homogenous to an academic specification. It relies on and is open to all students, scholars, and practitioners for contributions, as well as edits, and thus utilizes a crowdsource data gathering methodology. The internet can be used to expand the "who" of information sharing as it is a way to consolidate local knowledge into a global database. Lazer, Mergel, Ziniel, Esterling, and Neblo (2011) examined the design of webpages in the US House of Representatives to explore the role that three institutional mechanisms have in relation to organizing collective effort in problem solving: market, hierarchy, and network. Focusing on informal networks, they examine how the system pools together the experiences of various offices' use of their official websites. Market, network, and hierarchy have their distinctive logics in organizing human activity, and each plays an important role for knowledge sharing and collective learning. Vendors play a critical role in aggregating experiences and standardizing practice through their provision of services to multiple offices. Multiple hierarchies govern office behavior, with both the administration of the House and the powers within the House (through the parties) playing key roles.

There were two pathways by which offices affect each other in the study: interpersonal communication and passive observation (Lazer et al., 2011). Attentional networks (passive observation) played a larger role than interpersonal networks (Lazer et al., 2011). The relative unimportance of interpersonal networks is explained through two factors: longevity in position and longevity in career. Both of these are scare for the individuals in charge of websites in congressional offices (Lazer et al., 2011). On the other hand, the importance of attentional networks is explained by the nature of the innovation, where merely observing what other congressional offices do with their websites is easier and cheaper.

The Use of Information and Communication Technology in Networks

We have seen enormous developments in ICT over the last two decades. Organizations use ICT to increase knowledge utilization and improve decision-making and problem-solving. To solve complex problems, networks in public administration often find solutions in a combination of practice-based (every day challenges, tacit knowledge) and evidence-based (research driven, explicit knowledge) innovations (Agranoff, 2007; Ahuja, 2000; Binz-Scharf et al., 2012; Huang, 2014). Innovation can be the product of a successful knowledge sharing network (Considine & Lewis, 2007). The central node utilizes collective trust and openness (lowered risk) in order to produce a positive outcome. In this case, while advice (mostly formal) networks are usable, it is the strategic information networks using ICTs that allow for the greatest success in innovation, service production, and performance (Brown, O'Toole, & Brudney, 1998; Chen & Lee, 2018; Considine & Lewis, 2007).

ICT is critical for knowledge sharing in organizations and networks. ICTs such as webinars, cloud systems, video conferencing systems, and the intranet provide solutions across the network, thus eliminating the need for individual solutions (Mergel, 2016). Overlapping use of ICTs in networks can impede knowledge sharing. Overlapping systems require increasing compatibility in order to ensure the smooth transfer of knowledge from one actor to another (Hu & Kapucu, 2014). When organizations keep channels of communication open and learn from one another, they gain second hand experience. This allows them to develop and maintain a network and improve public service production (or co-production) and delivery (Pardo et al., 2006; Nebus, 2006).

Innovation can be found in many forms, including the knowledge network itself. As mentioned before, the Participedia project allows for collaboration around the world, through the use of an open source code platform. Individuals join the data process and become members of a new network by posting information to be added to the global knowledgebase (Fung & Warren, 2011). This is considered innovative as it allows for new solutions to traditional problems using technology. Fung and Warren (2011) discussed the use of crowd sourced data to predict flu trends (based on localized google searches on flu symptoms), document accountability within elections (as seen in the Kenyan elections), and even track migratory animals.

Information is critical for networks as much as networks are critical for information sharing. It is also how to use that information when collaborating with other organizations in a network to provide public value and evaluate the network's performance (Agranoff, 2007, 2008; Brown et al., 1998). When public organizations lack the necessary information to create public value, they rely on the private sector, which possess the information and resources to form a collaborative effort to create change or create public value (Donahue & Zeckhauser, 2011). It is not only critical to collect information and data, but also to use in managing knowledge in order to understand how networks change and sustain over time (Suitor, Wellman, & Morgan, 1997).

ICTs can enable large-scale participation in problem solving or information sharing. The Participedia project, as outlined by Fung and Warren (2011), is demonstrative of a 'tangled problem' which involves the use of third parties and public input in order to solve it. Tangled problems can be classified as moderately ill-defined or problems that lay between complex and simple problems (Dawes et al., 2009). Often in public-private collaborations, there are impediments to knowledge exchange given the nature of the competing interest. In regard to information exchange, potential competing interests between the public and private sector might emerge as private entities aim for profit maximization (Donahue & Zeckhauser, 2011). Tools such as the Participedia project can help to overcome these issues of information exchange, as

> new information technologies can enable collaborative research on a large scale in areas in which the variety of phenomena is high, knowledge of the phenomena is widely held, and the technical and educational barriers for knowledge contribution are relatively low.
>
> (Fung & Warren, 2011, p. 346)

In a recent report, the Urban Institute (La Vigne et al., 2017) highlighted core elements of data sharing for crime prevention for government agencies at different levels and jurisdictions. Critical resources for data integration and interoperability included in the report are the following: resources, technology, cultural interoperability and political support, sufficient staffing in each organization in the network, shared goals and cultural interoperability, shared mental models, and leadership support from the central administration of each actor in the network. A framework and structure for data and knowledge sharing, partner identification, and relationship management are also critical for data integration and knowledge sharing.

Knowledge-Sharing Barriers in Networks

Knowledge sharing processes in multi-organizational public-sector settings face difficulty across agencies, as each has its own cultures, incentives, risks, and barriers for sharing and trust (Evans & Campos, 2012; Pardo et al., 2006). Knowledge, innovations, and discoveries are actively sought out based on individual choices, not passively transported through social systems (Binz-Scharf et al., 2012). Searching and acquiring innovative knowledge has costs, risks, and trade-offs for individual actors in the network. Actors make calculations about transaction costs and weighs the trade-offs of expertise versus trustworthiness, information quality versus source accessibility, and information quality versus the costs and time to obtain that information (Nebus, 2006). Actors may also worry that admitting ignorance within a network may expose its vulnerability and negatively impact reputation (Binz-Scharf et al., 2012).

Structural issues, such as lack of legal or policy guidance, are prevalent barriers for knowledge (especially explicit) sharing in networks. Organizations that are involved in PSKNs must mind policy and legal constraints (including cost allocation, jurisdiction issues), competing policy agendas and priorities (Dawes et al., 2009, p. 398), technological, organizational, and institutional situations within each participating organization, as well as the existing interorganizational relationships (Pardo et al., 2006). A theory of network formation, discussed earlier in the book, analyzes who people contact when they need an advice and suggests that the advice seeker, when possessing rich information on potential alters, decides who to contact by trading off expected knowledge value versus the cost of obtaining it (Nebus, 2006). Additionally, the loss of autonomy and competitive edge are also organizational concerns (Popp et al., 2014).

The nature of knowledge itself can be a hindrance to knowledge-sharing. Contrary to explicit knowledge, which is highly encodable, directly observed, captured, and expressed by formal technique, tacit knowledge can be difficult to codify, and often requires person-to-person contact (Nebus, 2006). Other knowledge characteristics that concern public organizations are privacy, confidentiality, security concerns, ambiguity about statutory authority to collect, share, or release and exemption of information (Podolny & Page, 1998). Some potential barriers to information sharing are based off ignorance. People oftentimes do not like to admit that they do not know something, so it can prove to be difficult to seek help. Another obstacle would consist of possible ramifications outside the network such as the reputation of the particular group or network (Binz-Scharf et al., 2012).

Recent research focuses on the movement away from a "need to know" toward a "need to share" network culture. The elusive nature of knowledge can cause considerable difficulty for public sector knowledge networks. It is dangerous to assume that meanings are clear, context is understood, and quality is acceptable to all participants. As a potentially sharable resource, knowledge varies in several essential respects—codifiability, embeddedness, and dynamics. Each variation demands substantially different treatment within a network. They are a form of cross-boundary exchange in a network. The boundaries of organizations, jurisdictions, and sectors present the most obvious challenges, but the subtler boundaries related to ideology, professional norms, cultural differences, differences in cognitive frames and institutional divisions can be equally problematic.

Trust comes in different forms that work best under different conditions. Lack of sufficient trust- and lack of the right kind of trust—can be powerful inhibitors to PSKNs. Risk is inevitable in PSKNs and is perceived and handled differently by different players. The processes of PSKN engagement build professional networks, organizational connections, and reusable capabilities regardless of the level of substantive network success. Acquiring legal authority for a PSKN is a necessity, but there is no one-size-fits-all approach to structuring formal authority. Regardless of structure, mobilizing political support helps. Policy barriers are the greatest obstacles to substantive success in building PSKNs, but often they can be navigated by early intervention, focused action, and consistent attention. Organizational barriers are serious, but amenable to innovation and creative management. Early experience sets the tone and direction of cross-boundary relationships- unrealistic, incorrect, or misaligned expectations, processes, incentives, and assumptions are hard to change once set. Learning and adaptation are essential to PSKN development and survival. Technology is also necessary but not sufficient for success (Dawes et al., 2009).

Although these concerns regarding effective knowledge sharing exist in public organizations that are not participating in PSKN's, they become exponentially more important as the communication flow begins to travel in a direction different from the formal structure of the organization (Considine & Lewis, 2007). This includes lateral and horizontal flow through interorganizational avenues. When there is no policy to direct this flow, the trust within the relationship among actors will guide their advice seeking (Binz-Scharf et al., 2012), as the network is based on trust and the more the trust within a relationship, the lower the transaction costs of that knowledge-sharing, and the lower the risks (Pardo et al., 2006). Therefore, it is important for organizations to establish activities that help professionals to connect to one another and deepen their relationships among agency actors. These deep relational ties facilitate instrumental use of knowledge, especially of the tacit variety, which is the most difficult to share (Hansen, 1999). Trust is listed as a mediating factor within the conceptual model of knowledge management.

Knowledge sharing is a result of personal relationships, social capital, and investment in trust building. Organizations can invest and build social capital by convening individuals, information use in problem-solving, managing personnel resources, and managing material resources (Díez-Vial & Montoro-Sánchez, 2014; Dawes et al., 2009). Intentionally designed mechanisms, institutional and network capacity, policy and legal frameworks in the form of an interorganizational structure, as well as leadership support, can assist in knowledge sharing despite its difficulties in networks. Recently developed ICT utilization within these sociotechnical systems can also assist in knowledge sharing in networks. Network learning and adaptation can assist in eliminating some of the barriers mentioned earlier as well.

Knowledge Sharing and Network Learning

As networks work with knowledge creation, use, and innovation, they are expected to learn as they develop and address complex issues. Direct and indirect ties can impact network knowledge sharing, creativity and innovation as structural holes, or disconnections among network members. These can negatively impact network learning and knowledge sharing (Ahuja, 2000; Borgatti & Cross, 2003). Knowledge sharing and learning can occur both in formal and informal settings (Powell, 1998). Knowledge networks are considered learning organizations that require adaptation (Dawes et al., 2009). Agranoff (2008) suggested, in terms of translation of tacit knowledge, that "rather than focusing on operationalizing tacit knowledge, greater emphasis needs to be placed on new ways of talking, fresh forms of interacting, and novel ways of distinguishing and connecting" (p. 166).

Understanding network level learning can assist in our understanding of network level effectiveness (Provan & Milward, 1995). Network learning should focus not on network as a context for organizational learning, but rather learning as a system. More critical question would be how we can utilize knowledge management and information sharing strategies to improve network learning. Leach et al. added that it is important to address where learning occurs, and how learning occurs in networks, in addition to answering the classic questions of who learns, what they learn, and consequences of learning within the policy context (Bennett & Howlett, 1992), learning, (Leach, Weible, Vince, Siddiki, & Calanni, 2014). Tracking these five elements of learning in networks would be a good contribution. Howlett, Mukherjee, and Koppenjan (2017) highlighted the availability of multiple 'brokers' and their critical position in a policy network to facilitate learning. (Policy learning goes beyond the coverage of the chapter).

Frank, Penuel, and Krause (2015) explored how interorganizational networks, especially subgroups, affect policies and practices in organizations through implementation and successful change management. They provide managers with "know-how" flows that will contribute to organizational change and management. Frank et al. (2015) defined know-how as "the accumulated practical skill or expertise that allows one to do something smoothly and efficiently" (p. 378). They find that know-how is essential for learning, communicating and coordinating. This is similar to teachers in a classroom, because the school system works in a very hierarchical way, teachers often find themselves going past their job descriptions and having informal ways of coordinating tasks. Whether it is with other teachers, these networks are created informally, and on a local level, regardless of who is at the top. Schools are similar to other organizations whose workers draw on networks to adapt innovations to local contexts. Managers play a substantial role in the distribution of resources and sharing knowledge and know-how. It is their responsibility to build an environment that will help ensure better policy and practices. The study also found that implementing know-how is crucial for managers when determining the distribution of resources.

Organizational, group, and individual level learning have been studied substantially in organization studies. Network learning is a relatively new topic of interest. Network learning can be defined as learning from members of the networks and outside stakeholders to improve network performance and generate innovative ideas or/and usable knowledge. It

> **Network Learning**
>
> The natural process by which network actors learn from one another and share knowledge. Organizational learning across network members leads to network-level changes.

is not just organizational or individual actor level learning in interorganizational setting, rather a system or network level learning. Knight (2002) defined network learning as "learning by a group of organizations as a group" (p. 428). Network learning is also different from learning in a network or interorganizational learning. Network learning will cause a behavioral change of the network and not of individual members of it. Network learning requires advanced level learning as well as linkages to a goal that is larger than an individual or organizational level goal or mission (Engel, Woolley, Jing, Chabris, & Malone, 2014; Newig, Gunther, & Pahl-Wost, 2010). It is considered a prerequisite to organizational level learning (Schulz & Geithner, 2010). Scholars also found that the level of engagement, diversity of participants, and high level of trust help network learning and resilience, as discussed in Chapter 4. Network members who will want to increase network or system level learning "should devote adequate time and resources to cultivating interpersonal trust and procedural fairness" (Leach et al., 2014, p. 611). They also highlighted that knowledge acquisition and learning can lead to behavioral change and institutional rearrangements. Connectivity or being part of a network is considered an important and positive contribution element of learning and innovation in or through networks (Krätke, 2010).

Social network analysis measures such as density, betweenness centrality, and structural holes can provide additional analytical tools to investigate knowledge sharing, information exchange, and network learning. Basics of networks and network analysis were provided in Chapter 3. Chapters 10 through 14 provide some application examples including knowledge sharing and learning in networks.

Conclusion

Knowledge management is crucial to understanding how a network operates and how collaboration can move forward. Without the sharing of knowledge, trust is hard to build. Lack of knowledge sharing might hinder network success of even cause a potential collapse. Knowing the type of knowledge, tacit or explicit, will help us design different management and information sharing strategies for better knowledge sharing and network learning. Managing or sharing tacit knowledge in networks is much more difficult compared to explicit knowledge.

Knowledge management and information-sharing is a complex and multifaceted issue. Before managing knowledge, one should differentiate between explicit and tacit. The explicit knowledge can be directly observed while the tacit knowledge is complex, hard to articulate. There are various tools for knowledge sharing such as: data bases, corporate libraries, intranets, sharing best practices, training programs, creating virtual organizations. In the process of knowledge management technology may be used and citizen participation may be involved.

For the knowledge management to be successful, public management networks need to focus on not only getting information but also sharing it. As knowledge management continues to improve, strategies, tools, and successful tips relating to its progress are becoming evident. While sharing information is imperative to furthering our knowledge capacity, it is important to remember that both risk and trust are critical components for its success. Relationship building and shared worldviews among members are significant for effective tacit knowledge management. Mangers and leaders in networks should promote a culture of openness, trust, inclusiveness, and respect to different ideas and competing interests to embrace knowledge creation and use for effective network governance. Still, there is a lot to be learned on knowledge management in networks. The next chapter addresses power and decision-making in networks.

References

Agranoff, R. (2007). *Managing within networks: Adding value to public organizations.* Washington, DC: Georgetown University Press.

Agranoff, R. (2008). Collaboration for knowledge learning from public management networks. In L. B. Bingham & R. O'Leary (Eds.), *Big ideas in collaborative public management* (pp. 36–54). Armonk, NY: M. E. Sharpe.

Ahuja, G. (2000). Collaboration networks, structural holes, and innovation: A longitudinal study. *Administrative Science Quarterly, 45*(3), 425–455.

Augier, M., & Vendelo, M. T. (1999). Networks, cognition and management of tacit knowledge. *Journal of Knowledge Management, 3*(4), 252–261.

Bennett, C. J., & Howlett, M. (1992). The lessons of learning: Reconciling theories of policy learning and policy change. *Policy Sciences, 25*, 275–294.

Binz-Scharf, M. C., Lazer, D., & Mergel, I. (2012). Searching for answers networks of practice among public administrators. *The American Review of Public Administration, 42*(2), 202–225.

Borgatti, S. P., & Cross, R. (2003). A relational view of information seeking and learning in social networks. *Management Science, 49*(4), 432–445.

Brown, J. S., & Duguid, P. (2000). *The social life of information.* Boston, MA: Harvard Business School Press.

Brown, J. S., & Duguid, P. (2001). Knowledge and organization: A social-practice perspective. *Organization Science, 12*(2), 40–57.

Brown, M. M., O'Toole, L. J. Jr., & Brudney, J. L. (1998). Implementing information technology in government: An empirical assessment of the role of local partnerships. *Journal of Public Administration Research and Theory, 8*(4), 499–525.

Chen, Y., & Lee, J. (2018). Collaborative data networks for public service: Governance, management, and performance. *Public Management Review, 20*(5), 672–690.

Considine, M., & Lewis, J. M. (2007). Innovation and innovators inside government: From institutions to networks. *Governance, 20*(4), 581–607.

Dawes, S. S., Cresswell, A. M., & Pardo, T. A. (2009). From "need to know" to "need to share": Tangled problems, information boundaries, and the building of public sector knowledge networks. *Public Administration Review, 69*(3), 392–402.

Díez-Vial, I., & Montoro-Sánchez, Á. (2014). Social capital as a driver of local knowledge exchange: A social network analysis. *Knowledge Management Research & Practice, 12*(3), 276–288.

Donahue, J. D., & Zeckhauser, R. J. (2011). *Collaborative governance: Private roles for public goals in turbulent times.* Princeton, NJ: Princeton University Press.

Eglene, O., Dawes, S. S., & Schneider, C. A. (2007). Authority and leadership patterns in public sector knowledge networks. *The American Review of Public Administration, 37*(1), 91–113.

Engel, D., Woolley, A. W., Jing, L. X., Chabris, C. F., & Malone, T. W. (2014). Reading the mind in the eyes or reading between the lines? Theory of mind predicts collective intelligence equally well online and face-to-face. *PLoS One, 9*(12), e115212.

Evans, A. M., & Campos, A. (2012). Open government initiatives: Challenges of citizen participation. *Journal of Policy Analysis and Management, 32*(1), 172–203.

Flyvbjerg, B. (2001). *Making social science matter: Why social inquiry fails and how it can succeed again.* Cambridge, UK: Cambridge University Press.

Frank, K. A., Penuel, W. R., & Krause, A. (2015). What is "good" social network for policy implementation? The flow of know-how for organizational change. *Journal of Policy Analysis and Management, 34*(2), 378–402.

Fung, A., & Warren, M. E. (2011). The Participedia project: An introduction. *International Public Management Journal, 14*(3), 341–362.

Hansen, M. T. (1999). The search-transfer problem: The role of weak ties in sharing knowledge across organization subunits. *Administrative Science Quarterly, 44*(1), 82–111.

Hartley, J., & Benington, J. (2006). Copy and paste, or graft and transplant? Knowledge sharing through inter-organizational networks. *Public Money & Management, 26*(2), 101–108.

Howlett, M., Mukherjee, I., & Koppenjan, J. (2017). Policy learning and policy networks in theory and practice: The role of policy brokers in the Indonesian biodiesel policy network. *Policy and Society, 36*(2), 233–250.

Hu, Q., & Kapucu, N. (2014). Information communication technology (ICT) utilization for effective emergency management networks. *Public Management Review, 18*(3), 323–348.

Huang, K. (2014). Knowledge sharing in a third-party-governed health and human services network. *Public Administration Review, 74*(5), 587–598.

Kapucu, N. (2012). Classrooms as communities of practice: Designing and facilitating learning in a networked environment. *Journal of Public Affairs Education, 18*(3), 585–610.

Klijn, E-H., Steijn, B., & Edelenbos, J. (2010). The impact of network management on outcomes in governance networks. *Public Administration, 88*(4), 1063–1082.

Knight, L. (2002). Network learning: Exploring learning by interorganizational networks. *Human Relations, 55*(4), 427.

Krätke, S. (2010). Regional knowledge networks: A network analysis approach to the interlinking of knowledge resources. *European Urban and Regional Studies, 17*(1), 83–97.

La Vigne, N., Paddock, E., Irvin-Erickson, Y., Kim, K., Peterson, B., & Bieler, S. (2017). *A blueprint for interagency and cross-jurisdictional data sharing.* Washington, DC: Urban Institute.

Lazer, D., Mergel, I., Ziniel, C., Esterling, K. M., & Neblo, M. A. (2011). The multiple institutional logics of innovation. *International Public Management Journal, 14*(3), 311–340.

Leach, W. D., Weible, C. M., Vince, S. R., Siddiki, S. N., & Calanni, J. C. (2014). Fostering learning through collaboration: Knowledge acquisition and belief change in marine aquaculture partnerships. *Journal of Public Administration Research and Theory, 24*(3), 591–622.

Mergel, I. A. (2016). *The social intranet: Insights on managing and sharing knowledge internally.* Washington, DC: IBM Center for the Business of Government.

Mergel, I. A., Lazer, D. M., & Binz-Scharf, M. C. (2008). Lending a helping hand: Voluntary engagement in a network of professionals. *International Journal of Learning and Change, 3*(1), 5–22.

Nebus, J. (2006). Building collegial information networks: A theory of advice network generation. *Academy of Management Review, 31*(3), 615–637.

Newig, J., Gunther, D., & Pahl-Wost, C. (2010). Synapses in the network: Learning in governance networks in the context of environmental management. *Ecology and Society, 15*(4), 24–40.

Nonino, F. (2013). The network dimensions of intra-organizational social capital. *Journal of Management & Organization, 19*(4), 454–477.

Nowell, B. (2009). Out of sync and unaware? Exploring the effects of problem frame alignment and discordance in community collaboratives. *Journal of Public Administration Research and Theory, 20*(1), 91–116.

Pardo, T. A., Cresswell, A. M., Thompson, F., & Zhang, J. (2006). Knowledge sharing in cross-boundary information system development in the public sector. *Information Technology and Management, 7*(4), 293–313.

Podolny, J. M., & Page, K. L. (1998). Network forms of organization. *Annual Review of Sociology, 24*(1), 57–76.

Popp, J. K., Milward, B. H., MacKean, G., Casebeer, A., & Lindstorm, R. (2014). *Interorganizational networks: A review of the literature to inform practice.* Washington, DC: IBM Center for the Business of Government.

Powell, W. W. (1998). Learning from collaboration: Knowledge and network in the biotechnology and pharmaceutical industries. *California Management Review, 40*(3), 228–240.

Provan, K. G., & Milward, H. B. (1995). A preliminary theory of network effectiveness: A comparative study of four mental health systems. *Administrative Science Quarterly, 40*(1), 1–33.

Provan, K. G., & Milward, H. B. (2001). Do networks really work? A framework for evaluating public-sector organizational networks. *Public Administration Review, 61*(4), 414–423.

Schulz, K., & Geithner, S. (2010). Between exchange and development: Organizational learning in schools through inter-organizational networks. *Learning Organization, 17*(1), 69–85.

Soltani, I., & Lavafan, A. (2014). The impact of knowledge management on competitive advantage considering the mediating role of organizational agility case study: The hospitality industry in Isfahan. *International Journal of Management & Information Technology, 9*(1), 2278–5612.

Suitor, J. J., Wellman, B., & Morgan, D. L. (1997). It's about time: How, why, and when networks change. *Social Networks, 19*(1), 1–7.

Weber, E. P., & Khademian, A. M. (2008). Wicked problems, knowledge challenges, and collaborative capacity builders in network settings. *Public Administration Review, 68*(2), 334–349.

Wenger, E. P. (2005). *Communities of practice: Learning, meaning, and identity.* Cambridge, UK: Cambridge University Press.

Yi, H., Berry, F. S., & Chen, W. (2018). Management innovation and policy diffusion through leadership transfer networks: An agent network diffusion model. *Journal of Public Administration Research and Theory, 28*(4), 457–474.

7 Power and Decision-Making in Interorganizational Networks

Power is relevant to our discussion as network governance involves multiple organizations from different sectors and jurisdictions in collective decision-making and public service delivery. Yet, studies on power relationships, power imbalances, and network effectiveness in interorganizational context remain limited. An organization wishing to influence stakeholders needs to have power to do so in a network setting. Public policies are designed and implemented through networks actors with intertwined ties and differentiated power, world-view, and resources. Power imbalances need to be mitigated and monitored for an interorganizational network to be successful (Bardach, 1998; Purdy, 2012). This chapter focuses on power and its impact on collective decision-making in interorganizational networks. It expands upon power relations, the complexity of decision-making in networks, and the role of leadership in promoting public interest and effective network governance. The chapter also identifies key factors that contribute to effective power structures and decision-making in interorganizational networks. The following questions are considered when we discuss the role of power in interorganizational network:

- How do power relations impact decision-making in interorganizational networks?
- Why are power and power relations critical?
- How does network leadership facilitate ways of engaging partners from different sectors?
- How can power imbalances be eased in collective decision-making?
- How does network composition influence power sharing/relationships within networks?
- How does power sharing influence network effectiveness? How do public leaders and government agencies balance their power relationships when working with non-state actors in a network?

Sources of Power in Hierarchical Structures and Interorganizational Networks

Different from the hierarchical control and centralized command structure, a network is a more flexible organizational structure for communication, resource allocation, interorganizational collaboration, and decision-making (Figure 7.1). A flexible collaborative network approach is crucial for engaging nonprofit organizations, faith-based organizations, and businesses in responding to immediate and critical community and societal needs.

Within hierarchical decision-making context, *power* is defined as "the capability to get what you want or to fulfill your identity" (March, 1994, p. 141). Dahl (1957) defined power as a process: if A has power over B then A can get B to do something that it would not do otherwise.

> ### Power within Networks
>
> Power within a network is determined by a node's relations with others and position in network.

Power distribution, power relations, power imbalance, power use, and source of power play a substantial role in organization theory (Kramer & Neale, 1998; Pfeffer, 1992). An individual's characteristics are useful for explaining personal power in an organization. These include charisma, expertise, gender, education, formal role or position in the organization, control of critical resources and information, and potential gatekeeping function in an organization (Nohria, 1992). Raven and French (1959) identified five bases of power within organizational context: coercive (punishing noncompliance), reward (rewarding compliance), legitimate (formal responsibility), referent (sense of perceived acceptance), and expert (knowledge or expertise). They later added information, or the ability to control information, as a source of power. These six bases of power remain applicable in network environments as well.

Organizational attributes such as prior experience, culture, resources, position, and capacity, as well as authority and legitimacy, are key sources of power for both hierarchical and network arrangements (Bardach, 1998; Kapucu & Demiroz, 2011; Klijn & Koppenjan, 2016; Purdy, 2012). Authority refers to judgment or decision-making power granted to an actor as a result of them inhabiting a socially accepted position. The state and its agencies exercise their authority through a legal system and bureaucratic organization based on expertise. Different from authority, resourcefulness, or aspects such as human resources, size of the organization, financial resources, experience, expertise, can also be considered sources of power. For example, an organization with

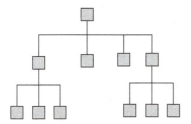
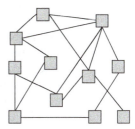

Figure 7.1 Hierarchical and Network Organization

extensive experience in dealing with disasters will take a more accepted and appreciated leadership role in disaster/emergency management networks than an organization with less experience (Kapucu & Demiroz, 2011; Kapucu & Van Wart, 2006). Organizations, if they are part of larger discourses or play a role in legitimization, such as public diplomacy can also claim power in interorganizational networks (Benson, 1975; Purdy, 2012).

The traditional attributes of an individual have been useful for explaining personal power in organizations. However, power relations in networks demand additional perspectives. Huxham and Beech (2008) elaborated that power in networks is similar to March's analysis (1994), by highlighting an organization's capacity to "influence, control, or resist the activities of others" (p. 555). This definition is more relevant to our discussion on network governance and interorganizational networks involving collective decision-making for public service delivery. An organization trying to influence other stakeholders needs to have enough power and, simultaneously, power imbalances need to be monitored for the success of an interorganizational network arrangement (Kelman, Hong, & Turbitt, 2013; Purdy, 2012).

A network approach to power provides additional insight in determining power. Network research often focuses on relations and the structure of those relationships (Provan & Lemaire, 2012; Scott, 2013; Scott & Davis, 2007). An organization's position in a network determines, in part, the challenges or opportunities that it will face. Therefore, identifying an organization's position within a network is critical for predicting power relations, as well as the performance of an actor in an interorganizational setting. Castells (2011) used "networked power," defining it as "the form of power exercised by certain nodes over other nodes within the network" (p. 781). The location in the network provides access to resources and, more importantly, to information and knowledge. The power imbalance within a network affects the way the knowledge is shared. Organizations in the network have or accumulate power based on their access to critical resources (broadly defined) or control of the resources needed by others (Emerson, 1962; Klijn & Koppenjan, 2016).

In addition to the position, power in networks can be derived from informal relationships (social capital) and the structure of relationships. Organizations could mobilize resources through social relationships (Galaskiewicz, 1979). What happens in an interorganizational setting is also, in part, a function of the structure of relations among the actors. Past research either investigated individual behavior that reflected power within organizations or focused on macro-level analysis of how power is structurally positioned within networks and organizations. Therefore, integration of the micro-macro perspectives and discussions on both structural and behavioral aspects of power within networks is needed (Brass & Burkhardt, 1993). Structural power is generated by "structural positions that serve as a basis for the exercise of power: formal (hierarchical level) and informal (network position)" (Brass & Burkhardt, 1993, p. 444). Structural power helps us understand the power dynamics in a network based on the position of an actor. Behavioral power is tactics and actions used to exercise power such as assertiveness, rationality, and information exchange (Brass & Burkhardt, 1993). Structural and behavioral bases of power are not competing explanations of power but are in fact complementary as "structure arises from the actions of people, and these actions are shaped by structure" (Brass & Burkhardt, 1993, p. 443).

Power within networks needs to be studied, identified, and examined to understand its role in building, functioning, and sustaining networks (Edelenbos & Klijn, 2007). If executed in a balanced way, power can help build trust. In addition to power and trust, we bring structural, behavioral power, and homophily) as important features that help to explain connections and ties within networks (Berardo & Lubell, 2016; McPherson, Smith-Lovin, & Cook, 2001). Homophily, or actors' similarity, might impact the structure of a network. For example, nonprofit organizations might easily join a network with other nonprofits in addressing a social concern. Positional attributes of an actor will be an important factor the way the organizations practice power.

In addition to conceptual explanation of power in networks, network analysis tools and method can also be useful in analysis power in networks. Brass and Burkhardt (1992), for example, utilize degree centrality (actor with many relations or links), betweenness centrality (central connection links other actors), and closeness centrality (immediate access to core actors in the networks) measures as a way of determining someone's power in the network. They also use structural sources of power in the system as formal (hierarchical) and informal (social capital). Formal power is attached to the position or position of an organization in the network (Pfeffer, 1992; Scott & Davis, 2007). Formal power can also be based on a design or structure of a network. We do not claim in this chapter that network position from a structural point of view is the only reason determining power, but it can be an important explanation in addition to the individual organizational characteristics. A network perspective can be useful for understanding power dynamics and strategies gain or control power.

Studying Power Relations in Networks

In this section of the chapter, we discuss why studying power is complex in networks and propose different angles from which to examine power relations in interorganizational networks. Power is a complex organizational and network-positional attribute to investigate because of several related variables and dimensions. Power in networks is even more difficulty to examine. The attributes of networks such as strengths of ties, number of participants, trust and social capital, goal consensus, and network type may influence the behavior of power sharing among organizations.

Power can be considered an independent variable as well as a dependent variable. In the following sections, we will address sources of power, power distribution, power imbalances, and potential conflict caused by power issues in interorganizational networks and the role of power relations in network effectiveness. The role of network governance in addressing power imbalances and dealing with conflict is also addressed. Failure in effective network governance can cause power issues in networks as well.

Complexity of Power Relations and Decision-making in Networks

In complex policy fields requiring networked or coordinated solutions, there are multiple agencies usually with conflicting goals, agendas, and interests. How might power be accommodated under these conditions? Coordinated action can be accomplished by the standardization of tasks and having specific, network level goals (Kelman et al., 2013; Thompson, 2007). In a shared power environment, since no single organization has information and the ability to address complex public challenges alone, multiple organizations work collaboratively to improve collective service delivery and decision-making. Networks raise substantial concerns about power imbalance, power sharing, accountability, and legitimacy and creating complexity in network arrangements.

Network governance involves formal as well as informal structures. This makes understanding and analyzing dynamic power relations in networks challenging. Traditional sources of power are limited in explaining the role, imbalance, and use of power in networks. A relational perspective of power is better suited in network perspectives for explaining power dynamics in networks. Organizations with power can monopolize their capacity and influence in networks leading to differentiated power among participants. Relational aspects of power require insights into the network's internal and environmental context. We address relational aspect of power by addressing position of an organization, its resourcefulness, source of power (such as legal authority), resource availability, and legitimacy (Table 7.1).

Networks are created to address a specific issue and increased resources for network through connections and do not replace hierarchical structure for individual organizations. Networks are becoming larger parts of individual organizations but are external to these actors who remain largely the same in terms of their own internal organization. Government agencies collaborate with other agencies and/or nonprofit and private organizations with their existing structures. This additional collaboration creates another layer of complexity in terms of network governance. Past literature has addressed power imbalances and power sources by examining organizational attributes such as prior experience, capacity, and resources. These core elements need to be investigated within complex network environment.

Power Relations in Networks

Power is included as core elements of effective management and leadership in network scholarship (e.g., O'Toole, 2015). The initiation and activation of networks and building capacity all require an understanding of power dynamics.

Table 7.1 Examining Power Relations and Use in Interorganizational Network

Stages	*Exercise and Sources of Power in Interorganizational Networks*		
	Relationship & Structure	*Resources & Capacity*	*Legitimacy & Trust*
Formation	Selection of stakeholders Members of the network Number of participants Prior experience	Organizational resources Representatives Expertise, roles, functions Capabilities	Membership to the network with known organizations Vested interest Mission fit
Development	Engagement in network development Regular interaction in decision-making Position in the network Decision-making authority	How the resources are shared Protocols for resources sharing	Frequent communication Position to lead agency Joint initiatives Communication with the lead agency
Sustainability	Shared outcomes Goal consensus Use of network position as power Institutional rules, norms	Information sharing Joint examination of the core issues Organization of meetings and dissemination of minutes	Issue prioritization Identifying ways to address issues, Identifying resources to address issues

Among the three identified areas of network research in the book (policy networks, collaborative networks, and governance networks) all three include concepts of power (Hu, Khosa, & Kapucu, 2016; Kapucu, Hu, & Khosa, 2017). In the context of network governance (specific to interorganizational networks), multiple types of power questions deserve scrutiny.

Analyzing power in networks from dyad, node, and network levels can be expanded to the community level. However, this expansion can bring complexity and chaos to our understanding and analysis of networks. Level of analysis and unit of analysis can be of substantial concern, but analysis at community level, as well as decentralized perspectives, provide useful information.

Network attributes and composition, such as strengths of ties, number of participates, trust, social capital, goal consensus, and network type influence power relations and power imbalances in networks. Network structural configuration such as density, centralization, connectedness and different governance forms also influence the power relations and sharing within interorganizational networks. Relational power is considered an attribute of relations rather than that of an actor or organization. Actors with resources and knowledge can have a visible influence on the structure of the network and can be a major contributor of success in the network (Henry, 2011). Networks can also provide opportunities for boundary spanners and bridging structural holes can be source of a power advantage for actors in the network (Burt, 1992).

There are important basics of power to keep in mind when analyzing an interorganizational network. First, an organization that is more central in the network will have more power (e.g., Brass & Burkhardt, 1992; Choi & Robertson, 2014; Scott & Davis, 2007). Second, organizations with more resources in the network might have more power, control and authority, in decision-making (e.g., Kelman et al., 2013; Klijn & Koppenjan, 2016; Pfeffer & Slancik, 1978).

Unlike a hierarchy, there is no single actor in charge in a network. Some members of the network might have more power than others. In addition to formal power, informal power may play an important role in networks (Keast, Mandell, Brown, & Woolcock, 2004). Relationships, roles, and positions in a network, as well as structure of a network, can impact power relations and power sharing in interorganizational arrangements. Organizational resources, attributes, and prior experience, as well as institutional norms, rules, and environmental risks can be sources of power imbalance in a hierarchical structure. Network management and leadership can play critical role in addressing the power relations and imbalances in a network. These issues are addressed in the following sections of the chapter.

Power Imbalance in Networks

Organizations join the network with different levels of resources and capacity, thereby making power imbalance unavoidable (Klijn & Koppenjan, 2016; Popp, MacKean, Casebeer, Milward, & Lindstrom, 2014). Ansell and Gash (2008, 2018) treated power asymmetries as one of the initial conditions of network design and formation. Emerson, Nabatchi, and Balogh (2012), in their collaborative governance framework and collaborative regimes, considered power as one element of the broader system context. For them, positional power of participants can hinder or facilitate success of coordinated network action. Bryson, Crosby, and Stone (2006, 2015) in their collaborative governance framework, treated power imbalances as one of the factors that can influence collaboration processes and direction of network structure. Early transparent communication, joint development of shared goals, and buy-in for public interest might mitigate potential problems and help resolve conflict. Bryson et al. (2006) proposed that the success of interorganizational collaboration is impacted by preparing resources to deal with power imbalances before they worsen.

Organizations, with different attributes, may play different roles and take different positions based on resource availability in networks. Power sources and imbalances can influence how organizations form their ties and cause some conflicts (Crosby & Bryson, 2005). Conflicts and tensions usually involve power imbalances, competing logics, struggles between autonomy and interdependence, disagreement on problem severity, and the strategies and tactics used to address the shared problem. Klijn and Koppenjan (2016) related public managers' ability to handle both substantive (e.g., differences in perceptions of the nature of the problem) and strategic complexity (e.g., the differences in perceptions, objectives, and strategies of interdependent actors) to effectively sustaining networks.

It is hard to generalize for every type of network, but we can emphasize some elements of the source of power in networks and the exercise of power during different stages of networks (Table 7.1). First, during the formation stage of a network, selection of stakeholders, members, and number of participants are critical for network relationship and structure. Organizational representatives with resources, expertise, and capabilities can contribute to capacity during formation phase. Affiliation to a known organization in the network, vested interest in the policy issue, and mission fit will help legitimacy and trust during network formation phase. Second, during the development phase, regular engagement in decision-making, position in the network, and decision-making authority will be important elements in network structure. Collaborative capacity is influenced by the way the resources are shared and by the protocols on resource sharing. Regular communication, having a lead agency position, participation to joint initiatives, and regular communication with a lead agency can assist in building trust and legitimacy. Finally, joint agenda setting, developing shared outcomes, reaching goal consensus, and identifying institutional rules and norms will facilitate effective structure and relationship during the sustainability phase of networks. Regular information sharing, joint examination of core issues, and shared decision-making will facilitate building capacity and resources during this phase. During the sustainability phase, joint issue periodization, collectively addressing the issues, and identifying resources needed to address these issues will be critical in keeping trust and legitimacy in the network.

An organization with resources and capacity that participates in a network might be considered powerful. However, in earlier stages of network formation and development, an organization that initiates and invites others to participate in a network may be considered more powerful. An organization facilitating network activities (such as NAO) might gain additional power based on its role and position in the network as well. Not all organizations are interdependent at the same level with reciprocal trust. Organizations usually have dual interests in networks: one is organizational priorities and goals while the other is the network mission and goal(s). This duality may cause conflict and make power a vital element in network setting.

As mentioned earlier, the greater the discrepancies of centrality among actors, the greater the likelihood of pathological power imbalances. A densely connected network can prevent the dominance of a select few in the network (e.g., Brass & Burkhardt, 1992; Kelman et al., 2013). Higher density in networks signals less reliance on individual organizations, greater potential for resource pooling, and trust in a greater number of network members. If organizations have many reciprocated ties in the network, it is hard for one organization to have power over others (e.g., Castells, 2011; Choi & Robertson, 2014; Nohria, 1992; Purdy, 2012). Homophily also plays a role in reinforcing this network density, as it provides a strong foundation from which to build trust and social capital upon. An interorganizational network formed with similar organizations, in terms of culture or capacity, will be effective in collective decision-making and facilitating power differences (e.g., Berardo & Lubell, 2016; McPherson et al., 2001).

Power Sharing in Networks

Organizational power and centrality depend on the nature and the context of the network (Hoffman, Stearns, & Shrader, 1990; Keast et al., 2004). Sharing power among organizations in a network setting is challenging because of the inherent power imbalance and complex nature of power relations in networks. Having a facilitative lead agency or NAO in an interorganizational network can help facilitate coordination and reduce conflicts and competition by balancing power asymmetry (Alter, 1990). Benson (1975) characterizes interorganizational network as inherently political bodies in which organizations obtain and distribute resources and share information in this system of power relations. This perspective assumes interorganizational equilibrium for power sharing based on consensus, mutual respect, and reciprocal trust. Consensus among network members can be established based on clarification of role and scope, level of commitment for participation. The nature of tasks and the way the tasks are accomplished, as well as positive evaluation, or perceived organizational effectiveness, by other members in the network can contribute to power sharing and network effectiveness. Work coordination assists functional coordination among organizations in the network. Organizations' position in the network will determine their ability to obtain, share, and/or control resources.

Power is needed to involve stakeholders from different sectors. Public sector organizations sometime initiate the collaboration as well as regularly participate in these collaborations. These can include emergency management and community economic development networks. This role might raise a question of balancing state/public agencies in dealing with interorganizational networks. A balanced way of using power will help the legitimacy of the network and help keep less resourceful organizations engaged as well. Instead of focusing on one organization, or formal structures making core decisions, we need to shift our attention to how organizations and their strategies operate and evolve within complex environments of networks (Bryson, Sancino, Benington, & Sørensen, 2017). This perspective included informal and other institutional arrangements in networks and power relations in decision-making. This perspective has potential to contribute to the fast-growing body of knowledge in network governance and building capacity for network effectiveness (Provan, Veazie, Staten, & Teufel-Shone, 2005).

Organizations position themselves in the network in order to safeguard themselves and gain advantageous positions and power in obtaining resources (Pfeffer & Slancik, 1978; Weick, 2005). This perspective represents resource dependence and power relations in networks. Organizations can use two mechanisms, network extension (increase resource alternatives by creating additional links with actors in the network) and network consolidation (reduce alternative resources by partnering with other actors/organizations) to increase their resourcefulness and reduce resource dependence to others. These two perspectives represent exchange relationships and potential power arrangements among network members. Resource dependency theory assumes that organizations might avoid interorganizational networks that limit their power of autonomic decision-making and other forms of organizational autonomy. Provan and Milward (1995) addressed resource dependency by focusing on the interorganizational network, instead of the individual organizations in the network. They highlighted that networks with a centralized decision-making agency are more effective than distributed network structure, based on their research of mental health service delivery networks. Of course, the relationship between network structure and effectiveness is influenced by external environmental factors, as well such as stability and uncertainty, as mentioned in Chapter 3.

Ran and Qi (2017) proposed a contingency framework regarding power sharing and effectiveness of network governance. They highlight the contingency factors in effective collaborative arrangements instead of power sharing and power imbalances alone. They acknowledge the potential role of power imbalances as one of the major causes of conflict in network relationships. The relationship between power sharing and effectiveness of network governance is examined through six contingencies as moderating factors: institutional environment (similar to systems perspective links networks to a broader context), network mission (mission differentiation among network members and goal consensus), types of networks (informal-formal, mandated-voluntary, bottom up-top down), previous experience (expertise, tenure, legitimacy), diffusion of power sources (sources of power, authority, resources and legitimacy), and cost-benefit (potential cost for collaboration).

Collective and inclusive decision-making and inclusion of smaller organizations in said decision-making is a key element of maintaining a balanced exercise of power in a network. A balanced facilitation of power use will help the legitimacy of the network and help less resourceful organizations become engaged (e.g., Bryson et al., 2017; Huxham & Vangen, 2000). Organizations' geographic proximity in a network might help facilitate sharing power (e.g., Choi & Rebertson, 2014; Hoffman et al., 1990; Nohria, 1992). Organizations that can easily reach one another and achieve face-to-face interpersonal communication can ease tensions and avoid issues of interpretation that may arise over electronic communication.

Since power relations and resource sharing in a network can influence network effectiveness, public managers need to pay close attention to power issues to achieve a greater collaborative outcome. Managers need to identify network participants and activate resources from the participants (activation), establish network rules, collaborative goals or vision (framing), mobilize resources and gain support (mobilizing), and build and strengthen strong relationships and address conflicts (synthesizing) (Agranoff & McGuire, 2003). In networks, the perceptions and attitudes of actors change from that of a bureaucratic mode of governance toward more horizontal governance to achieve preferable outcomes in network collaboration (Isett & Miranda, 2015). Thus, the internal and external network stakeholders need to collectively identify multilevel outcomes in setting the monitoring and evaluation mechanism (Graddy & Chen, 2006; Lazega, Jourda, Mounier, & Stofer, 2008), including effective communication channels among actors in the networks and jurisdictions the actors are located (Isett & Miranda, 2015).

Power and Network Effectiveness

Power has a negative connotation for many. However, it can be a source of success if successfully diagnosed and addressed, it can be beneficial for network performance. As the foci of networks are nodes and ties, the emphasis on the relational structure is necessary in understanding how relationships between actors transfer into effectiveness. This can range from resource allocation (e.g., information, financial resource, materials, expertise, and services) (Carlsson & Sandstrom, 2008; Provan, Fish, & Sydow, 2007), relationships and communication (Berardo & Lubell, 2016; Carlsson & Sandstrom, 2008; Siciliano, 2015), and the politics among actors (Choi & Robertson, 2014; Graddy & Chen, 2006; Henry, 2011). As complexity can be assumed from the network governance, the relationships between actors are not static and can be changed over time. As ignoring power imbalance can be costly for network success, the power issue needs to be addressed carefully in terms of conflict, competition, process, and consensus building or integration.

The key consideration of the relational structure of the network is that there are transactional costs, which is the cost the actors face in joining the network. This leads to potential members comparing the benefits of collaborating to the risks (Berardo & Lubell, 2016). On the network level, the literature points out the trade-off between density and centralization (Provan et al., 2007). High levels of density may lead to the higher costs in maintaining the relationships, when such relationships seem to have limited relations to the network goals (Raab, Mannak, & Cambre, 2013). Lower centralization may lead to the fragmentation and structural holes, reflecting the difficulty to coordinate with other actors (Provan et al., 2007). Despite the recommendations regarding centralization as one of key factors for effective network performance (Carlsson & Sandstrom, 2008), too much centralization may also lead to the decreased likelihood of network learning (Isett & Miranda, 2015; Provan et al., 2007).

Conflicts are another form of costs that network actors risk. Network members not only have the network-based goals but also organizational-based goals.

Thus, the different values, goals, and interests between network members and the whole network is possible. In this sense, the cost in cooperating for collective goals may lead to the decreased individual/organizational interests/values (Carlsson & Sandstrom, 2008). Substantial costs during the network formation are inevitable, as building relationships between actors takes time (Carlsson & Sandstrom, 2008). This means that the power-seeking behavior in protecting individual/organizational values/interests, or even establishing him/her/itself as the gatekeeper, is possible (Graddy & Chen, 2006; Roberts, 1997). This might be especially the case, when coalition for power-seeking will be organized among members share ideological homophily (Henry, 2011).

In the competitive environment for funding and performance measurement among teachers (Siciliano, 2015), the benefits of useful advice and future cooperation can be overlooked by weighting the individual costs of losing face and strengthening "opponents" through collaboration. This leads to the decreased sharing of ideas between teachers, which in turn creates negative consequence for students learning. Thus, power bargaining is required in balancing power and solving conflict within the network (Choi & Robertson, 2014; Saz-Carranza, Iborra, & Albareda, 2016). This process will eventually decrease the transaction costs among network members (Carlsson & Sandstrom, 2008). Overall, relational structure can be changed over time, and literature also suggests that it can also affect network performance when combined with other factors such as governance forms, network age, and contextual system stability (Raab et al., 2013).

Thomson and Perry (2006) argue that the 'black box' representing the internal processes necessary for effective network collaboration and power sharing are governance, administration, organizational autonomy, mutuality, and the norms of trust and reciprocity. Without a firm understanding of these five principles, the collaboration effort will fail. The first two processes of governance and administration, subgrouped as the structure dimensions, look at the ability of the group to come together for decisions, the relationship and structure of the network, and how administrative decisions can be made across agencies in the network. Thomson and Perry (2006) advocated for a paradigm shift among those in collaborative networks. The traditional ideas of a hierarchy and firmly established roles do not work in this model. Organizational autonomy, another dimension to working with networks, is important to recognize, as each entity retains its identity and personalized goals as it enters a network. While conflict may arise due to the nature of independent organizations and their unique demands, it is also important to have mutually beneficial relationships (Lazega et al., 2008). Without a mutually beneficial relationship, only few are seen to gain from collaboration, leaving little reason to be part of a network. Likewise, there must be a sense of trust and reciprocity among those involved. Trust, one of the keystones of networks, must be established in order to work together. Reciprocity, on the other hand, is a product of trust. If one agency trusts another to reciprocate effort, services, resources, and information, the network will function effectively.

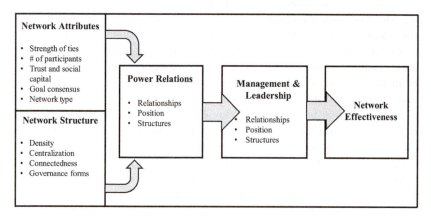

Figure 7.2 Power Relations, Structure, and Network Effectiveness

Figure 7.2 demonstrate some of the core elements and discussion in this section on network relations, structure, and network effectiveness through network governance. Centralized integration of the decision-making process from power relations perspective (e.g., prioritizing and defining problems), and the diversity of resources, expertise, values, and backgrounds of the network members (i.e., heterogeneity) are key determinants for effective network performance (Carlsson & Sandstrom, 2008). This implies the importance of some sort of "control" of the network. However, network governance is a time-consuming process, which may need some time to address power issues, to weave trust, values, and goals collectively (Raab et al., 2013). This means that the capacity of the network is not only the ability and instruments (e.g., the supermajority vote; steering committee; joint activities) to manage resources, conflicts, and levels of relationships (Choi & Robertson, 2014; Raab et al., 2013), but also the emergence of network learning, which will eventually enhance experiences in facilitating healthy network process and governance (Provan et al., 2007). Thus, power relations and network effectiveness should be treated as multilevel outcomes: organization/participant-level (i.e., individual/organizational goals); network-level (i.e., processes/relational structure goals); and community-level (i.e., result-based goals or collective impact) (Raab et al., 2013).

Leadership in Promoting the Public Interest in Networks

Power imbalance in networks might require careful facilitation and leadership for promoting and protecting public interest. Leaders in public organizations are increasingly asked to engage organizations from the private and nonprofit sectors in a collaborative or network fashion to solve complex societal problems such as natural disasters, homelessness, and food insecurity (Bingham, Nabatchi, & O'Leary, 2005; Lukensmeyer, 2013). Although employing interorganizational arrangements through collaborations and networks can lead to benefits, including reduced transaction costs and increased information sharing, and collaborative capacity (Bingham et al., 2005), scholars have observed a variety of leadership challenges associated with interorganizational arrangements (Willem & Lucidarme, 2014). This issue can be especially critical in terms of power relations and legitimacy of actors from different sectors in a society.

The development phase of networks typically centers on building the necessary components to begin addressing the shared problem. Several factors are relevant to the development and growth of networks. These include, but are not limited to, trust (Popp et al., 2014; Vangen & Huxham, 2003), power (Popp et al., 2014), and the capacity of the lead organization (Evans et al., 2014). With regards to trust, scholars (e.g., Popp et al., 2014; Vangen & Huxham, 2003) consistently note that the success of networks hinges upon the degree of trust among network participants. Another key factor that influences the development of a network or any interorganizational arrangement is the issue of power. According to Popp et al. (2014), when developing a network, leaders should pay attention to power differences. Specifically, efforts need to be made to ensure that the lead organization is not a dominant force and that organizations with less power are included in the decision-making process to avoid co-option by more powerful actors. Evans et al. (2014) underscored the need for the lead organization to have the capacity to develop the interorganizational arrangement. They specifically point out that "unless the lead organization leaders can articulate the values, purpose, and goals of the effort in terms understandable and compelling to their staff and the broader community, people may view the effort with confusion, cynicism or even suspicion" (Evans et al., 2014, p. 10).

To understand the leadership concept in networks, it is important to analyze how authority and power are distributed among the actors. In collaborative bodies, decisions and agreements are based on consensus, because participating administrators and professionals are partners, not superiors or subordinates. However, an individual still needs to come forward and help orchestrate a vision, follow through on the work plan, contact key partners, orchestrate meetings, and so on (Agranoff, 2007). In many collaborations, an organization is given positional leader legitimacy through their formal designation as a lead organization. Individuals within the lead organization enact leadership and gain greater legitimacy to do so through working on behalf of the lead organization (Huxham & Vangen, 2000). Grants and contracting arrangements, in which governments may serve as the lead organization, would be an example of this kind of authority usage.

Whether or not there is a lead organization, most collaborations give a positional leader role to a management committee, board, or steering group comprising individuals representing organizations associated with the collaboration. These individuals formally have joint decision-making power with respect to the direction of the collaboration. However, many collaborations appoint a member of one of the participating organizations to the individual positional leader role of chair or convener of the committee, board, or group

(Huxham & Vangen, 2000). In some cases, most commonly in community collaborations, the chair is rotated among members as a way to share the power (and the workload) associated with the position. This sharing brings its own set of leadership problems because of its difficulty in maintaining continuity and responsibility for direction. In many collaborations, the individual playing the most significant role in leading the collaborative agenda is the partnership manager, director, or chief executive, who is usually not actually a member of the collaboration (Huxham & Vangen, 2000).

Leaders of external stakeholders also frequently play roles in leading the direction of collaborations. The power of external positional leaders to influence may also stem from their positions in local society—elected mayors are always likely to have a large influence—or even from their positions in other influential local partnerships (Huxham & Vangen, 2000). After identifying the participants who use or influence the leadership authority and power, the next step will be to understand how they use this authority and power, as well as behaviors and strategies.

Network leadership is needed to solve power imbalances and solve potential conflicts for the sake of effective network coordination. It is the role of leadership to create a culture of collaboration in addressing potential conflict of interest, based on power differentials, in accomplishing the shared goals of the network for public interest. This gives an opportunity to public managers to act in a network boundary spanner, network administrative, or broker role. If the leadership in network is successful, power can facilitate collective effectiveness instead of hindering. Having strong power, as well as balanced stakeholder inclusion, requires leadership skills.

Informal leaders in networks, whether in support or in opposition of formal leaders, are great at providing innovative ideas, fostering communication, and ensuring that stakeholders' preferences are considered. When good formal and informal leaders function ideally, the organization is "humanized," providing useful and early feedback: enhancing worker motivation through the facilitation of sense making and stakeholder engagement (Lukensmeyer, 2013; Roberts, 1997; Van Wart, 2012).

Conclusion

Network governance requires the control of power in network to ensure that collaboration is effective and sustainable. Networks also require flexibility to shift the bureaucratic mode of government toward network governance, which requires dealing with the complexities of multilevel relationships, and the context and outcomes of the network. This chapter highlighted the role of power sharing for effective network governance. The primary role of interorganizational power is controlling the flow of resources for effective collective action. Regardless of the source of power, position, as a source of relational power, plays a substantial role in determining the role of an organization in the network. What is critical, though, is the exercise of power in the network and facilitative role of leadership to benefit public interest. The position can be a negative element if a power imbalance is present. If mitigated carefully, it can serve as a major factor for effective collaborative arrangements. We will revisit the role of power dynamics when we discuss the cases and applications of network perspectives in the application chapters.

References

Agranoff, R. (2007). *Managing within networks: Adding value to public organizations.* Washington, DC: Georgetown University Press.

Agranoff, R., & McGuire, M. (2003). *Collaborative public management: New strategies for local governments.* Washington, DC: Georgetown University Press.

Alter, C. (1990). An exploratory study of conflict and coordination in interorganizational service delivery system. *Academy of Management Journal, 33*(3), 478–502.

Ansell, C., & Gash, A. (2008). Collaborative governance in theory and practice. *Journal of Public Administration Research and Theory, 18*(4), 543–571.

Ansell, C., & Gash, A. (2018). Collaborative platforms as a governance strategy. *Journal of Public Administration Research and Theory, 28*(1), 16–32.

Bardach, E. (1998). *Getting agencies to work together: The practice and theory of managerial craftsmanship.* Washington, DC: Brookings Institution Press.

Benson, J. K. (1975). The interorganizational network as a political economy. *Administrative Science Quarterly, 20*(2), 229–249.

Berardo, R., & Lubell, M. (2016). Understanding what shapes a polycentric governance system. *Public Administration Review, 76*(5), 738–751.

Bingham, L. B., Nabatchi, T., & O'Leary, R. (2005). The new governance: Practices and processes for stakeholder and citizen participation in the work of government. *Public Administration Review, 65*(5), 547–558.

Brass, J. D., & Burkhardt, M. E. (1992). Centrality and power in organizations. In N. Nohria & R. G. Eccles (Eds.), *Networks and organizations, structure, form and action* (pp. 191–215). Boston, MA: Harvard Business School Press.

Brass, J. D., & Burkhardt, M. E. (1993). Potential power and power use: An investigation of structure. *Academy of Management Journal, 36*(3), 441–470.

Bryson, J. M., Crosby, B. C., & Stone, M. M. (2006). The design and implementation of cross-sector collaborations: Propositions from the literature. *Public Administration Review, 66*(Suppl. 1), 44–55.

Bryson, J. M., Crosby, B. C., & Stone, M. M. (2015). Designing and implementing cross-sector collaborations: Needed and challenging. *Public Administration Review, 75*(5), 647–663.

Bryson, J. M., Sancino, A., Benington, J., & Sørensen, E. (2017). Towards a multi-actor theory of public value co-creation. *Public Management Review, 19*(5), 640–654.

Burt, R. S. (1992). *Structural holes.* Cambridge, MA: Harvard University Press.

Carlsson, L., & Sandstrom, A. (2008). Network governance of the commons. *International Journal of the Commons, 2*(1), 35–54.

Castells, M. (2011). A network theory of power. *International Journal of Communication, 5,* 773–787.

Choi, T., & Robertson, P. J. (2014). Caucuses in collaborative governance: Modeling the effects of structure, power, and problem complexity. *International Public Management Journal, 17*(2), 224–254.

Crosby, B. C., & Bryson, J. M. (2005). *Leadership for the common good: Tackling public problems in a shared-power world*. San Francisco, CA: Jossey-Bass.

Dahl, R. A. (1957). The concept of power. *Behavioral Science, 2*(3), 201–215.

Edelenbos, J., & Klijn E-H. (2007). Trust in complex decision-making networks: A theoretical and empirical explanation. *Administration and Society, 39*(1), 25–50.

Emerson, K., Nabatchi, T., & Balogh, S. (2012). An integrative framework for collaborative governance. *Journal of Public Administration Research and Theory, 22*(1), 1–29.

Emerson, R. M. (1962). Power-dependence relations. *American Sociological Review, 27*(1), 31–41.

Evans, S. D., Rosen, A., Kesten, S. M., & Moore, W. (2014). Miami thrives: Weaving a poverty reduction network. *American Journal of Community Psychology, 53*(3), 357–368.

Galaskiewicz, J. (1979). *Exchange networks and community politics*. Beverly Hills, CA: Sage Publications.

Graddy, E. A., & Chen, B. (2006). Influences on the size and scope of networks for social service delivery. *Journal of Public Administration Research and Theory, 16*(4), 533–552.

Henry, A. D. (2011). Ideology, power, and the structure of policy networks. *Policy Studies Journal, 39*(3), 361–383.

Hoffman, A. N., Stearns, T. M., & Shrader, C. B. (1990). Structure, context, and centrality in interorganizational networks. *Journal of Business Research, 20*, 333–347.

Hu, Q., Khosa, S., & Kapucu, N. (2016). The intellectual structure of empirical network research in public administration. *Journal of Public Administration Research and Theory, 26*(4), 593–612.

Huxham, C., & Beech, N. (2008). Inter-organizational power. In S. Cropper, M. Ebers, M. C. Huxham, & P. S. Ring (Eds.), *The handbook of inter-organizational relations* (pp. 555–579). Oxford: Oxford University Press.

Huxham, C., & Vangen, S. (2000). Leadership in the shaping and implementation of collaboration agendas: How things happen in a (not quite) joined-up world. *Academy of Management Journal, 43*(6), 1159–1166.

Isett, K. R., & Miranda, J. (2015). Watching sausage being made: Lessons learned from the co-production of governance in a behavioral health system. *Public Management Review, 17*(1), 35–56.

Kapucu, N., & Demiroz, F. (2011). Measuring performance for collaborative public management using network analysis methods and tools. *Public Performance and Management Review, 34*(4), 551–581.

Kapucu, N., Hu, Q., & Khosa, S. (2017). The state of network research in public administration. *Administration & Society, 49*(8), 1087–1120.

Kapucu, N., & Van Wart, M. (2006). The emerging role of the public sector in managing extreme events: Lessons learned. Lead article. *Administration & Society, 38*(3), 279–308.

Keast, R., Mandell, M. P., Brown, K., & Woolcock, G. (2004). Network structures: Working differently and changing expectations. *Public Administration Review, 64*(3), 363–371.

Kelman, S., Hong, S., & Turbitt, I. (2013). Are there managerial practices associated with the outcomes of an interagency service delivery collaboration? Evidence from British crime and disorder reduction partnerships. *Journal of Public Administration Research and Theory, 23*, 609–630.

Klijn, E. H., & Koppenjan, J. (2016). *Governance networks in the public* sector. New York, NY: Routledge.

Kramer, R. M., & Neale, M. A. (1998). *Power and influence in organization.* Thousand Oaks, CA: Sage Publications.

Lazega, E., Jourda, M. T., Mounier, L., & Stofer, R. (2008). Catching up with big fish in the big pond? Multilevel network analysis through linked design. *Social Networks, 30*(2), 159–176.

Lukensmeyer, C. J. (2013). *Bringing citizen voices to the table: A guide for public managers.* San Francisco, CA: Jossey Bass.

March, J. G. (1994). *A primer on decision making: How decisions happen.* New York, NY: The Free Press.

McPherson, M., Smith-Lovin, L., & Cook, J. M. (2001). Birds of a feather: Homophily in social networks. *Annual Review of Sociology, 27,* 415–444.

Nohria, N. (1992). Introduction: Is the network perspective a useful way of studying organizations? In N. Nohria & R. G. Eccles (Eds.), *Networks and organizations, structure, form and action* (pp. 1–22). Boston, MA: Harvard Business School Press.

O'Toole, L. J. (2015). Networks and networking: The public administrative agendas. *Public Administration Review, 75*(2), 361–371.

Pfeffer, J. (1992). *Managing with power: Politics and influence in organizations.* Boston, MA: Harvard Business School Press.

Pfeffer, J., & Slancik, G. (1978). *The external control of organizations: A resource dependence perspective.* New York, NY: Harper and Row.

Popp, J., MacKean, G., Casebeer, A., Milward, H. B., & Lindstrom, R. (2014). *Interorganizational networks: A review of the literature to inform practice.* Washington, DC: IBM Center for the Business of Government.

Provan, K. G., Fish, A., & Sydow, J. (2007). Interorganizational networks at the network level: A review of the empirical literature on whole networks. *Journal of Management, 33*(3), 479–516.

Provan, K. G., & Lemaire, R. H. (2012). Core concepts and key ideas for understanding public sector organizational networks: Using research to inform scholarship and practice. *Public Administration Review, 72*(5), 638–648.

Provan, K. G., & Milward, H. B. (1995). A preliminary theory of network effectiveness: A comparative study of four mental health systems. *Administrative Science Quarterly, 40*(1), 1–33.

Provan, K. G., Veazie, M. A., Staten, L. K., & Teufel-Shone, N. I. (2005). The use of network analysis to strengthen community partnerships. *Public Administration Review, 65*(5), 603–613.

Purdy, J. M. (2012). A framework for assessing power in collaborative governance processes. *Public Administration Review, 72*(3), 409–417.

Raab, J., Mannak, R. S., & Cambre, B. (2013). Combining structure, governance, and context: A configurational approach to network effectiveness. *Journal of Public Administration Research and Theory, 25*(2), 479–511.

Ran, B., & Qi, H. (2017). Contingencies of power sharing in collaborative governance. *American Review of Public Administration.* doi:10.1177/0275074017745355

Raven, B. H., & French, J. (1959). The bases of social power. In D. Cartwright (Ed.), *Studies in social power* (pp. 150–167). Ann Arbor, MI: Institute for Social Research.

Roberts, N. (1997). Public deliberation: An alternative approach to crafting policy and setting direction. *Public Administration Review, 57*(2), 124–132.

Saz-Carranza, A., Iborra, S., & Albareda, A. (2016). The power dynamics of mandated network administrative organizations. *Public Administration Review*, *76*(3), 449–462.

Scott, J. (2013). *Social network analysis*. Los Angeles, CA: Sage Publications.

Scott, R. W., & Davis, G. F. (2007). *Organizations and organizing: Rational, natural, and open system perspectives*. Upper Saddle River, NJ: Pearson.

Siciliano, M. D. (2015). Advice networks in public organizations: The role of structure, internal competition, and individual attributes. *Public Administration Review*, *75*(4), 548–559.

Thompson, J. D. (2007). *Organizations in action: Social science bases of administrative theory*. New Brunswick, NJ: Transaction Publisher.

Thomson, A. M., & Perry, J. L. (2006). Collaboration processes: Inside the black box. *Public Administration Review*, *66*(Suppl. 1), 20–32.

Vangen, S., & Huxham, C. (2003). Nurturing collaborative relations: Building trust in interorganizational collaboration. *Journal of Applied Behavioral Science*, *39*(1), 5–31.

Van Wart, M. (2012). *Leadership in public organizations: An introduction*. New York, NY: Taylor & Francis.

Weick, K. E. (2005). Organizing and failures of imagination. *International Public Management Journal*, *8*(3), 425–438.

Willem, A., & Lucidarme, S. (2014). Pitfalls and challenges for trust and effectiveness in collaborative networks. *Public Management Review*, *16*(5), 733–760.

8 Legitimacy and Accountability in Networks

Legitimacy and accountability are important parts of network governance scholarship and practice. These aspects play important roles in addressing the effectiveness of interorganizational arrangements. Chapter 8 discusses network legitimacy and accountability issues in network governance. It examines the characteristics and nature of network accountability systems and proposes a network accountability perspective that includes both formal and informal accountability. It also provides recommendations about how to ensure network members assume accountability in pursuing collaborative goals as part of a participatory network governance. The following questions are examined in the chapter:

- What is network legitimacy?
- What is the latest development within academic and practitioner communities regarding ways to make networks accountable?
- How is accountability defined within the network context? Should we have different standards of accountability for participant organizations in networks? Whom do we hold accountable?
- Why is accountability in a network setting different from a traditional one?
- What is formal accountability? What is informal accountability? Can these both be used in addressing network governance issues?

Network Legitimacy

Considering the growing interest in collaboration, there is an increasing demand for new perspectives and research related to legitimacy and accountability in relation to network performance and effectiveness. A major shortcoming of the existing literature is a lack of research on legitimacy building in networks. *Network legitimacy*, as defined from a network perspective, is the perceived acceptance of network activities and mission based

> **Network Legitimacy**
>
> The perceived acceptance of the network's mission, goals, norms, and values.

on shared goals, common norms, and values by members of a network and public at large. Legitimacy is an important concept for networks and can be a critical variable for empirical research. We will begin by discussing the importance of legitimacy in networks and then address the different dimensions of legitimacy in network settings.

Some argue that state actors are losing legitimacy because they are "clumsy, bureaucratic, and path dependent and, in part, because of the control of information and implementation structure by private actors (Peters & Pierre, 1998, p. 255). However, concerns about legitimacy are not only relevant for state actors but for other actors in networks as well. Legitimacy building is not only central to the evolution of social systems but is also a key component of successful organizational networks (Provan, Kenis, & Human, 2008). Legitimacy is defined by Provan et al. (2008) as a "generalized perception that the actions of a network are desirable, proper, or within some system of norms, values, beliefs, and definitions" (p. 122).

Network managers and leaders can start with building internal legitimacy among member organizations and later proceed to external groups. This is called inside-out strategy (Provan, Lamb, & Doyle, 2004, p. 119). Outside-in strategies for legitimacy building start with external legitimacy building then translate to the network itself (Provan et al., 2004, p. 119). Success of legitimacy building for both strategies rests with achieving an optimal balance between internal and external legitimacy. As Provan and colleagues (2004) observed "[s]trong and early inside-out strategy may, in the long run, be more successful for network survival because it first attends to the often problematic issue of building support and legitimacy among network members who may neither have experience working with each other nor trust that interaction will be mutually beneficial" (p. 119).

Legitimacy is critical for social systems, including organizations and networks. However, the concept of legitimacy, in terms of networks, has received limited attention (Popp, Milward, MacKean, Casebeer, & Lindstorm, 2014; Provan et al., 2008). Any state-sponsored agency may face challenges to its legitimacy. The Department of Homeland Security (DHS) was created after 9/11 with the purpose of "connecting the dots," primarily among intelligence agencies. Collaboration among intelligence agencies was an attractive justification for both policy makers and public at large. A major window of opportunity, in the form of 9/11, helped the agency establish its legitimacy and build upon it further (Kapucu, 2009). This might not be the case for all newly created organizations in the public sector. Legitimacy is much more challenging in network development, evolution, and sustainability for both participants and stakeholders of a network. From an institutional theory perspective, an organization must build legitimacy using elements such as structure, processes, and strategies before investing resources and capacity in a network (Suchman, 1995). Building legitimacy for a sole organization, guided by law and policy, may be easy. Network-based organization is not easily understood, and therefore is perceived as less legitimate compared to traditional legal bureaucratic structures. Success of a network will depend on building a legitimate and trusted interorganizational system that involves all stakeholders.

There are three distinct dimensions of networks that need to be considered in addressing legitimacy issues: network-as-form, network-as-interaction, and network-as-entity (Provan et al., 2008). In network-as-form, the important factor is the sector-wide establishment of networks and its acceptance as a legitimate form of organizing by the stakeholders. Network-as-entity aims to create reasonable level of recognition for the network-as-form of legitimacy. Building network legitimacy in network-as-interaction identify cooperative interactions between all organizations in a network as a legitimate activity in order for effective functioning of networks (Provan et al., 2008).

Legitimacy in Network-As-Form

Networks are a relatively new form of organizing. In this dimension of legitimacy, it is important to know the "sector- or area-wide diffusion of networks" (Provan et al., 2008, p. 125). In instances where diffusion of networks is wide (health and human services for example), it is more than likely for stakeholders to understand the need for, accept, and promote the use of networks, even in the absence of performance-based criteria indicating their effectiveness (Provan et al., 2008). Where there is low diffusion, networks are not understood or appreciated by the participant stakeholders, and the likelihood of their use is reduced. Networks in these areas are perceived as uncertain and risky. It is imperative to establish legitimacy for network-as-form prior to, and during, the formation and development of the network to remove uncertainty and confusion regarding the costs and benefits of the process (see Chapter 4).

Legitimacy in Network-As-Entity

Network-As-Entity refers to shared goals, integrated activities, and a clear network structure. The primary rationale of establishing network-as-entity legitimacy is to create a reasonable level of recognition for the network, so that participants function and treat the network as a whole, unified structure, as opposed to a clustering of individual organizations. The emphasis then is placed upon coordinating and managing the network to provide a seamless integration of services. Nonprofit organizations and public entities can form a coalition to end homelessness, for example. Legitimacy for network-as-entity depends primarily upon its governance structure, i.e., whether it has a loose arrangement, single entity coordination, or a separate legal entity set up solely for that purpose. The most critical stages of building legitimacy for the network-as-entity are during formation and early network growth, where uncertainty regarding what the network is, and who it represents, is primary for both outsiders and member organizations (Provan et al., 2008). Under this form, accountability can be addressed from a formal perspective.

Legitimacy in Network-As-Interaction

Agencies routinely legitimize cooperative interactions by establishing trust. Legitimacy through network-as-interaction is completed through a series of transactions and information sharing, culminating in more collaborative ties and interactions. Problems arise when time and expenditures are not placed into creating relationships with other non-network agencies and when there is resistance to the establishment of ties. Ties and relationships help to legitimize cooperative interaction and smooth the way for new interactions and relationships. Network-as-interaction retains its critical nature from formation into maturity (Provan et al., 2008). Legitimacy through interaction implies that organizations that had prior working experiences and high level of trust will participate in networks more easily than the ones without prior experience. The level of interaction will help reduce transaction cost as well as encourage power sharing. This form also implies that more emphasis on informal accountability mechanisms is needed in evaluating performance.

While the three dimensions we have addressed are useful, lacking one or more of these dimensions may result in legitimacy shortages that can collapse the network or seriously impact its effectiveness (Provan et al., 2008). Though other research on legitimacy of networks does not utilize the three dimensions we mentioned, implications for network legitimacy are similar. For example, some contend that legitimacy originates from expectations rather than experience (Donahue & Zeckhauser, 2011). Donahue and Zeckhauser note the flow of information between the private and public sector and use the phrase "reputational externalities" to reflect that flow of reputations from one sector to another. In addition, "utilizing the private sector to produce public value can foster legitimacy in a variety of contexts" (Donahue & Zeckhauser, 2011, p. 123) as one organization's reputation may help another in the network. For example, the "success of collaboration with charter schools and public parks make them more amenable to private sector production in other areas" (Donahue & Zeckhauser, 2011, p. 154). FEMA's or Red Cross's experience in dealing with disasters give them privilege in networks as well as contribute legitimacy of other actors in the collaborative response system. They do not need to educate partners or network participants about their roles and responsibilities in dealing with emergencies and disasters. The legal system and the policy documents provide them legitimacy and acceptance by others want to work with them in assisting communities after disasters. The importance of legitimacy building as a means of success can be seen in health networks for the uninsured. In this case, "legitimacy building was critical for explaining how the network evolved and the effectiveness of the network in sustaining itself and building a patient base" (Provan et al., 2004, p. 117).

Legitimacy can be perceived differently for voluntary networks versus mandated networks. Legitimacy issues in a mandated network are more challenging compared to voluntary networks (Provan et al., 2008). In mandated networks, some members might resist active participation. The US government created a plan to adopt health information technology in the 2009 Health Information Technology for Economic and Clinical Health Act. The policy mandated building a nationwide health information communication infrastructure with wide participation of organizations within the health sector. The network received substantial challenges for participation and did not make a substantial progress as quickly as expected from the act (Patel, Swain, King, & Furukawa, 2013). Emergency management networks might be exceptions to this issue in mandated network because of vested interests and the urgency involved in this type of collaboration in response to disasters and crises (Kapucu, 2009).

For a network to appear as legitimate, it must be perceived as acting within an already preestablished realm of conduct that is acceptable in its community and society. In doing such, legitimacy pushes organizations toward "structural conformity with others in their class, lead[s] young organizations to conform to the expectations of key external constituencies and are a critical element in the adoption of innovative organizational practices" (Provan et al., 2008, p. 121). When the government rewards contracts to nonprofit or for-profit organizations, it transfers power to the agents as specified by law or policy, however the transfer of the legitimacy does not come as easy (Milward & Provan, 2000; Milward, Provan, Fish, Isett, & Huang, 2010). The organizations "operating under contract have time limited legitimacy" (Milward & Provan, 2000, p. 366).

Whether the network itself is voluntary or mandatory also impacts network legitimacy. Fully mandated networks are those required by law or policy and because of this, they are automatically granted legitimacy in a society. Voluntary networks have to study and emulate existing structures and behave according to preestablished norms and expectations in order to obtain legitimacy. In the attempts of the voluntary networks to gain legitimacy, attention is given to the fusion of pressure and legitimacy. While networks comprise individual organizations working collaboratively for mutual goals, they are not subject to the same legitimacy pressures that sole entities face (Provan et al., 2008). Voluntary, or emerging, networks play substantial roles in response to and recovery from disasters. The US Federal government provides policies and frameworks to facilitate network arrangements in response to emergencies and crises. These frameworks and policies are perceived as mandates by local and state agencies. These policies and frameworks in addition to local level plans help participating non-governmental agencies for their legitimacy in participating response and recovery networks (see Chapter 10 for emergency and crisis management networks).

Hybrid Nature of the Network Accountability

Networks have become more unique in their structure, generating a need for multiple methods of assessing accountability (Kapucu & Demiroz, 2011). There is also a need to identify difficulties in network performance measurement. Since partnerships and collaborative arrangements increased substantially at all levels of government. (See Chapter 9 for details of network performance evaluation.) The US Government Accountability Office (GAO) has recently developed interest in evaluating accountability of networks and partnerships. GAO (2005) defined collaboration as "any joint activity that is intended to produce more public value than could be produced when the organizations act alone" (2005, p. 2). The report highlights ways for federal agencies to work better collaboratively and identify key practices that can enhance and sustain this relationship.

Many of the challenges that these organizations face include missions that are not compatible and may even conflict with one another. They struggle to reach a consensus, and many times find themselves unable to function because of procedures in place that deter finding a solution. This is also due to agencies not using their tools and resources to the best of their ability (GAO, 2005). Through review of federal collaborations such as, Healthy People 2010, wildland fire management, and US Department of Veterans Affairs (VA) and US Department of Defense (DOD) health resource sharing, the GAO's report identified key strategies in accomplishing collaborative results. Those include defining a clear outcome, establishing and reinforcing joint strategies, identifying needs for resources, identifying roles and responsibilities, developing policies and procedures that work across agency boundaries, developing ways to monitor and report results, reinforce agency accountability through reports, and reinforce individual accountability through performance management systems (GAO, 2005, p. 6).

It is not easy to find a comprehensive model that responds to all of the questions related to network accountability. From a traditional perspective, accountability can be defined as "the obligation to give an account of one's action to someone else, often balanced by a responsibility of that other to seek an account" (Scott, 2006, p. 175). The obligations are identified by explicit standards (law, administrative regulations, bureaucratic checks and balances, and contractual obligations) or implicit norms (professional norms, social values, beliefs, and assumptions). Within the evaluation process for accountability, one important aspect is the identification of indicators. Measurable indicators allow organizational analysts to compare an organization to itself over time, or a similar organization, or network standards (Brandsma & Schillemans, 2012; Bingham & O'Leary, 2008; Milward et al., 2010; Siegel, Clayton, & Kovoor, 1990). How are indicators developed for the context applied to network arrangements? This question has gained substantial interest but not much progress.

Accountability, traditionally, was analyzed from four different types of relationships: legal (law constructed constraints and controls that mandate the agency perform certain activities); bureaucratic/hierarchical (guidance provided by administrative rules at the top of the hierarchy or bureaucracy); political (democratic pressures that come from outside stakeholders for responsiveness); and professional (peer expectations on job performance and expertise, norms, and ethical principles). The relationships change based on the source (internal or external) and degree of control involved (high or low). Legal and hierarchical accountability relationships entail a high degree of control (Romzek & Dubnick, 1987). However, legal accountability involves degrees of control that are external to the agency, whereas, hierarchical relationships have a high degree of internal control. Political and professional relationships have a low degree of control. Political entails a low degree of external control and professional has a low degree of internal control (Page, 2004). Table 8.1 provides basic types of accountability in a single agency setting and provides some level of control for accountability.

Koliba, Meek, and Zia (2010) highlighted eight different accountability types in terms of actors to whom accountability must be rendered in complex network arrangements: Elected representatives, citizens, legal, bureaucratic, professionals, owners/shareholders, consumers, and collaborators. Accountability structures within a networked environment necessitate a certain measure of interdependency between those to whom accounts should be rendered and those rendering the accounts. Similar to building legitimacy, accountability in networks is also challenging. A discussion on accountability is necessary, as it is an essential element in network governance design, processes, and implementation. Page (2004) highlighted the critical role of state-sponsored human service collaboratives in accomplishing public service missions and result oriented accountability. He recommended these collaborative network arrangements need to develop the capacity to track results for accountability measures with four platforms: "external authorization, internal inclusion,

Table 8.1 Types of Accountability

Legal	Legal, policy constraints and controls of agencies in the public sector.
	Legal accountability involves high degree of external control.
Bureaucratic	Guidance and regulations, organizational policies provided within a bureaucratic structure and implemented by executives in the agency.
	Bureaucratic accountability involves a high degree of internal control.
Political	Democratic pressure and demand from citizens for political accountability and responsiveness in dealing public's business.
	Political accountability involves a low degree of external control.
Professional	Professional job performance expatiations, norms, and ethical principles.
	Professional accountability involves a low degree of internal control.

Source: Adapted from Page, 2004; Romzek & Dubnick, 1987

results measurement, and managing for results" (p. 593). Accountability measures and evaluation strategies specific to networks are discussed in chapter
nine, including the definition of network effectiveness, the approaches to evaluate network performance from multidimensional perspective, and the use of
network analysis tools for assessing performance.

Network capacity for accountability rests on four platforms: external authorization defined as "the capacity to manage expectations and to respond to the
demands of political stakeholders"; internal inclusion defined as "the capacity
to manage expectations and to respond to the demands of professional colleagues and collaborative partners"; results measurement defined as "the capacity to identify the collaborative's mission, goals, and indicators of progress,
and to track data that document changes in progress over time"; and finally
managing for results defined as "the capacity to use data about results strategically to assess progress and to improve policies and operations in the future"
(Page, 2004, p. 593). Each of these platforms is expected to enhance network
accountability for results and facilitate ways to measure them effectively.

Actors in the network must be responsive and responsible to certain constituencies in network accountability structures. Actors are those responsible
for evaluating the performance of agents who are being held accountable.
Accountability types and network accountability are depicted in Table 8.2. We
highlight that members of the network are still accountable as an individual
organization, yet greater complexity, in terms of accountability, is added once
an organization joins a network. The table expands on democratic, legal, market, and administrative accountability types discussed in the literature. Bureaucratic, professional, and legal accountability subcategories are included as part
of administrative accountability. The table includes network accountability as
a new addition to accountability discussion in addition to accountability types,
frameworks, standards, and norms.

The democratic frame of accountability is divided in to three components.
Elected representative accountability authorizes elected representatives to
work as the primary actors in the lawmaking and executive divisions of democratic government. Citizen accountability directly ensures public institutions
are accountable through horizontal ties such as feasible participation regulations and deliberative forums. Legal accountability ensures the execution of
sound judgments within an organization within the bounds of already existing
law and policy. Stakeholder accountability, which calls for the alignment of
performance measures with profitability, and consumer accountability, which
enables consumers to choose between alternative goods and services, constitute the market frame of accountability. Efficiency, market share, innovation,
affordability, quality, and satisfaction are used as some examples of accountability measures (Koliba et al., 2010).

The administrative frame of accountability consists of bureaucratic accountability, professional accountability and legal accountability structures and
procedures. Bureaucratic accountability structures are characterized by traditional hierarchical structures, such as unity of command and span of control.

Table 8.2 Accountability Types and Network Accountability

Type of Accountability	To Whom Actors Are Accountable	Institutional Framework	Formal Standards	Informal Norms
Democratic Accountability	Citizens, elected officials, representatives, and media	Elections, vote of confidence, public's trust	Laws, statutes, rules, and regulations	Public values, interest, policy goals, fairness, representation, and legitimacy
Legal Accountability	Courts	Legal system	Laws, statutes, contracts, and agreements	Due process, precedence, rights, reasonableness, and legitimacy
Market Accountability	Shareholders, consumers	Regulations, consumer law	Performance measures	Efficiency, market share, innovation, affordability, quality, and satisfaction
Administrative Accountability	*Bureaucratic*: principles and supervisors *Professional*: colleagues and peers *Legal*: judicial system	Organizational structure, rules Associations Law, rules and regulations	Administrative procedures, budgets, org charts, performance measures Code of ethics, performance standards, certificates Legal standards	Organizational goals, standards, power, span of control Professional norms, expertise, competence Respect for the legal system, expectations
Network Accountability	Collaborators, network actors, partners, peers, and stakeholders	Networks, horizontal arrangements	MOUs, contracts, negotiations, decision-making procedures	Trust, reciprocity, social capital, relationships, negotiation and consensus building

Source: Adapted from Klijn & Koppenjan, 2016, 2014; Koliba et al., 2010; Page, 2004; Romzek & Dubnick, 1987.

Administrative procedures, budgets, organizational structure/charts, and performance measures are used as formal accountability indicators. Organizational goals, standards, power, span of control can be seen as informal norms for bureaucratic accountability (Koliba et al., 2010). Professional accountability structures rely on expertise or special skills of professionals such as code of ethics, performance standards, and certifications. As part of bureaucratic accountability, courts and judicial system plays a role based on laws, regulations, legal standards, and respect to legal system from the parties involves.

Finally, collaborative, or *network accountability*, structures exist through that actors interact with each other as peers or partners organized around collective efforts (Koliba et al., 2010). Network accountability perspective allows for the combining of democratic, legal, market and administrative factors based on our multilayer accountability perspective we identified in the chapter. Network accountability can be seen in terms of trade-offs between accountability types. Trade-offs may happen between democracy

> **Network Accountability**
>
> Establishing responsibility through formal standards and informal norms in a network setting.

and market accountabilities, democracy and administrative accountabilities, or intra-administrative accountabilities. In a network setting actors are accountable to collaborators, other actors, partners, peers, and stakeholders. Institutional framework can include, in addition to legal system, rules and regulations, and organizational structures, networks and horizontal arrangements at a system level. MOUs, contracts, negotiations, decision-making procedures can provide formal measures for network accountability. Trust, reciprocity, social capital, relationships, negotiation, and consensus building brings informal norms as additional measurement for network accountability.

Accountability in a network setting is a multilevel construct analyzed at organizational, network, and community level processes and structures. Network accountability involves organizational level accountability and the network as a distinctive entity. Each organization in the network is accountable for its own actions and accountable to the network as a system. Accountability is not measured by any one organization within the network but is based upon the actions of the new whole.

There are new tools and technology available for identifying accountability measures and outcomes for network arrangements (Kapucu & Demiroz, 2011; Linden, 2010; Popp et al., 2014). The network is typically represented by the public, private, nonprofit sector organizations with shared power and responsibilities (Mandell & Keast, 2007, p. 577). Cross-sector networks recognize various accountability characteristics for each sector. The public sector is accountable to citizens, interest groups, and elected officials for policy goals and implementation, as well as meeting public needs in creating or delivering public services or value. The nonprofit sector is accountable to citizens, interest groups, boards of directors, and clients for fulfilling missions. The private sector is accountable to owners and shareholders, customers, and corporate boards of directors for profits.

Networks can be classified as cooperative, coordinative, or collaborative (Mandell & Keast, 2007). In cooperative and coordinative networks, traditional performance measurement tools for accountability may be appropriate because participants in these types of networks remain independent. On the other hand, since participants in collaborative networks are interdependent, traditional measurement tools are inadequate for measuring their performance for accountability. Collaborative networks consist of organizations from multiple sectors, and their effectiveness depends on high levels of trust and intense reciprocal relationships between actors. Evaluating the effectiveness of collaborative networks requires different set of assumptions, perspectives, and measures for accountability.

Network Accountability

Accountability is critical, as it contributes to network effectiveness and building and maintaining legitimacy (Klijn & Koppenjan, 2016; Popp et al., 2014). Since network governance may involve the public sector to collaborate with non-state stakeholders, make and/or implement public policies, and manage programs, knowing who is in charge and who is accountable is critical. Network structure might impact network accountability mechanisms differently. Network accountability in lead organizations or NAO structure, can be easier than shared governing network structure, as it has less clearly defined structure and shared goals for collective effort. The number of participants can also influence accountability mechanism in network. An increased number of participant actors might make accountability system more complex and challenging.

Network accountability is challenging in practice for several reasons. First, it may be difficult to reach a consensus between partners about which outcomes to measure and which data to use. Second, some collaborators will fear that they will not perform well either because of doubt in their own capacity, or that conditions beyond their control will prevent them from meeting stated network performance goals. The third concern is that measuring certain issues may lead to the neglect of other important objectives that are harder to measure. Fourth, new measurement tools are not well-developed and tested in network accountability. Fifth, a complete mental reorientation is also necessary for public managers and their authorizers, stakeholders, staff, collaborators, and citizens themselves. Finally, clarification as to "who should be accountable to whom and for what results" is required (Page, 2004, p. 592).

Accountability exists when interdependency occurs between those rendering accounts and those to whom they are rendered (Koliba et al., 2010; Scott, 2006). Accountability is strengthened when there is a strong measure of interdependency between those who seek to give information and those who seek account of the information given (Klijn & Koppenjan, 2016; Koliba et al., 2010). Accountability structures often act as feedback loops to organizations that play a critical role in assisting in effective network governance. The governance perspective argues that "traditional channels of accountability have been replaced by several different processes of electoral control such as 'stakeholderism' and consumer choice" (Peters & Pierre, 1998, p. 228). On the other hand, New Public Management New Public Governance schools argue that through relating "public service more directly to the market demand instead of political decisions about quality and quantity, service providers receive immediate information about their performance" (Peters & Pierre, 1998, p. 228). Emphasizing the accountability among stakeholders is imperative.

Stakeholder theory, like network perspective, states that an organization has various stakeholders who influence and are influenced by it. A stakeholder is most popularly defined as a "group or individual who can affect or is affected by the achievement of the organization's objectives" (Freeman, 1984, p. 46; Simmons, 2003). Stakeholder accountability in networks is a central idea in collaborative public-private sector partnerships. For example, in a partnership between universities and pharmaceutical companies their partnership "raises important issues of governance and research integrity" (Simmons, 2003, p. 585). However, the systematic incorporation of stakeholders can "enhance effectiveness, social responsibility and stakeholder commitment" (Simmons, 2003, p. 585). Through well-developed stakeholder engagement, which incorporates the concepts of organizational justice, integrity, and morality all stakeholder needs are addressed, and an imbalance between the partners is avoided.

Accountability involving stakeholder engagement in networks can be vertical or horizontal. While vertical refers to being accountable to an organization at a higher level in the hierarchy, horizontal accountability refers to establishing accountability system to other actors in the network (Klijn & Koppenjan, 2016). Individual organizations constitute collaborative networks, but the effectiveness of any one organization in the network cannot indicate the effectiveness of the network. Although individual successes may be significant to the head of an organization represented in the network, these successes do not, by themselves, illustrate a success of the network.

Acar, Guo, and Yang (2011) noted that "there exists a relatively high level of agreement as to the basic elements or questions pertinent to the specification of an accountability scheme or system, namely, who should be held accountable, to whom, for what, how, and with what consequences [emphasis in original]" (p. 2). To move beyond these general principles, Acar et al. (2011) focused on two dimensions (to whom? and for what?) and employed a bottom-up approach to theory building that sought to probe the "practical" meaning of accountability via interviews with experts involved in partnerships between K-12 public and private schools and/or nonprofit organizations (pp. 2–4). In terms of "accountability for what," Acar et al. (2011) found that partnerships between schools and nonprofit organizations should be accountable for their explicit mission, goals, and objectives (p. 11). In terms of "accountability to whom," the respective partnership should be accountable to their target population (students and parents), followed by accountability to partners and community (pp. 12–13). Although Acar et al. (2011) focused on a specific partnership domain and overlooks certain dimensions of accountability (such as how, and with what consequences), this does not mean that it cannot be used to determine poor or good accountability.

Accountability is "multifaceted" and "multidimensional" in the context K-12 public school partnerships. Within this category, the dimensions of measurements, outcomes, and impacts receive the most attention. The partnerships in education are accountable mainly for student achievement goals and objectives while being held accountable to students, partners, and the community. The importance of result-oriented and client-based views of accountability is reflective of other partnerships based on a common goal (Acar et al., 2011). Provan and Milward (2001) highlighted that participants in networks may have varied roles, responsibilities, and functions that occur simultaneously at different levels. Because of this, stakeholders need to evaluate them at the community, network, and organizational levels. Participants and stakeholder goals may be varied, yet effective networks organizers can aim to minimally satisfy needs at macro levels (network and participating organization), while continuously being mindful of micro level needs (community level/client needs).

Accountability mechanisms in a network setting are fragmented and not easy to address and identify. In a traditional policy making process or bureaucratic structure, accountability is accomplished by tracking outcomes or service delivery performance. In a network setting, decisions on performance are made by means of negotiation and compromise. It is difficult to hold participants fully accountable most of the time (Acar et al., 2011; Klijn & Koppenjan, 2016, 2014). The following section briefly addresses formal and informal accountability for network arrangements.

Formal Network Accountability

In a network setting, there can be many different accountability mechanism and standards that exist (Klijn & Koppenjan, 2016). Public managers or organizational representatives, in an interdependent network setting, might develop a different understanding of accountability. Formal network accountability can be arranged within the lead agency or by the network administrative type. It will be difficult to develop formal accountability in a shared responsibility network type without a strong actor facilitating the network action because of conflicting interests and goals of participating agencies. This type might be more appropriate for informal network accountability (discussed in the following section). Regardless of the types of accountability, an accountability mechanism designed for horizontal networks should allow for transparency and legitimacy to develop in the network, ultimately helping build an accountable system.

Horizontal network accountability does not replace traditional vertical accountability. How can network accountability mechanism include elements from both? Networks are traditionally formed to address complex societal and policy issues. The complexity of the issue addressed by the network makes accountability even more challenging. Klijn and Koppenjan (2016) recommended the following to help develop an accountability system for networks: open information exchange, openness and flexibility to different standards, openness to negotiation of the accountability measures and standards, transparency and openness to other partners, maintaining flexibility, learning, and adaptability and, finally, openness to network intervention by external stakeholders. The accountability system design elements can include the following: positions (which roles are available), boundaries (exit and access rules), scope (delineation of activities), the use of information, the division of authority, way of decision-making and conflict regulation (decision rules), and the division of costs, benefits, and risks, rules regarding products and codes of behavior (Ostrom, 1990; Klijn & Koppenjan, 2014).

MOUs, contracts, and decision-making procedures are critical for formal accountability. Ehren and Godfrey (2017) provided an example of the impact that external accountability has on internal quality control and mandated inter-organizational networks. Using a case study, they examined external accountability and control of an educational network and how the school system is held accountable by the English Inspectorate of Education, under the UK Department for Education, through Regional Schools Commissioners. They concluded that accountability measures led to increased centralized control on curriculum, assessment, and school performance improvement. An established regional structure helped in accomplishing the accountability measures in this case. Since the performance measures developed around individual school performance, it is hard to develop a direct link between the network outcome and the accountability measure. However, this case still provides some valuable lessons for network accountability in a formal arrangement.

Informal Network Accountability

Informal network accountability mechanisms are as critical as formal network accountability mechanisms arrangements for network governance. Even though we do not have well-developed formal accountability systems for networks, informal accountability based on trust, relationships, rewards, and sanctions can be critical for effective network governance. Romzek, LeRoux, Johnston, Kempf, and Piatak (2014) discussed the ability of social connections that professionals share to help "foster relationships that provide mutual benefit, reduce transaction costs of future collaboration, and solidify a sense of shared norms and mutual accountability among collaborative network participants" (p. 817).

Romzek et al. (2014) explained informal accountability as

> Collaborative service delivery networks involve professionals with a common orientation, informal accountability is facilitated because it may flow naturally from the shared perspectives of the network individuals. Just as these interpersonal relationships are informal, so are some network organizations' expectations; these are expectations that are typically not included in formal contracts and agreements, and they often involve interpersonal behaviors. These interpersonal behaviors are discretionary

rather than mandated by official agreements. So, too, are the dynamics of informal accountability.

(p. 817)

Romzek, LeRoux, and Blackmar (2012) linked informal accountability to other accountability types by tapping into a shared normative view, with respect for other professionals in the collaborative network. If the shared normative views and respect for colleagues in the network are strong enough, it can serve accountability goals of the network better than formalized accountability discussed earlier. Informal accountability can be critical for legitimacy among informal networks, as well as addressing power relations in network. Trust, reciprocity, social capital, relationships, negotiation, and consensus building are critical elements of informal accountability in networks. Informal accountability does not replace formal accountability. Depending on the context and network development stages and network types, network managers and leaders can decide the level of formality for the accountability mechanisms.

Network Governance and Accountability

The difficulty in building legitimacy and establishing accountability systems reflects the challenges in maintaining a positive reputation for networks and effective network governance. A network accountability system can help foster trust among internal and external stakeholders, which promotes the utilization of networks in collective decision-making, as well as implementation of public services. Networks imply participatory governance both internally, among stakeholders or partners, as well as externally, between the network and regulatory body, funders, or supporters. A collaborative nature is critical for network accountability and building internal, as well as external, legitimacy. The collaborative nature of networks was highlighted as "the processes and structures of public policy decision-making and management that engage people constructively across the boundaries of public agencies, levels of government, and/or the public, private and civic spheres" (Emerson, Nabatchi, & Balogh, 2012, p. 2). The inclusive nature of network governance and collective decision-making help build social capital and increase trust among network participants in addition to reducing conflict, increasing knowledge sharing, and creating sense of ownership (Bryson, Crosby, & Stone, 2006). Network governance, especially lead organization or network administrative organization types, provide a 'collaborative platform' (Ansell & Gash, 2017) for a consensus-oriented collective decision-making and effective network governance. Network governance addresses the importance of the process in addition to outcome or output for accountability.

In network governance, each actor (partner) will be part of consensus-based collective decision-making, apart from specific agency identity, goal, and mission. This joint-decision-making effort requires a set mechanism (different network arrangement, for example), and network leadership for successful facilitation of accountability. Effective facilitation and encouragement of voluntary participation for higher levels of accountability and legitimacy requires transparency and the promotion of legitimacy (Ansell & Gash, 2012). In addition to network capacity and structure, trust, quality of relationship, mutual respect, resourcefulness of participating stakeholders, credibility, and legitimacy are important elements to be considered for effective accountability mechanism for network governance.

Figure 8.1 depicts the key elements of network governance and accountability. The brief model suggests preexisting relationships, legitimacy, resources, shared goals, and governance structure as network capacity elements. Accountability measures can be formal and informal as already discussed. Network accountability aims to reach shared goals of the partnership, benefit the organizations in the network, network itself, and the community the network serves.

Milward and Provan (2000) captured the significance of accountability in network governance by emphasizing the relationships between a clear network accountability structure and network effectiveness. This perspective reflects more complicated accountability challenge in designing the platform for stakeholder participation and needs further investigation.

The importance of network accountability and effectiveness were highlighted by Milward and Provan (2000) by synthesizing the lessons learnt on network governance from their ten years of research experience in health and human services networks. The primary question they asked was "how can effective institutions be designed in a world of shared power where few organizations have the power to accomplish their missions alone?" (p. 360). They highlight four key points: the effective network governance needs not only clear principal-agent structure (via some centralized, lead organization mechanism), but also direct financial control, the availability of sufficient resources, and network stability for social learning and trust-building (in contrast with frequent competition).

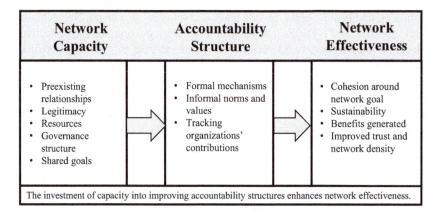

Network Capacity	Accountability Structure	Network Effectiveness
• Preexisting relationships • Legitimacy • Resources • Governance structure • Shared goals	• Formal mechanisms • Informal norms and values • Tracking organizations' contributions	• Cohesion around network goal • Sustainability • Benefits generated • Improved trust and network density
The investment of capacity into improving accountability structures enhances network effectiveness.		

Figure 8.1 Network Accountability and Network Governance

O'Toole (1997) suggested that network governance's accountability structure is more nuanced than the hierarchical, bureaucratic governmental structure. This reflects the conflict of interests between individuals and the public (responsibility issue), the challenges in inviting the public to engage in the network (responsiveness issue), and the network's time-consuming nature for civic learning, trust-building, and network capacity building (civic deliberative trust issue). Despite these challenges, O'Toole (1997) proposed that the emergence of network governance is inevitable and may also raise opportunities for administrators in enhancing public deliberative trust and public values and designing the accountability structure which genuinely serves the public, though these tasks are difficult due to the complexity of the network and its context. Network governance complements the existing policy and administrative structures in organizational setting for accountability rather than replacing it.

Ensuring the clear principal-agent structure and balancing individual organizations' self-interests and goals and network's collective interests and goals are significant for effective network governance. We also need to highlight the importance of the temporal factor as a key variable for network learning and trust-building (Milward & Provan, 2000; Milward et al., 2010; O'Toole, 1997). However, while Milward and Provan (2000) argued that some lead organization structure is needed for effective performance, O'Toole (1997) suggested that self-organizing network structure can achieve similar levels of network performance. This implies that different contexts, policy domains, and political jurisdictions may play important roles in determining network's outcomes.

The participatory and inclusive nature of network governance has added a level of complexity to the already complex issue of accountability. How does this participatory nature of networks reflect the hybrid nature of the accountability system? The participatory nature of network governance invites flexibility, transparency, creativity, and innovation in policy development and implementation, as well as service delivery, despite the order and control focus of hierarchical systems. This perspective brings together individual, organizational, network, and community resources in addressing complex policy and societal problems. All members of the collaborative action are collectively accountable, identifying policy and management issues, making decisions, implementation, and evaluations of the outcomes.

Conclusion

Since most of the complex policy decisions are made by collaborative structures and several public service programs are delivered by partnerships and networks, accountability for effective network governance is critical. Network arrangements do not remove organizational or bureaucratic structure. Rather, they co-exist and create duality in accountability system. The multisectoral nature of network governance, including state and non-state actors, co-production of policies or co-delivering services makes an accountability system in networks complex and challenging. As they are loosely coupled, informal networks also make it difficult to develop an accountability structure with clear standards. Accountability structure, or lack thereof, will impact the legitimacy of networks as well. In the chapter, legitimacy and accountability for effective network governance were considered in some degree for potential collaborative efforts. The hybridized accountability regime examined democratic, market, legal, and administrative accountability frames.

This chapter suggests that the importance of accountability and highlights the challenge in maintaining a positive reputation for legitimacy and accountability and selecting appropriate evaluating tools. Accountability and evaluation in networks foster trust that promotes legitimacy and the utilization of networks in decision-making, in the implementation of services, and in other collaborative actions. At the most fundamental level, trust between individuals, government, nonprofit organizations, and public and private sectors is needed to navigate through the maze of societal problems in communities. There is ample room for new research in each topic, which suggests that the surge of research surrounding legitimacy, accountability, and evaluation in network theory will continue. Although it is generally accepted that traditional performance evaluation and accountability tools are not appropriate for collaborative networks, there is not a generally agreed method of how to develop accountability within a collaborative network structure. Stakeholders' involvement in network arrangements can maintain organizational accountability standards. Stakeholders can also develop accountability mechanisms and standards for the network collectively. Even though there is hope for developing collective accountability mechanisms for networks, there is still substantial research is needed both from theoretical and empirical perspectives. The following chapter will shed some light on evaluating network performance.

References

Acar, M., Guo, C., & Yang, K. (2011). Accountability in voluntary partnerships: To whom and for what? *Public Organization Review*. doi:10.1007/s11115-011-0169-0

Ansell, C., & Gash, A. (2012). Stewards, mediators, and catalysts: Toward a model of collaborative leadership. *The Innovation Journal: The Public Sector Innovation Journal, 17*(1), article 7.

Ansell, C., & Gash, A. (2017). Collaborative platforms as a governance strategy. *Journal of Public Administration Research and Theory, 18*, 543–571.

Bingham, L. B., & O'Leary, R. (2008). *Big ideas in collaborative public management.* New York, NY: M. E. Sharpe.

Brandsma, G. J., & Schillemans, T. (2012). The accountability cube: Measuring accountability. *Journal of Public Administration Research and Theory, 23*(4), 953–975.

Bryson, J. M., Crosby, B. C., & Stone, M. M. (2006). The design and implementation of cross-sector collaborations: Propositions from the literature. *Public Administration Review, 66*(Suppl. 1), 44–55.

Donahue, J. D., & Zeckhauser, R. J. (2011). *Collaborative governance: Private roles for public goals in turbulent times.* Princeton, NJ: Princeton University Press.

Ehren, M. C. M., & Godfrey, D. (2017). External accountability of collaborative arrangements: A case study of a multi academy trust in England. *Educational Assessment, Evaluation and Accountability*. doi:10.1007/s11092-017-9267-z

Emerson, K., Nabatchi, T., & Balogh, S. (2012). An integrative framework for collaborative governance. *Journal of Public Administration Research and Theory, 22*(1), 1–29.

Freeman, R. E. (1984). *Strategic management: A stakeholder approach*. Boston, MA: Pitman Publishing.

Kapucu, N. (2009). Interorganizational coordination in complex environments of disasters: The evolution of intergovernmental disaster response systems. *Journal of Homeland Security and Emergency Management, 6*(1), article 47.

Kapucu, N., & Demiroz, F. (2011). Measuring performance for collaborative public management using network analysis methods and tools. *Public Performance and Management Review, 34*(4), 551–581.

Klijn, E. H., & Koppenjan, J. (2014). Accountable networks. In M. Bovens, M. Goodin, & T. Schillemans (Eds.), *The Oxford handbook of public accountability* (pp. 242–258). Oxford: Oxford University Press.

Klijn, E. H., & Koppenjan, J. (2016). *Governance networks in the public sector*. New York, NY: Routledge.

Koliba, C., Meek, J. C., & Zia, A. (2010). *Governance networks in public administration and public policy*. New York, NY: CRC Press.

Linden, R. M. (2010). *Leading across boundaries: Creating collaborative agencies in a networked world*. San Francisco: Jossey-Bass.

Mandell, M., & Keast, R. L. (2007). Evaluating network arrangements: Toward revised performance measures. *Public Performance & Management Review, 30*(4), 574–597.

Milward, H. B., & Provan, K. G. (2000). Governing the hollow state. *Journal of Public Administration Research and Theory, 10*(4), 359–379.

Milward, H. B., Provan, K. G., Fish, A., Isett, K. R., & Huang, K. (2010). Governance and collaboration: An evolutionary study of two mental health networks. *Journal of Public Administration Research and Theory, 20*(Suppl. 1), i125–i141.

Ostrom, E. (1990). *Governing the commons: The evolution of institutions for collective action*. Cambridge, UK: Cambridge University Press.

O'Toole, L. J. (1997). The implications for democracy in a networked bureaucratic world. *Journal of Public Administration Research and Theory, 7*(3), 443–459.

Page, S. (2004). Measuring accountability for results in interagency collaboratives. *Public Administration Review, 64*(5), 591–606.

Patel, V., Swain, M. J., King, J., & Furukawa, M. F. (2013). Physician capability to electronically exchange clinical information. *American Journal of Managed Care, 19*(10), 835–843.

Peters, B. G., & Pierre, J. (1998). Governance without government? Rethinking public administration. *Journal of Public Administration Research and Theory, 8*(2), 223–243.

Popp, J. K., Milward, B. H., MacKean, G., Casebeer, A., & Lindstorm, R. (2014). *Interorganizational networks: A review of the literature to inform practice*. Washington, DC: IBM Center for the Business of Government.

Provan, K. G., Kenis, P., & Human, S. E. (2008). Legitimacy building in organizational networks. In L. Bingham & R. O'Leary (Eds.), *Big ideas in collaborative public management*. New York, NY: M. E. Sharpe.

Provan, K. G., Lamb, G., & Doyle, M. (2004). Building legitimacy and the early growth of health networks for the uninsured. *Health Care Management Review*, *29*(2), 117–128.

Provan, K., & Milward, H. B. (2001). Do networks really work? A framework for evaluating public sector organizational networks. *Public Administration Review*, *61*(4), 414–423.

Romzek, B. S., & Dubnick, M. J. (1987). Accountability in the public sector: Lessons from the challenger tragedy. *Public Administration Review*, *47*(3), 227–238.

Romzek, B. S., LeRoux, K., & Blackmar, J. M. (2012). A preliminary theory of informal accountability among network organizational actors. *Public Administration Review*, *72*(3), 442–453. doi:10.1111/j.1540-6210.2011.02547.x

Romzek, B. S., LeRoux, K., Johnston, J., Kempf, R. J., & Piatak, J. C. (2014). Informal accountability in multisector service delivery collaborations. *Journal of Public Administration Research and Theory*, *24*(4), 813–842.

Scott, C. (2006). Spontaneous accountability. In M. W. Dowdle (Ed.), *Public accountability: Designs, dilemmas and experiences* (pp. 174–194). Cambridge, UK: Cambridge University Press.

Siegel, G. B., Clayton, R., & Kovoor, S. (1990). Modeling inter-organizational effectiveness. *Public Performance & Management Review*, *13*(3), 215–222.

Simmons, J. (2003). Rules of engagement: Towards effectiveness and equity in public private sector collaboration. *Public Management Review*, *5*(4), 585–596.

Suchman, M. C. (1995). Managing legitimacy: Strategic and innovative approaches. *Academy of Management Review*, *20*(3), 571–610.

U. S. Government Accountability Office. (2005). *Practices that can help enhance and sustain collaboration among federal agencies*, GAO-06–15. Washington, DC: United States Government Accountability Office. Retrieved from https://www.gao.gov/assets/250/248219.pdf

9 Network Performance and Evaluation

An important question in network research is whether interorganizational networks produce positive results as intended (Agranoff, 2007). Although a vague concept, network effectiveness has been the subject of increasing interest (Turrini, Cristofoli, Frosini, & Nasi, 2010; Raab, Mannak, & Cambré, 2015). The performance of interorganizational networks can be evaluated from different theoretical perspectives. In this chapter, we define network effectiveness and discuss the approaches to evaluate network performance. We conceptualize network effectiveness at multidimensional levels and introduce a multilevel approach to evaluate network performance at the organizational, network, and community levels. We also cover network analysis tools for assessing performance. This chapter addresses the following questions:

* Why is it challenging to evaluate network performance?
* What are the key dimensions of network effectiveness?
* What are the tools and approaches to evaluate network performance?
* What is a multilevel approach to network effectiveness?

The Multidimensional Nature of Network Performance

Evaluating network performance can run into conceptual and methodological challenges. Defining network performance is context-specific and contingent upon the goals of the network, the dynamic interactions among organizations, the consensus reached by network participants, and the expectations of key stakeholders (Herranz, 2010). Interorganizational networks function to achieve multiple, sometimes vague, goals, with different organizational cultures and structures, the influence of complex environments, and a wide range of stakeholders (Herranz, 2010; Provan & Milward, 2001; Walker, Farley, & Polin, 2012). Another challenge is that there is a lack of performance measures that apply to network arrangements, as existing measures often focus on individual organizations (Callahan & Kloby, 2007; Mandell & Keast, 2007). Network performance can be measured at the levels of individuals, organizations, and communities (Provan & Milward, 2001). Another contributing factor to the complexity of network performance is the intertwined relationship between collaboration processes and outcomes, which is discussed here.

Processes and Outcomes

Cross-sector collaboration among public, nonprofit, and for-profit organizations has become crucial for delivering public services (Donahue & Zeckhauser, 2011; Milward, 1996). Therefore, understanding the processes and outcomes of interorganizational collaboration has gained more importance. We cannot address network outcomes without discussing the process of interorganizational collaboration. Although, scholars have called attention to the differences between "process performance (i.e., the results of the collaborative process)" and "productivity performance (i.e., the resulting outcomes of collaborative action)" (Emerson & Nabatchi, 2015). Process is one of the key dimension of collaboration (Ansell & Gash, 2008; Thomson, Perry, & Miller, 2009). Thomson et al. (2009) defined collaboration as an interactive process in which "autonomous actors interact through formal and informal negotiation, jointly creating rules and structures" (p. 23).

The performance of interorganizational networks can be evaluated from a process perspective. Ansell and Gash, in their research on collaborative governance, argued that collaborative process is iterative. This process not only involves having face-to-face dialogues, building trust, developing commitment and shared understanding, but also includes "immediate outcomes" such as small wins and the development of strategic plans (2008, p. 550). It is not easy to separate network outcomes from the process, due to the complex nature of interorganizational relations. Collaboration is considered effective when process outcomes are achieved. Expected process outcomes include, but are not limited to, facilitative communication, shared values and goals of network members, trust building, and organizational learning (Herranz, 2010).

Collaboration processes should be linked to the network outcomes. Researchers have conducted empirical studies on the relationship between collaboration processes and collaborative outcomes. Five outcome variables were used to measure collaborative outcomes, including perceived effectiveness in achieving goals, perceived increase in quality of partners' working relationships, perceived broadening of partners' views, perceived increase in partner interactions (network density), and perceived increase in equitable influence/power have often been used (Thomson, Perry, & Miller, 2008). The collaboration process is multidimensional, composed of five key dimensions: governance, administration, organizational autonomy, mutuality, and norms (Thompson et al., 2008). According to their empirical work, administration and trust influence perceived effectiveness in achieving goals (Thomson et al., 2008). They noted that good administrative structure with clear roles, task coordination, and goal agreement is important for achieving collaborative goals (Thomson et al., 2008). Trust contributes to collaborative outcomes by lowering transaction costs and facilitating coordination (Thomson et al., 2008).

Factors Influencing Network Effectiveness

Given the intertwined relationship between processes and outcomes, we do not intend to differentiate between the two in this book. Instead, we use the concept of *network effectiveness* to evaluate and measure network performance. We build on existing research on network effectiveness to further explain why evaluating network performance is complex. We focus on three key groups of factors that influence network effectiveness,

> **Network Effectiveness**
>
> The extent to which a network achieves its organizational, community, or network level goals.

including contextual factors, structural characteristics of networks, and network functioning factors (Provan & Milward, 1995; Turrini et al., 2010; Raab et al., 2015). Adapting existing frameworks of network effectiveness, Table 9.1 presents the key variables to consider when explaining network effectiveness.

Contextual Factors

A variety of external and contextual factors can influence network effectiveness. For instance, the uncertainty and changes in the external environment can influence how a network functions and performs. The relationship can be a nonlinear, suggesting that networked organizations respond to and adapt to the changing environment (Turrini et al., 2010). Resource availability matters to a network because organizations in a network need resources to operate and coordinate. Scarce financial resources limit organizations from investing in interorganizational coordination. Another important environmental factor is the support that member organizations receive from the larger community (Guo & Acar, 2005). Social capital developed over past collaborations influence the trust building among member organizations and ultimately the performance of the network (Turrini et al., 2010).

Structural Characteristics of Networks

The size, age, and composition of a network influence its performance. As the network becomes bigger and more heterogeneous, the cost of coordination increases. On the other hand, large and heterogeneous networks may produce diverse ideas and solutions (Sandström & Carlsson, 2008). Yet, few empirical studies have systematically tested the direction of relationships between network composition, size, and age, and network performance (Turrini et al., 2010). Other structural characteristics of networks, such as formalization, stability, integration, closure, and clustering, can affect network performance. The formalization of networks enables the adoption of

Table 9.1 Factors Influencing Network Effectiveness

Three Groups of Factors	Variables	Brief Description
Contextual Factors: The influence of external environment	System stability	Changes in the external environment
	Resource munificence	Resource availability to the network, such as financial resources
	Cohesion and support from the community	Social capital, and community support
Structural Characteristics of Networks	Size of the network	The number of member organizations
	Composition of member organizations	The diversity and heterogeneity of member organizations
	Age of the network	The number of years network has existed
	Formalization and accountability	Use of formal rules, organized meetings, and formal decision-making processes
	Network inner stability	The length of management tenure and the level of competitiveness among personnel
	Network integration	The degree of integration through density, centralization, or clique overlap
	External control	The influence of constituents and stakeholders
Network Functioning Factors	Traditional management	Management competency and behaviors
	Managerial networking behavior	Interactions with a diverse range of external stakeholder groups
	Network management and leadership	Managerial behaviors to build commitment, steer the network process, address conflicts, and mobilize resources.
	Network governance structures	Different modes of governance

Sources: Provan & Milward, 1995; Turrini et al., 2010; Raab et al., 2015

performance measures. Network stability (e.g., having committed management) also plays a positive role in achieving network effectiveness and network integration, as centralized coordination tends to promote network effectiveness (Provan & Milward, 1995; Turrini et al., 2010). Network closure—often measured by network density and centralization—influences network performance (Provan & Milward, 1995; Sandström & Carlsson, 2008). A centralized network enables organizations to establish priorities in a timely manner (Sandström & Carlsson, 2008). Yi's research on clean energy governance networks suggested that network structures—both bridging (measured by the network-level average degree centrality) and bonding (measured by network-level average clustering coefficient)—contribute to job growth in renewal energy industry and state-level renewable energy capacity (Yi, 2018).

Network Functioning Factors

Among the network functioning factors, we focus on three key ones: network governance structures, networking behaviors of leadership, and network management and leadership. Provan and Kenis (2008) suggested three types of network governance structures: participant-governed or shared governance (members of the network collectively govern the networks), governance by a lead organization (a lead organization in the network coordinate network-level decision-making and major activities), and governance by a network administrative organization (NAO). Multiple contingency factors affect the network's performance. This includes the level of trust between participants of a network, size of a network, level of goal consensus, and "need for network-level competencies" (Provan & Kenis, 2008, p. 240). The effectiveness of shared governance requires high levels of trust, few participants, and goal consensus (Provan & Kenis, 2008). In summary, the functioning of networks depends on the alignment of governance structure with the attributes and context of networks.

Other researchers also tested the relationship between network governance and effectiveness by considering the influence of contingency factors on governance roles. Different from Provan and Kenis's three governance modes, Span et al. asserted that there are three governance roles on a continuum from top-down (commissioner) to bottom-up (facilitator), with an intermediate area (co-producer) (Span, Luijkx, Schols, & Schalk, 2012). These three roles are developed based on eight dimensions: main actor, steering mechanism, boundary setting, formality of dependency, alignment, responsibility for goals, vision, and monitoring mechanism. Contingency factors include network age, network size, network diversity, service customization, network stability, and complexity. Based on these contingency factors, networks can be categorized into four types: simple and stable (the network is old and small with homogeneous actors, and the network only needs to provide low customized services); simple but dynamic (the network is young and large with homogeneous actors, and the network provides low customized services); complex and stable (the network is old and small with heterogeneous actors, and the network provides highly customized services), and complex and dynamic (the network is young and large with homogeneous actors, and the network provides highly customized services). A top-down commissioner role is more effective for simple and stable public networks and the bottom-up facilitator role is more effective for complex and dynamic public networks, while a coproducer role is better for simple and dynamic networks as well as complex and stable public networks (Span et al., 2012). Yet, empirical testing of these propositions is warranted.

In addition to network governance, networking behaviors, network management, and leadership also play key roles in achieving effectiveness. Scholars have highlighted the value of networking behaviors among leadership for higher network performance (Meier & O'Toole, 2001; O'Toole, Meier, & Nicholson-Crotty, 2005). For instance, schools with superintendents who interacted frequently with outside stakeholder actors (business leaders, other superintendents, Texas legislators, and the Texas Education Agency) had consistently higher student performance outcomes than schools with superintendents who had lower level of interactions (Meier & O'Toole, 2001).

As we discussed in Chapter 5, network management is another key determinant of network effectiveness. In order to achieve high performance, network managers need to solve conflicts, build connections, and mobilize resources (Agranoff & McGuire, 2001). There are various managerial strategies for managing networks such as, arranging, connecting, exploring, and establishing process rules (Klijn et al., 2014). The arranging strategy facilitates interaction, connecting strategy is to link actors in networks, while the exploring strategy develops new content and the process rule creates temporary procedures that guide the behavior of the actors (Klijn et al., 2014). The use of managerial strategies can facilitate network processes and dynamics, bridging divergent perspectives, overcome barriers to collaboration, and contribute to network effectiveness (Klijn et al., 2014).

Herranz (2010) discussed different network coordination strategies and how different coordination strategies can achieve different outcomes. There are three strategic approaches to network coordination: "bureaucratically-oriented network coordination," "entrepreneurially-oriented network coordination," and "community-oriented network coordination" (Herranz, 2010, pp. 320–324). The bureaucratically oriented network coordination is characterized by its focus on formalization, centrality, rules, standards, network stability. He argued that "bureaucratically oriented network coordination" can be used to achieve the following performance outcomes: meeting legal requirements, providing stability in service delivery, and demonstrating accountability (Herranz, 2010). The "entrepreneurially oriented network coordination" is often connected with maximizing public value, maximizing financial resources, and innovation" (Herranz, 2010, p. 323). The "community-oriented network coordination" is hypothesized to establish collaborative capacity by means of trust and voluntary reciprocity. This coordination strategy emphasizes the process of building relationships rather than other network outcomes (Herranz, 2010). Depending on the goals of the network, managers and leaders may need to use different coordination strategies or combinations of these strategies.

A Theory-Driven Approach and a Logical Approach to Conceptualize Network Performance

As shown in Figure 9.1, there are different approaches to conceptualizing and evaluating network performance. This section introduces two approaches to conceptualize *network performance*: A theory-driven approach and a logical approach. Let us start with a theory-drive approach to understand what network

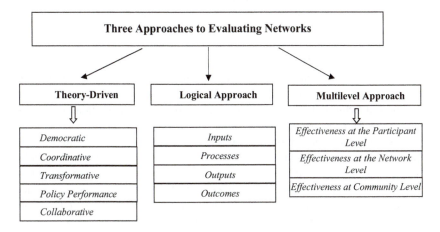

Figure 9.1 Different Approaches to Network Performance and Evaluation

performance means. Skelcher and Sullivan (2008) proposed a set of five performance domains covering the democratic, coordinative, transformative, policy, and sustainability dimensions of collaboration. Each of these dimensions allow researchers to develop insights into the measurement of performance (Skelcher & Sullivan, 2008). Democratic performance, built upon democratic theory, focuses on fundamental democratic values and principles, such as legitimacy, consent, and accountability (Skelcher & Sullivan, 2008). Democratic performance is important for networks as it relates to network legitimacy and accountability (discussed in Chapter 8), although empirical studies remain limited on this dimension.

Coordinative performance of collaboration addresses the expectation that collaboration performs by connecting disparate actors and mobilize them to take part in coordinative action. Power/resource-dependency and exchange theories are helpful to measure the degree of coordinative performance of collaboration, by "explaining patterns of authority exercised over resource flows" (Skelcher & Sullivan, 2008, p. 754). Among these five dimensions, coordinative performance has received most attention in network research, due to the goal of most interorganizational networks in improving coordination and strengthening partnerships.

Transformative performance focuses on the potential of a network to create synergy and the potential of member organizations to "exercise path-breaking behavior" (Skelcher & Sullivan, 2008, p. 754). Institutional theory provides for a useful tool for understanding the extent to which external forces, peer pressure, and professional values motivate network actors to participate in path-breaking behavior (Skelcher & Sullivan, 2008).

Policy performance evaluates the extent to which policy goals have been achieved (Skelcher & Sullivan, 2008). The policy performance dimension is built on two schools of thought: policy network theory and the Dutch school of network theory. Policy network theory emphasizes the structures and patterns of interactions among policy actors, and the Dutch school of network literature focus on the "steering" role network managers in achieving policy goals (Skelcher & Sullivan, 2008).

The final theoretical perspective on collaborative performance addresses the sustainability of network itself (Chapter 4). Both interdependency theory and post-structural discourse theory are used to explain the sustainability performance (Skelcher & Sullivan, 2008). Interdependency theory can explain the rise of connections among network actors and the use of rules to manage and sustain the relations among network members. Discourse theory can help analyze the sustainability performance of networks by assessing "the extent to which a hegemonic discourse is realized, and the institutional arrangements associated with it are naturalized" (Skelcher & Sullivan, 2008, p. 764). Some researchers have used size of network members and stability of network structure to capture the network-level effectiveness (Provan & Milward, 2001).

A theory-driven approach is important in helping researchers and policy makers conceptualize the complex and multidimensional nature of network performance. While many empirical network studies have been conducted on coordinative performance and policy performance, and sustainability performance, especially in the context of emergency management and social service relatively few empirical studies have focused on the democratic and transformative dimensions of performance. Few empirical studies have been conducted to further conceptualize and operationalize these three dimensions in the domain of network performance.

A Logic Model Approach to Network Performance

Originating from performance evaluation, a logical approach provides a model to conceptualize network coordination and performance (Herranz, 2010). A logic model includes four key components: inputs (e.g., financial investments and human capital), (b) processes (e.g., services coordination and provision), (c) outputs (e.g., tangible intermediate products or services), and (d) outcomes (e.g., expected changes in the short, medium, and long term) (Herranz, 2010, p. 62). The logic model presents a simplified framework to examine complex relationships in networks, to develop performance indicators, and to offer step-by-step approach to understand the process and outcomes of inter-organizational networks (Koliba, Meek, & Zia, 2010).

Inputs can originate internally or externally (Koliba et al., 2010). Internal inputs include resources such as financial investment, human capital, and organizational goals. External inputs include policy tools, rules, norms, and network goals. Processes include interactions among organizations. For instance, organizations build different ties with one another to share information and resources, refer clients, and provide joint services (Herranz, 2010). In the process, networks choose governance structures. Managers and leaders

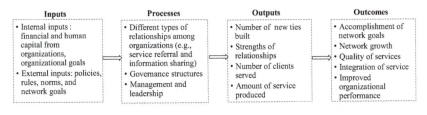

Figure 9.2 Logic Model Network Performance and Evaluation

work across organizational boundaries to mobilize resources, addresses differ-ences, and build coalitions. Outputs are immediate measurable products, such as the number of clients served, the amount of service produced. It also includes network-level outputs that covers examines the number of new ties built in the network, and strengths of relationships (Herranz, 2010). Outcomes are con-nected to goals of the network and its member organizations. It also includes network growth. More importantly, outcomes often measure whether service has been improved or better integrated (Koliba et al., 2010) (Figure 9.2).

A Multilevel Approach to Network Effectiveness

This section first discusses a multilevel approach to network effectiveness—the evaluation of network performance at the organizational, network, and community levels (Provan & Milward, 2001). Then, it introduces the use of social network analysis for evaluating network performance.

Evaluating Network Performance at Different Levels

Networks are examined at multiple levels such as: dyads, actors, groups and whole networks and network can be analyzed at the micro, meso, and macro levels (Borgatti, Everett, & Johnson, 2013; Kilduff & Brass, 2010; Mandell & Keast, 2007, p. 585). As Provan and Milward noted in their seminal work on network effectives, networks need to be evaluated at different levels: commu-nity, network, and organization/participant levels (2001, p. 414). Three com-ponents are involved with these levels: principal organizations/administration; agent and clients. Interactions between three levels are required for an effective network, but network effectiveness at one level does not guarantee effective-ness at the other two levels (Provan & Milward, 2001).

Effectiveness at the Organization/Participant Level

The effectiveness of network at the individual level can be evaluated using four criteria: "client outcomes, legitimacy, resource acquisition, and cost" (Provan & Milward, 2001, p. 420). For small and less-established organizations, joining a publicly funded network may provide more legitimacy. In addition, organizations can get more resources by engaging in a network. Organizations, even larger ones, can reduce their costs and enhance client outcomes through network involvement and tapping into network resources and learning. Service networks can integrate resources from individual organizations and help network members to provide a broad range of needed services more efficiently and effectively (Provan & Milward, 2001). When evaluating network performance, one should ask the following questions: Does your organization gain more resources after joining the service network? Does your organization reduce the cost of service delivery after joining the service network? Does your organization gain more legitimacy? Does your organization improve efficiency of service delivery? Does your organization improve quality of services provided to clients?

Effectiveness at the Network Level

The first way to evaluate network effectiveness is to examine "the ebb and flow of agencies to and from the network" by measuring the numbers of network members that join and stay engaged (Provan & Milward, 2001, p. 418). A stable number of members can reflect the stability and function of the network. The second way of evaluating network-level effectiveness is to examine the extent to which the network fulfills the actual needs of clients. To evaluate the strength of network members' relationships is the third way to assess network effectiveness. In an effective network, many organizations have multiplex relationships, meaning that they are connected to one another through different types of programs or client services or through general information sharing and friendship. The last way of assessing network-level effectiveness is to judge whether its administrative structure can obtain and distribute resources in ways that maximize resources utilization within a network (Provan & Milward, 2001). Questions can be asked: How many organizations join the network and stay engaged in the network? Does the service network improve service integration across organizational boundaries? What types of relations do organizations have with one another? Does the governance structure support the function of the service network?

Network Effectiveness at the Community Level

The satisfaction of clients and other community-interest groups provide important legitimacy and external support for networks. To evaluate the effectiveness of a network at the community level, the main measures are the impact on the clients' well-being, the total cost of service, public satisfaction about the service, and growth of social capital (Provan & Milward, 2001). These questions should be asked: Does community social capital change after the network is formed? Does the service network improve clients' well-being? How much does it cost for the network to deliver the service? Another way to evaluate network effectiveness is to link the community-level network effectiveness to *collective impact*. Instead of making isolated individual impact on communities, collective action of network actors can make collective impact (Kania & Kramer, 2011). For example, in Cincinnati, to address student performance cri-

---

Collective Impact

The positive effect generated by the network at the community level.

---

sis in greater Cincinnati and northern Kentucky, Strive, a nonprofit organization has brought together more than 300 community leaders, government officials, educators, school district representatives, heads of foundations, and advocacy groups. These network actors focus on the entire educational community and set goals to be obtained by the entire community (Kania & Kramer, 2011). These goals cannot be achieved by any individual organization's isolated efforts but requires collective effort. Therefore, the extent to which these goals are accomplished can be used as measures of community-level network effectiveness.

Network effectiveness at the three levels is interdependent, as the outcome at one level may influence the outcome at other levels. Various stakeholder groups may have different priority levels of network effectiveness, making leading, integrating, and balancing network effectiveness at three levels an uneasy task (Provan & Milward, 2001).

Network Analysis to Assess Network Performance

Traditional performance measures focus on individual organizations; therefore, it is imperative to find new ways to measure performance, structural patterns and processes of interorganizational networks (Kapucu & Demiroz, 2011; Mandell & Keast, 2007). Developing appropriate performance measures for interorganizational networks is a challenging undertaking (Walker et al., 2012). Networks have their own unique attributes, and thus additional tools are needed to measure their performance. Social network analysis allows researchers to evaluate network performance at individual, dyadic, group, and network levels.

Interorganizational relations are examined to evaluate the effectiveness of a collaborative network. Network members can use their relations more effectively if they understand their existing relations and if they are able to build new relations with other members when needed. Since members are interdependent, they must assist their partners. Otherwise, a member may hamper the coordination of the whole network (Kapucu & Demiroz, 2011). Organizations can better engage with their stakeholders by understanding the relations among organizations, and central and peripheral roles played by organizational stakeholders (Prell, Klaus, & Reed, 2009). Furthermore, social network analysis can help enhance interorganizational effectiveness of a network by identifying high and low performers in a network and the reasons behind performance discrepancies.

Social network analysis focuses on how different actors are connected to one another through relations. A detailed introduction of the network measures has been provided in Chapter 2. Many network concepts are meaningful for studying network performance, such as strong ties, weak ties, homophily, centrality (both degree and betweenness,) and centralization.

Centrality measures (degree, closeness, betweenness, and eigenvector) that are used to identify important actors in a network are indicators of the amount of collaboration and cooperation, connectivity, and communication. Those concepts are also the objectives of creating network structure. Centrality measures "reveals the organizations that are able to interact with others not only in a small group but also in the network as a whole" (Kapucu & Demiroz, 2011, p. 560). The performance of September 11 and Hurricane Katrina response networks have been examined using network analysis techniques. They compared the levels of the collaboration and networking identified in the plans- Federal Response Plan (FRP), National Response Plan (NRP)— and the implementation of these plans in response to disasters. The FRP and NRP illustrate every aspect of how the federal government should respond to a disaster by identifying the functional responsibilities of each agency and department of the federal government. The UCINET program was used to evaluate the relationships among the agencies that responded to these catastrophic disasters.

The study results stated that "the September 11 response network performance differed from the FRP network and the Hurricane Katrina response network outcomes showed different structures from those of the NPR. The structural differences between these formal versus informal and planned versus actual networks demonstrate the utility of providing measures of network outcomes" (Kapucu & Demiroz, 2011, p. 573). On the other hand, two factors are necessary for a healthy network performance evaluation in this approach. "First, there should be an identifiable planned network structure that can be compared against the actual network, as is the case for disaster response networks. Second, there should be reports or other reliable data sources that identify network actors, and their collaborative actions" (Kapucu & Demiroz, 2011, p. 573).

Conclusion

Understanding network performance is crucial for public mangers to identify issues or conflicts to solve and develop proper strategies to achieve network goals. Performance data provide substantial information for strategy development, day-to-day operations, resource allocation, and service delivery. Performance management is more complex and difficult in interorganizational networks than a single organization because many organizations join the network with different expectations, goals, expectations, and divergent organizational cultures. In this chapter, we discussed the factors that can influence network performance, introduced three approaches to conceptualize network effectiveness, and put weight on the multilevel approach to network performance. Due to the multilevel nature of networks, network performance can be evaluated at individual organizational level, network level, and community level (Provan & Milward, 2001). In addition, we discussed the use of network analysis to evaluate network performance, which continues to evolve to provide evaluation measures, tools, and techniques for interorganizational networks.

References

Agranoff, R. (2007). *Managing within networks: Adding value to public organizations.* Washington, DC: Georgetown University Press.

Agranoff, R., & McGuire, M. (2001). Big questions in public network management research. *Journal of Public Administration Research and Theory, 11*(3), 295–326.

Ansell, C., & Gash, A. (2008). Collaborative governance in theory and practice. *Journal of Public Administration Research and Theory, 18*(4), 543–571.

Borgatti, S. P., Everett, M. G., & Johnson, J. C. (2013). *Analyzing social networks.* Los Angeles, CA: Sage Publications.

Callahan, C., & Kloby, K. (2007). Collaboration meets the performance measurement challenge. *Public Manager, 36*(2), 9–12.

Donahue, J. D., & Zeckhauser, R. J. (2011). *Collaborative governance: Private roles for public goals in turbulent times.* Princeton, NJ: Princeton University Press.

Emerson, K., & Nabatchi, T. (2015). *Collaborative governance regimes.* Washington, DC: Georgetown University Press.

Guo, C., & Acar, M. (2005). Understanding collaboration among nonprofit organizations: Combining resource dependency, institutional, and network perspectives. *Nonprofit & Voluntary Sector Quarterly, 34*(3), 340–361.

Herranz, J. (2010). Network performance and coordination: A theoretical review and framework. *Public Performance and Management Review, 33*(3), 311–341.

Kania, J., & Kramer, M. (2011). Collective impact. *Stanford Social Innovation Review, 9*(1), 36–41.

Kapucu, N., & Demiroz, F. (2011). Measuring performance for collaborative public management using network analysis methods and tools. *Public Performance and Management Review, 34*(4), 551–581.

Kilduff, M., & Brass, D. J. (2010). Organizational social network research: Core ideas and key debates. *The Academy of Management Annals, 4*(1), 317–357.

Klijn, E-H., Ysa, T., Sierra, V., Berman, E. M., Edelenbos, J., & Chen, D. Y. (2014). The influence of network management and complexity on network performance in Taiwan, Spain and the Netherlands. *Public Management Review.* doi:10.1080/1471 9037.2014.957340

Koliba, C., Meek, J. C., & Zia, A. (2010). *Governance networks in public administration and public policy.* New York, NY: CRC Press.

Mandell, M., & Keast, R. L. (2007). Evaluating network arrangements: Toward revised performance measures. *Public Performance & Management Review, 30*(4), 574–597.

Meier, K. J., & O'Toole, L. J. (2001). Managerial strategies and behavior in networks: A model with evidence from U.S. public education. *Journal of Public Administration Theory and Research, 11*(3), 271–294.

Milward, H. B. (1996). Symposium on the hollow state: Capacity, control and performance in interorganizational settings. *Journal of Public Administration Research and Theory*, 6(2), 193–195.

O'Toole, L. J., Meier, K. J., & Nicholson-Crotty, S. (2005). Managing upward, downward, and outward: Networks, hierarchical relationships, and performance. *Public Management Review*, 7(1), 45–68.

Prell, C., Klaus, H., & Reed, M. S. (2009). Stakeholder analysis and social network analysis in natural resource management. *Society and Natural Resources*, 22(6), 501–518.

Provan, K. G., & Kenis, P. (2008). Modes of network governance: Structure, management, and effectiveness. *Journal of Public Administration Research and Theory*, 18(2), 229–252.

Provan, K. G., & Milward, H. B. (1995). A preliminary theory of network effectiveness: A comparative study of four mental health systems. *Administrative Science Quarterly*, 40(1), 1–33.

Provan, K. G., & Milward, H. B. (2001). Do networks really work? A framework for evaluating public sector organizational networks. *Public Administration Review*, 61(4), 414–431.

Raab, J., Mannak, R. S., & Cambré, B. (2015). Combining structure, governance, and context: A configurational approach to network effectiveness. *Journal of Public Administration Research and Theory*, 25(2), 479–511.

Sandström, A., & Carlsson, L. (2008). The performance of policy networks: The relation between network structure and network performance. *The Policy Studies Journal*, 36(4), 494–524.

Skelcher, C., & Sullivan, H. (2008). Theory-driven approaches to analyzing collaborative performance. *Public Management Review*, 10(6), 751–771.

Span, K. C. L., Luijkx, K. G., Schols, J. M. G. A., & Schalk, R. (2012). The relationship between governance roles and performance in local public interorganizational networks: A conceptual analysis. *The American Review of Public Administration*, 42(2), 186–201.

Thomson, M. A., Perry, J. L., & Miller, T. K. (2008). Linking collaboration processes and outcomes: Foundations for advancing empirical theory. In L. B. Bingham & R. O'Leary (Eds.), *Big ideas in collaborative public management* (pp. 97–120). New York, NY: M. E. Sharpe.

Thomson, M. A., Perry, J. L., & Miller, T. K. (2009). Conceptualizing and measuring collaboration. *Journal of Public Administration Research and Theory*, 19(1), 23–56.

Turrini, A., Cristofoli, D., Frosini, F., & Nasi, G. (2010). Networking literature about determinants of network effectiveness. *Public Administration*, 88(2), 528–550.

Walker, K., Farley, E., & Polin, M. (2012). *Using data in multi-agency collaborations: Guiding performance to ensure accountability and improve programs*. Philadelphia, PA: Public/Private Ventures.

Yi, H. (2018). Network structure and governance performance: What makes a difference. *Public Administration Review*, 78(2), 195–205.

Section III

Applications

10 Networks in Emergency and Crisis Management

Earlier, we highlighted the importance of collaboration in addressing complex policy and social problems. Collaboration is imperative to deal with challenges faced during emergency and crisis events. It is believed that "emergency management is an ideal context" for studying interorganizational collaboration (McGuire & Silvia, 2010, p. 280). Over time, emergency and crisis management has grown from a highly centralized and hierarchical incident command system to the one that emphasizes partnerships, coordination, and collaboration (Waugh & Streib, 2006; Comfort, Waugh, & Cigler, 2012). This chapter highlights the importance of networks in emergency and crisis management, as emergency and crisis management often require different sectors to work together and coordinate their efforts. It outlines the nature of emergency and crisis management as a layered function, involving multiple networks of intergovernmental and cross-sector agencies. Furthermore, this chapter develops a framework for investigating contributing factors to effective interorganizational collaboration during disasters. The chapter illustrates how interorganizational networks are designed in response to disasters and discusses how to evaluate the performance of emergency and crisis management networks. In addition, it provides application examples of network analysis in emergency and crisis management. This chapter addresses the following questions:

- What does the emergency and crisis management system look like?
- Why are networks and coordination imperative in emergency and crisis management?
- What are the different types and structures of emergency and crisis management networks?
- How does one evaluate network performance in emergency and crisis management networks?
- What does crisis network leadership mean in emergency and crisis management networks?

Emergency and Crisis Management Networks: A Multilevel and Cross-Sector Emergency and Crisis Management System

Emergency and crisis management networks refer to interorganizational arrangements dealing with emergencies. The current US emergency and crisis management system is multilevel; involving federal, state, regional and local emergency management agencies and other government agencies, as well as nonprofit organizations, civic organizations, faith-based organizations, and businesses at community levels (as shown in Figure 10.1a). Each level of government plays a crucial role in managing emergencies and crises. At the federal level, Federal Emergency Management Agency (FEMA) within the Department of Homeland Security (DHS) coordinates efforts with other federal

> **Emergency & Crises Management Networks**
>
> Interorganizational arrangements dealing with emergencies and crises.

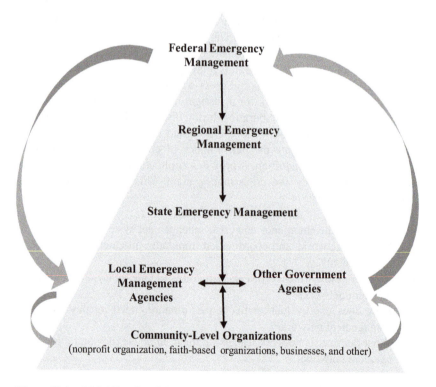

Figure 10.1a A Multilevel and Cross-Sector Emergency and Crisis Management System (adapted from Kapucu & Sadiq, 2016)

departments and agencies in all mission areas of disaster management: prevention, protection, mitigation, response, and recovery. To work with state and local emergency management agencies, FEMA established ten regional offices to coordinate disaster response efforts and allocate resources in collaborating with state and local governments (FEMA, 2018a).

State-level emergency management agencies work closely with both the federal, regional, and local emergency management agencies. For instance, in face of a disaster, the Florida Division of Emergency Management coordinates resources and assistance at the state level. It assesses and monitors the disaster and decides whether to request federal assistance to prepare, respond to, and recover from disasters. Local governments, especially county governments, play a crucial role in local emergency management (Waugh, 1994). The county office of emergency management often establishes close relationships with local public agencies, nonprofits, faith-based, and for-profit organizations to prepare for and to respond to disasters.

From an organizational network perspective, emergency and crisis management networks include a wide range of public agencies at different levels and across jurisdictional and other organizations across sector boundaries, working together to deal with emergencies (Kapucu & Demiroz, 2017; Lukensmeyer, 2007). As Figure 10.1b demonstrates, the network not only involves vertical relations among government organizations across all levels, but also includes the horizontal relations among emergency management organizations and other government organizations (represented by squares), nonprofit organizations (represented by diamonds), and private organizations (represented by

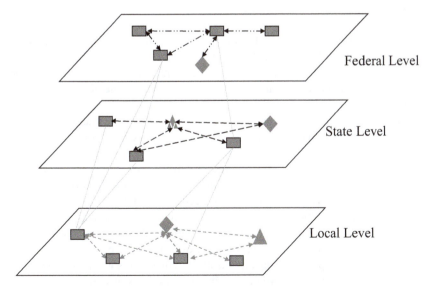

Figure 10.1b A Network Depiction of the Emergency and Crisis Management System

triangles). For instance, in response to the Pulse Nightclub shooting, 17 local government agencies, ten state government agencies, seven federal government agencies, 17 nonprofit organizations, six businesses, and one international government agency were involved in response efforts (City of Orlando Office of Emergency Management, 2016).

The Importance of Networks in Emergency and Crisis Management

A network approach to interorganizational coordination is critical for the effectiveness of emergency and crisis management (Comfort & Hasse, 2006; Nohrstedt, Bynander, Parker, & Hart, 2018; Waugh & Streib, 2006). On one hand, emergency management requires careful planning and systematic structuring of capacities and resources to prepare for scenarios. On the other hand, most emergencies and crises are low-probability but high-consequence events that occur and involve high levels of uncertainty, and potentially disastrous consequences (Waugh & Streib, 2006). Emergencies—from hurricanes to terrorist attacks—require immediate, well-coordinated response across jurisdictional, sectoral, and organizational boundaries.

Although the traditional command and control structure remains important for crisis management, a collaborative network approach is also necessary. The catastrophic failure in response to Hurricane Katrina in 2005 reflects the limitations of a rigid bureaucratic structure (Kettl, 2006). In the case of Katrina, the top-down chain of command constrains the timely exchange of critical information across government levels and jurisdictions, preventing managers from receiving operational feedback to adapt the system within dynamic environments of disasters (Comfort, 2007; Kettl, 2006). This top-down communication structure explained why intelligence agencies failed to share information nor predict prior to the September 11 terrorist attacks (Kapucu, 2006; Moynihan, 2005). The long vertical communication line also caused delays in evacuation and resource allocation, making it difficult for intergovernmental coordination in response to Hurricane Katrina in 2005 (Kettl, 2006).

Furthermore, the engagement of diverse organizations demands a network approach to coordinate emergency and crisis management efforts (Comfort, 2007). A hierarchical structure is needed to "provide the critical, unifying structure to the capacity of complex organizations;" however, emergency response "requires horizontal relationships to put that capacity to work" (Kettl, 2006, p. 279). Horizontal relations are needed to enable effective communication and coordination among a diverse range of organizations of heterogeneous size, backgrounds, and capacity (Comfort, 2007). Compared with the hierarchical (vertical) approach, a network (horizontal) approach focuses on relations among participating organizations. An interorganizational network allows organizations to develop multiple types of ties, which can foster the growth of trust and social capital, an important contributing factor for effective coordination (Kapucu & Hu, 2016). Flexible and frequent communication in a network can help organizations overcome organizational differences. In addition, a network structure allows flexibility in the dynamic context of emergencies and crises (Hu, Knox, & Kapucu, 2014).

Both a command-control bureaucratic structure and a network structure are reflected in the adoption of the Incident Command System (ICS) and the Emergence Support Function (ESF)-based system. These systems are built with guidance from federal policies, frameworks, and accreditation standards applicable to emergency management agencies. The ICS provides a hierarchical structure that operates around five functional sections: command, operation, planning, logistics, and finance/administration (FEMA, 2008, p. 1). When an incident occurs, the incident commander, with the support from command staff, including a public information officer, a safety officer, and a liaison officer, issues a unified command to all the involved agencies (Bigley & Roberts, 2001; Kapucu & Hu, 2016; Moynihan, 2009). The ICS highlights vertical chain of command, unified command, and hierarchy of authority to establish standard processes to achieve efficiency and effectiveness in incident management (FEMA, 2008). The ESF-based system, with a designated coordinator, and primary and support agencies, demonstrates an emphasis on horizontal organizational coordination, processes, and structures (Kapucu & Hu, 2016). The ESFs define the roles, responsibilities, and coordination structure among organizations through ESFs (FEMA, 2008). According to the ESFs, primary agencies and support agencies under each ESFs should coordinate with one another in response to disasters. Both the ICS and ESF-based system are of value to emergency and crisis management. A hybrid model of both systems is often adopted in practice for NIMS compliance and accreditation purposes (Kapucu & Hu, 2016).

In fact, a collaborative network approach has been highlighted in recent federal policies, initiatives, and guidelines to engage whole communities in emergency and crisis management (Hu et al., 2014). A federal example is the Urban Area Security Initiative (UASI), which aims to provide "high-threat and high-density" urban communities with funding to develop response capabilities and improve preparedness planning (Jordan, 2010). The UASI has promoted cross-jurisdictional collaboration in developing community capacity. At the state and local levels, comprehensive emergency management plans (CEMPs) guide intergovernmental and cross-sector coordination throughout all phases of emergency management. In addition, the Emergency Management Association Compact (EMAC)—a national interstate mutual aid agreement—facilitates the sharing of information, resources, and personnel across states in the face of disasters. EMAC played a crucial role in aiding and coordinating response efforts in disaster-impacted states (Kapucu, Augustin, & Garayev, 2009). At the local level, county government often establishes offices of emergency management and emergency operation centers to work with local other government agencies, nonprofit organizations, faith-based organizations, other community organizations, and businesses (Waugh, 2003).

Emergency and Crisis Management Networks

In the following section, we discuss different types of emergency and crisis management networks based on the relations among member organizations. We introduce different structures of emergency and crisis management networks and discuss the use of network analysis in analyzing the structure of emergency and crisis management networks.

Different Types of Emergency and Crisis Management Networks

There are different types of emergency and crisis management networks. As introduced in Chapter 3, networks can be grouped into different types using different criteria. The National Preparedness Goal identifies five mission areas: prevention, protection, mitigation, response, and recovery. Based on the different mission areas of emergency management (FEMA, 2018b), interorganizational emergency and crisis management networks can be categorized into preparedness networks, response networks, and recovery networks. At different mission areas, organizations focus their resources into different aspects of emergency management. Existing research has focused more on response networks, due to the constraints of data collection on the other stages of emergency response. The recent implementation of the National Disaster Recovery Framework (NDRF) should encourage more research on disaster recovery networks in the future.

Based on the content of interorganizational interactions, emergency management networks can be grouped into communication networks, knowledge sharing networks, resource allocation networks, and joint action networks. Many studies have examined communication networks and coordination networks (e.g., Comfort & Hasse, 2006), whereas fewer studies have delved into knowledge sharing and resource allocation networks.

In addition to one-mode networks, (organization-to-organization network) that only includes one type of node (organizations), emergency management networks can be two-mode. An example of a two-mode network, in the context of emergency and crisis management, is an affiliation network, involving organizations and the emergency support functions. An affiliation relation exists between the organization and the ESF(s) under which the organization is listed as primary or support agency in the NRF, or between recovery support functions (RSF) in the NDRF.

Another important grouping of emergency and crisis management networks is formal networks, or mandated networks, versus emergent networks. Formal networks are defined by the government policies, frameworks, and CEMPs. For instance, according to the NRF, there are primary agencies and support agencies for each of the 15 ESFs. Primary and support agencies should interact with one another to effectively respond to disasters. The formal network is composed of these primary and support agencies in addition to diverse types of interorganizational coordination. Similarly, at state and local levels, formal networks are defined through CEMPs. Emergent networks are formed in response to an actual disaster. Many organizations are involved in disaster response, plenty of which are emergent organizations and are not the primary or support agencies listed on government CEMPs or other policy documents. Including emergent organizations and/or groups into the formal disaster response and recovery networks is a challenge for emergency and crisis managers.

Structures of Emergency and Crisis Management Networks

A few scholars have examined the structures of emergency and crisis management networks, though most of the research is descriptive. Multiple network measures such as network density, network centralization, and clique analysis can be used to describe the overall network characteristics (Kapucu & Demiroz, 2011). Network density measures the extent to which emergency management organizations are connected, and network centralization measures the extent to which the network is dominated by a small number of organizations. Clique analysis assesses whether the network has closely connected subgroups (Comfort & Hasse, 2006). The existence of many cliques (subgroups) may influence the communication and coordination within an emergency and crisis management network (Comfort & Hasse, 2006).

Limited research has been conducted to identify the most effective network governance structure in emergency and crisis management context (Hu, Khosa, & Kapucu, 2016). Depending on the context of the emergency and crisis situations, attributes of the network, and characteristics of the member organizations, certain governance structures may function more effectively than others (Provan & Kenis, 2008). The nature of emergency and crisis management requires timely decision-making and quick action, and high-levels of coordination across jurisdictions and sectors. Compared with self-governed networks, lead and NAO modes have received more attention in research. To measure whether there is a dominant lead organization or administrative organization in the network, researchers can assess the level of network centralization and degree centrality (Jovita, Nurmandi, Mutiarin, & Purnomo, 2018). A recent empirical study of three subnetworks in German emergency response systems exhibited the combined features of participant-based/shared governance, lead mode, and NAO mode. In other words, certain features of shared governance (e.g., collaborative decision-making) can coexist with features of the other two governance modes (Berthod, Grothe-Hammer, Müller-Seitz, Raab, & Sydow, 2017).

Although there is no consensus on the optimal level of network density and centralization for emergency and crisis management, limited empirical research suggests that a certain level of density is needed for facilitating effective communication and trust building among organizations (Jovita et al., 2018). Scholars argued that the structure of emergency and crisis management networks takes on the form of "core-periphery" structure, with core organizations in the center and other participating organizations in the periphery

(Robinson, Eller, Gall, & Gerber, 2013). These core organizations tend to be governmental organizations that stay in the network and the peripheral set of organizations tend to be nonprofit organizations that join and leave the network in a more dynamic manner (Robinson et al., 2013). Based on interview data from experts in the field, a moderate core-periphery structure has been identified as an effective means of coordination, especially in response to wildfires (Nowell, Steelman, Velez, & Yang, 2018).

The structure of emergency and crisis management networks is not static, but dynamic. Networks adapt their structure and the composition of member organizations to meet the changes in the environment (Stallings & Quarantelli, 1985; Varda, Forgette, Banks, & Contractor, 2009). Empirical research examining the effective structure of emergency and crisis management network is limited. Network dynamism is another understudied area. Few scholars have collected longitudinal data to compare and assess the changes in network structures.

Performance Evaluation in Emergency and Crisis Management Networks

Traditional performance measures focus on organizational performance rather than overall network performance. For instance, some researchers proposed frameworks to evaluate the quality of local emergency policies and procedures (Henstra, 2010). A list of 30 elements and detailed rating systems were developed to evaluate local emergency management programs by examining preparedness, mitigation, response, and recovery efforts at local program level. The measures examine whether local governments have established plans, procedures and allocated resources to emergency management (Henstra, 2010). The list is comprehensive, ranging from staffing, planning, education, information management, to volunteer management (Henstra, 2010). However, these measures focus more on organizational level, rather than network-level (system) outcomes.

Scholars have proposed using a network approach to assess the performance of emergency and crisis management networks (Kapucu & Demiroz, 2011). Although network performance of emergency and crisis management networks can be measured at organizational, network, and community levels (Provan & Milward, 2001), current research has focused on organizational and network outcomes. From an organizational perspective, the position an organization holds in a network influences its access to information and resources, thus impacting its performance (Choi & Brower, 2006; Nowell & Steelman, 2015). An organization's embeddedness in a network, measured by organizational similarity in function and sector affiliation, can influence the frequency and efficacy of communication between organizations (Nowell & Steelman, 2015). Community-level network effectiveness in emergency and crisis management can be linked to different community disaster resilience measures. Community resilience measures examine social capital, community capital, and interorganizational partnership for effective response, recovery, and rebuilding resilient communities after a disaster (Cutter, Burton, & Emrich, 2010; FEMA, 2017; NAS, 2012).

There are multiple types of emergency and crisis management networks: formally designed networks (policy/legal networks) that are defined by the CEMPs; cognitive networks that are based on the perception of emergency managers, and actual networks that capture the interactions among organizations in disaster response (Choi & Brower, 2006). A group of scholars have focused on the whole network and compared the formally designed network with the actual response network to assess the overall network performance (e.g., Choi & Brower, 2006; Kapucu & Hu, 2016). These scholars assumed that greater similarity between the actual response network and the designed network leads to better outcomes. For instance, scholars have compared the key actors defined in government frameworks with the key actors identified in situation reports, after-action reports, and newspaper articles that captured the interactions among organizations in response to a disaster (Kapucu & Demiroz, 2011). The actual performance is considered effective if the key actors defined in framework or CEMPs match with the ones identified in the actual response (Kapucu & Demiroz, 2011). The response to Hurricane Katrina is full of examples of network coordination failures. One of the central actors, according to the plan, was Department of Transportation and Development (DOTD). However, the DOTD did not fulfill its responsibility due to lack of capacity and an unwillingness to participate (Kiefer & Montjoy, 2006).

An organization's position in policy/legal networks and cognitive networks positively correlated with their perceived influence (Choi & Brower, 2006). Research has shown that the relation in one network may influence the relation in another network (Kapucu & Hu, 2016). The connections during routine operations can influence interorganizational coordination in actual disaster response. Furthermore, organizations' interactions during disaster preparedness can influence interorganizational coordination in disaster response (Kapucu & Hu, 2016).

Although researchers have not reached a consensus on how to best evaluate the network-level performance of emergency and crisis management networks, five principles have been proposed to guide research (Nowell, Steelman, Velez, & Godette, 2017). First, network-level measures should focus on outcomes that require network-level efforts. This outcome cannot be something achieved by a single organization or a small group. Second, a single indicator is not sufficient to evaluate network-level outcomes. Instead, an index of multiple indicators is recommended to capture the complexity of networks. Third, network performance measures need to consider the actor-level performance that contributes to network-level goals and performance. Fourth, network performance measures need to be adapted to exogenous factors, such as the different types of incidents. Lastly, network performance measures should take into consideration the perspectives of all network members, because single informants may provide fragmented views about the network (Nowell et al., 2017).

Researchers have examined both facilitating factors and hindering factors to effective interorganizational networks in the context of disaster management (Kapucu & Demiroz, 2017; Moynihan, 2005). A multitude of factors, such as organizational capacities, capabilities of public managers, trust and social capital, communication mechanisms, technology use, and preexisting relations can contribute to the network performance. Organizational differences in cultures and missions, role ambiguity, and power differentials can hinder the performance of interorganizational networks (Kapucu & Demiroz, 2017). Other researchers examined the relations and dynamics among organizations and proposed that "general openness to collaborate, collaboration experience, mutuality, and coordination" can influence network output, and hence impacting network-level performance and organizational and network-level outcomes (Nolte & Boenigk, 2013, p. 148). In a study of the network performance of disaster relief organizations after the Haitian earthquake, researchers used network growth and reductions in service duplication to measure the network outcome and used organizational learning of best practices and new knowledge to measure organizational outcomes (Nolte & Boenigk, 2013).

Leadership in Emergency and Crisis Management Networks

Network leadership in the context of emergency and crisis management faces a different set of challenges (Boin & Hart, 2003). Leaders need to work with many organizations as boundary spanners, gate-keepers, or brokers, especially during large-scale disasters. Leaders face both political pressure and operational challenges, in face of an emergency or crisis. Leadership may need to have different competencies in response to the uncertain and complex environments of emergencies and crises (Kapucu & Van Wart, 2008). During emergencies and crises, it is a natural inclination to look up to leaders for action. However, leaders may not deliver immediate or clear direction due to the need to work across organizational, jurisdictional and sector boundaries (Boin & Hart, 2003). Therefore, scholars have highlighted unique attributes, competencies, or behaviors of network leadership (Kapucu & Van Wart, 2008; McGuire & Silvia, 2009).

The complex interorganizational structures within emergency and crisis management systems make coordination, decision-making, and the division of responsibility essential to effectiveness (Boin & Hart, 2003; Kapucu & Van Wart, 2006, 2008). Leadership competencies required for responding to emergencies and crises are not the same as those required for managing other routine scenarios (Van Wart & Kapucu, 2011). Within the complex network governance system of emergency and crisis management networks, one of the most critical skills administrators need is collaborative leadership.

Collaborative leadership refers to "the behaviors of public managers that facilitate productive interaction and move the participants in the network toward effective resolution of a problem" (McGuire & Silvia, 2009, p. 35).

Collaborative leadership plays a crucial role in spanning organizational boundaries and integrating resources for effective emergency and crisis management systems. Leaders representing individual organizations in emergency and crisis management system rely on networks for resources necessary to respond to emergencies. Furthermore, decisions in networks are based on consensus, due to participating stakeholders, administrators, and professionals as partners. In this system, legitimacy and trust are gained by working collaboratively to accomplish a common goal of saving lives and property (Boin & Hart, 2003; Kapucu & Van Wart, 2006).

Professional emergency managers repeatedly state that 'emergencies and crises are not good times to exchange business cards.' Leaders at different levels of government and communities within the emergency and crisis management system must be firm believers of relationship building and collaborative decision-making. They need to build cultural competency and technical interoperability to function effectively within the complex system of network governance. Otherwise, accomplishing the goal of effective response and recovery would not become reality under the stressful environment of emergencies and crises.

Among the 37 competencies of administrative leadership (Van Wart, 2005, 2012), researchers emphasized that certain competencies are directly related to crisis management and managing complexities, including "decisiveness, flexibility, informing, problem solving, managing change and creativity, personnel planning, motivating, building and managing teams, scanning the environment, strategic planning, networking and partnering, and organizational-level decision making" (Kapucu & Van Wart, 2008, p. 716). Among the list, "networking and partnering" deserves more attention, as it is crucial for leaders to build connections with other organizations through information and resource sharing or other types of interactions (Kapucu & Ustun, 2018). Developing these competencies can better prepare leaders for emergencies and crises.

In a national study of 500 emergency managers, researchers suggested that among the five dimensions of network leadership, the "mobilizing" and "synthesizing" dimensions of network leadership behaviors are more important to the effectiveness of emergency management networks (McGuire & Silvia, 2009). In an emergency management network, leaders not only need to serve as boundary spanners to mobilize resources from government at all levels, but also leverage community capacity and resources, as well resources from businesses and nonprofit organizations. "Synthesizing" different perspectives and priorities in a network setting is crucial to the function of emergency and crisis management networks. Leaders need to work on organizational differences, address power imbalances, and coordinate joint actions to prepare for or respond to an emergency. For instance, during disaster planning and preparation, state-level emergency mangers need to manage their vertical relationships with FEMA, local, and regional entities. They also need to manage their horizontal relationships with state entities such as state police and state national guard and other state governments through the EMAC

(Brooks, Bodeau, & Fedorowicz, 2012). State-level emergency managers serve as intermediaries between federal and local-level emergency managers and coordinate the distribution and allocation of resources from federal to local level (Brooks et al., 2012).

Application of Network Analysis: Key Actors and Network Structures

In this section, we first discuss how network analysis has been applied to studying the emergency response to large-scale disasters, such as the September 11 terrorist attacks and Hurricane Katrina. Scholars have used network analysis to identify the participating organizations, analyze the key actors, and examine the structure of emergency and crisis response networks (e.g., Kapucu, 2006; Kapucu & Demiroz, 2011; Comfort & Hasse, 2006).

Based on analysis of after-action reports, situation reports, newspaper reports, and interview data collected from the representatives of participating organizations, a total of 1,398 organizations, including 73 federal agencies, 1,176 nonprofit organizations, and 149 businesses, engaged in the immediate response after the attacks (Kapucu, 2006). Researchers not only calculated degree centrality to identify the key actors, based the national policy frameworks, but also identified the key actors for major ESF functions based on actual interactions among organizations, which were captured in different kind of documents (Kapucu & Demiroz, 2011). For instance, in response to the terrorist attacks, for ESF-5 Information and Planning, most of the organizations listed on the Federal Response Plan (FRP) participated in the actual response while FEMA played a central communicator role, as defined in the FRP.

In a study of the emergency response network after Hurricane Katrina, 535 organizations were identified in disaster response. Eight organizations, including FEMA, National Guard, the President of the United States, the Governor of Louisiana, New Orleans's Police Department, local hospitals, the government of Jefferson Parish, and the Mayor of New Orleans played central roles in response to Hurricane Katrina (Comfort & Hasse, 2006). Clique analysis suggested that there were 35 closely connected subgroups within the communication network, and the largest clique includes 11 federal and local government agencies. The presence of many cliques indicates the higher level of challenges of coordinating efforts in the network (Comfort & Hasse, 2006).

Given the importance of boundary spanners in emergency and crisis management networks, scholars have used network measures, such as betweenness centrality, to evaluate whether the organization can serve as information broker, bridger, or mediator (Comfort & Hasse, 2006; Fass, Velez, FitzGerald, Nowell, & Steelman, 2017). Yet, how organizations select information bridgers may change at the planning stage and during the actual incident. While trust, familiarity, and similarity influence an organization's selection of bridgers, more unexpected factors exert influence on an organizational behavior in seeking bridgers (Fass et al., 2017). Dominant organizations, with access to information and resources, may not necessarily be sought by other organizations. In fact, the number of bridging actors tend to decrease dramatically after a disaster (Jung, Song, & Feiock, 2017).

Researchers have noted the importance of studying network evolution, from tie formation to network development, sustainability, and resilience (Kapucu & Garayev, 2012; National Research Council, 2009). However, most of existing emergency management network studies have not collected longitudinal network data, with a few exceptions (e.g., Jung et al., 2017; Jung, Song, & Park, 2018). A group of scholars collected longitudinal data on interorganizational emergency management networks before and after typhoons in South Korea. They examined the formation and dynamics of collaboration ties (Jung et al., 2018).

We use the NRF as an example to illustrate how formal networks are defined based on government policies, frameworks, and plans as well as how formal affiliation network and interaction network can be drawn from the NRF. The website of FEMA (www.fema.gov/pdf/emergency/nrf/nrf-annexes-all.pdf) lists all the ESF functions and the corresponding coordinator, primary, and support agencies. The 15 ESFs include ESF #1—Transportation; ESF #2—Communications; ESF #3—Public Works and Engineering; ESF #4—Firefighting; ESF #5—Emergency Management; ESF #6—Mass Care, Emergency Assistance, Housing, and Human Services; ESF #7—Logistics Management and Resource Support; ESF #8—Public Health and Medical Services; ESF #9—Search Rescue; ESF #10—Oil and Hazardous Materials Response; ESF #11—Agriculture and Natural Resources; ESF #12—Energy; ESF #13—Public Safety and Security; ESF #14—Long-Term Community Recovery; and ESF #15—External Affairs (FEMA, 2008). See the appendix for the list of agencies. Figure 10.2 is the visual representation of a formal affiliation network (two-node) that is composed of 38 agencies, 15 ESFs, and the ties between the agencies and the

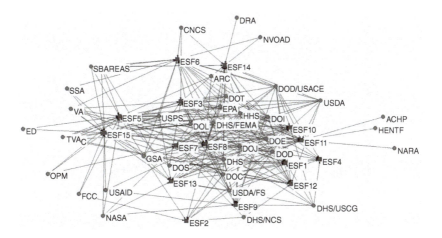

Figure 10.2 A Formal Affiliation Network Based on the NRF

ESFs. The figure is produced through the NetDraw Function of the software UCINET 6.0 for two-mode data (Borgatti, 2002; Borgatti, Everett, & Freeman, 2002). For instance, the ESF # 1 Transportation has 14 agencies that are listed as coordinator, primary, and support agencies. The Department of Transportation serves as the coordinator and the primary agencies. The 13 support agencies are listed here:

> The US Forest Service (USDA/FS)
> The Department of Commerce (DOC)
> The Department of Defense (DOD)
> The Department of Defense/Army Corps of Engineers (DOD/USACE)
> The Department of energy (DOE)
> The Department of Homeland Security (DHS)
> The Department of Homeland Security/Federal Emergency Management Agency (DHS/FEMA)
> The Department of Homeland Security/United States Coast Guard (DHS/USCG)
> The Department of the Interior (DOI)
> The Department of Justice (DOJ)
> The Department of State (DOS)
> General Services Administration (GSA)
> The US Postal Service (USPS)

Figure 10.3 is an organizational interaction network (one-node) that is composed of the 38 organizations listed on the NRF and the interactions among them. The interaction is coded based on whether the organizations are listed

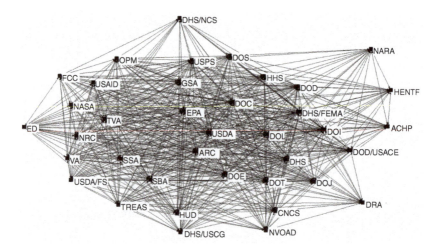

Figure 10.3 An Organizational Interaction Network Based on the NRF

under the same function. Organizations under the same function are supposed to interact with one another to fulfill the responsibilities. For instance, an interaction tie exists between the US Department of Housing and Urban Development (HUD) and the US Department of Agriculture (USDA), because both organizations are listed as support agencies under ESF #6—Mass Care, Emergency Assistance, Housing, and Human Services. Using the same dataset, we can run a network analysis to identify organizations that have highest scores on degree centrality, betweenness centrality, closeness centrality, and eigenvector (see Chapter 2 for a detailed discussion of the network measures). A total of 11 agencies, including HHS, DHS, and DHS/FEMA, have ties with all the other organizations because they are listed as either as coordinator, primary, or support agencies for all the ESFs. Compared with other organizations on the list, these organizations with high degree centrality tend to play more central roles in emergency responses due to their position in the network, access to information, resources, and other member organizations.

Conclusion

In this chapter, we introduced the multilevel and cross-sector emergency and crisis management system and highlighted that a network approach is useful for emergency and crisis management. A traditional, rigid bureaucratic structure does not suffice for timely information dissemination and exchange in response to the uncertain and evolving emergency environment. Horizontal relationships are important to overcome the differences in backgrounds brought by the diverse group of member organizations and to build trust in the long run, which can contribute to effective coordination in response to emergencies and crises. This chapter further discussed the different types of networks and noted that the studies on different stages of emergency management are unbalanced, with more focus on the response stage. In addition, compared with many studies on communication and coordination networks, knowledge networks and specific resource allocation networks are under-studied.

Evaluating network performance requires the measures to be developed through a more integrated approach and at a network level. Future research may go beyond the existing focus on the key actors and structural characteristics of emergency and crisis management networks. Advanced inferential analysis can help identify the hindering or facilitating factors to effectiveness of emergency and crisis management networks. In addition, as Chapter 4 highlighted, longitudinal data and advanced network analysis (e.g., stochastic actor-based model) are needed to examine the development, sustainability, and resilience of emergency and crisis management networks.

References

Berthod, O., Grothe-Hammer, M., Müller-Seitz, G., Raab, J., & Sydow, J. (2017). From high-reliability organizations to high-reliability networks: The dynamics of network governance in the face of emergency. *Journal of Public Administration Research and Theory, 27*(2), 352–371.

Bigley, G. A., & Roberts, K. H. (2001). The incident command system: High-reliability organizing for complex and volatile task environments. *Academy of Management, 44*(6), 1281–1299.

Boin, A., & Hart, P. (2003). Public leadership in times of crises: Mission impossible. *Public Administration Review, 63*(5), 544–553.

Borgatti, S. P. (2002). *NetDraw: Graph visualization software.* Harvard, MA: Analytic Technologies.

Borgatti, S. P., Everett, M. G., & Freeman, L. C. (2002). *UCINET 6 for windows: Software for social network analysis.* Harvard, MA: Analytic Technologies.

Brooks, J. M., Bodeau, D., & Fedorowicz, J. (2012). Network management in emergency response: Articulation practices of state-level managers—Interweaving up, down, and sideways. *Administration & Society, 45*(8), 911–948.

Choi, S. O., & Brower, R. S. (2006). When practice matters more than government plans: A network analysis of local emergency management. *Administration & Society, 37*(6), 651–678.

City of Orlando Office of Emergency Management. (2016). Pulse tragedy after action report (Unpublished document).

Comfort, L. K. (2007). Crisis management in hindsight: Cognition, communication, coordination, and control. *Public Administration Review, 67*(Suppl. 1), 189–197.

Comfort, L. K., & Hasse, T. W. (2006). Communication, coherence, and collective action: The impact of Hurricane Katrina on communication infrastructures. *Public Works Management & Policy, 10*(4), 328–343.

Comfort, L. K., Waugh, W. L., & Cigler, B. A. (2012). Emergency management research and practice in public administration: Emergency, evolution, expansion, and future directions. *Public Administration Review, 72*(4), 539–547.

Cutter, S. L., Burton, C. G., & Emrich, C. T. (2010). Disaster resilience indicators for benchmarking baseline conditions. *Journal of Homeland Security and Emergency Management, 7*(1), article 51.

Fass, A. J., Velez, A-L., FitzGerald, C., Nowell, B. L., & Steelman, T. A. (2017). Patterns of preferences and practice: Bridging actors in wildfire response networks in the American Northwest. *Disasters, 41*(3), 527–548.

Federal Emergency Management Agency (FEMA). (2008). *Emergency support function annexes: Introduction.* Retrieved from www.fema.gov/media-library-data/20130726-1825-25045-0604/emergency_support_function_annexes_introduction_2008_.pdf

Federal Emergency Management Agency (FEMA). (2017). *National risk index.* Retrieved June 5, 2018, from https://data.femadata.com/FIMA/NHRAP/National-RiskIndex/National_Risk_Index_Summary.pdf

Federal Emergency Management Agency (FEMA). (2018a). *FEMA regional office contact information.* Retrieved from the website www.fema.gov/fema-regional-office-contact-information

Federal Emergency Management Agency (FEMA). (2018b). *The four phases of emergency management.* Retrieved from https://training.fema.gov/emiweb/downloads/is10_unit3.doc

Henstra, D. (2010). Evaluating local government emergency management programs: What framework should public managers adopt? *Public Administration Review, 70*(2), 236–246.

Hu, Q., Khosa, S., & Kapucu, N. (2016). The intellectual structure of empirical social network research in public administration. *Journal of Public Administration Research and Theory, 26*(4), 593–612. doi:10.1093/jopart/muv032

Hu, Q., Knox, C. C., & Kapucu, N. (2014). What have we learned since September 11th? A network study of the Boston marathon bombings response. *Public Administration Review, 74*(6), 698–712.

Jordan, A. E. (2010). Collaborative relationships resulting from the urban area security initiative. *Journal of Homeland Security and Emergency Management, 7*(1), 38.

Jovita, H. D., Nurmandi, A., Mutiarin, D., & Purnomo, E. P. (2018). Why does network governance fail in managing post-disaster conditions in the Philippines? *Jàmbá: Journal of Disaster Risk Studies, 10*(1), a585. doi:10.4102/jamba. v10i1.585

Jung, K., Song, M., & Feiock, R. (2017). Isolated and broken bridges from interorganizational emergency management networks: An institutional collective action perspective. *Urban Affairs Review.* doi:10.1177/1078087417690257

Jung, K., Song, M., & Park, H. J. (2018). The dynamics of an interorganizational emergency management network: Interdependent and independent risk hypotheses. *Public Administration Review.* doi:10.1111/puar.12993

Kapucu, N. (2006). Interagency communication networks during emergencies: Boundary spanners in multi-agency coordination. *The American Review of Public Administration, 36*(2), 207–225.

Kapucu, N., Augustin, M. E., & Garayev, V. (2009). Interstate partnerships in emergency management: Emergency Management Assistance Compact (EMAC) in response to catastrophic disasters. *Public Administration Review, 69*(2), 297–313.

Kapucu, N., & Demiroz, F. (2011). Measuring performance for collaborative public management using network analysis methods and tools. *Public Performance and Management Review, 34*(4), 551–581.

Kapucu, N., & Demiroz, F. (2017). Interorganizational networks in disaster management. In E. C. Jones & A. J. Faas (Eds.), *Social network analysis of disaster response, recovery, and adaption* (pp. 28–38). Cambridge, MA: Butterworth-Heinemann.

Kapucu, N., & Garayev, V. (2012). Designing, managing, and sustaining functionally collaborative emergency management networks. *American Review of Public Administration, 43*(3), 312–330.

Kapucu, N., & Hu, Q. (2016). Understanding multiplexity of collaborative emergency management networks. *The American Review of Public Administration, 46*(4), 399–417.

Kapucu, N., & Sadiq, A. (2016). Disaster policies and governance: Promoting community resilience. *Politics and Governance, 4*(4). doi: 10.17645/pag.v4i4.829

Kapucu, N., & Ustun, Y. (2018). Collaborative crisis management and leadership in the public sector. *International Journal of Public Administration, 41*(7), 548–561.

Kapucu, N., & Van Wart, M. (2006). The emerging role of the public sector in managing extreme events: Lessons learned. *Administration & Society, 38*(3), 279–308.

Kapucu, N., & Van Wart, M. (2008). Making matters worse an anatomy of leadership failures in managing catastrophic events. *Administration & Society, 40*(7), 711–740.

Kettl, D. F. (2006). Is the worst yet to come? *Annals of the American Academy of Political and Social Science, 604*, 273–287.

Kiefer, J. J., & Montjoy, R. S. (2006). Incrementalism before the Storm: Network performance for the evacuation of New Orleans. *Public Administration Review, 66*(Special issue), 122–130.

Lukensmeyer, C. J. (2007). Large-scale citizen engagement and the rebuilding of New Orleans: A case study. *National Civic Review, 96*(3), 3–15.

McGuire, M., & Silvia, C. (2009). Does leadership in networks matter? Examining the effect of leadership behaviors on mangers perception of network effectiveness. *Public Performance & Management Review, 33*(1), 34–62.

McGuire, M., & Silvia, C. (2010). The effect of complexity, problem severity, and managerial capacity on intergovernmental collaboration: Evidence from local emergency management. *Public Administration Review, 70*(2), 279–288.

Moynihan, D. P. (2005). *Leveraging collaborative networks in infrequent emergency situations.* Retrieved from www.businessofgovernment.org/sites/default/files/IESituations.pdf

Moynihan, D. P. (2009). The network governance of crisis response: Case studies of incident command systems. *Journal of Public Administration Research and Theory, 19*(4), 895–915.

National Academies of Science (NAS). (2012). *Disaster resilience: A national imperative.* Washington, DC: The National Academies Press.

National Research Council (NRC). (2009). *Applications of social network analysis for building community disaster resilience.* Washington, DC: The National Academies Press.

Nohrstedt, D., Bynander, F., Parker, C., & Hart, P. (2018). Managing crises collaboratively: Prospects and problems—A systematic literature review. *Perspectives on Public Management and Governance, 1*(4), 257–271.

Nolte, M. I., & Boenigk, S. (2013). A study of ad hoc network performance in disaster response. *Nonprofit and Voluntary Sector Quarterly, 42*(1), 148–173.

Nowell, B., & Steelman, T. A. (2015). Communication under fire: The role of embeddedness in the emergence and efficacy of disaster response communication networks. *Journal of Public Administration Research and Theory, 25*(3), 929–952.

Nowell, B., Steelman, T. A., Velez, A., & Godette, S. K. (2017). Perspective matters: The challenges of performance measurement in wildfire response networks. In E. C. Jones & A. J. Faas (Eds.), *Social network analysis of disaster response, recovery, and adaption* (pp. 59–73). Cambridge, MA: Butterworth-Heinemann.

Nowell, B., Steelman, T. A., Velez, A., & Yang, Z. (2018). The structure of effective governance of disaster response networks: Insights from the field. *American Review of Public Administration, 48*(7), 699–715.

Provan, K. G., & Kenis, P. (2008). Modes of network governance: Structure, management, and effectiveness. *Journal of Public Administration Research and Theory, 18*(2), 229–252.

Provan, K. G., & Milward, H. B. (2001). Do networks really work? A framework for evaluating public sector organizational networks. *Public Administration Review, 61*(4), 414–431.

Robinson, S. E., Eller, W. S., Gall, M., & Gerber, B. J. (2013). The core and periphery of emergency management networks: A multi-modal assessment of two evacuation-hosting networks from 2000 to 2009. *Public Management Review, 15*(3), 344–362.

Stallings, R. A., & Quarantelli, E. L. (1985). Emergent citizen groups and emergency management. *Public Administration Review, 45*(Special issue), 93–100.

Van Wart, M. (2005). *Dynamics of leadership in public service.* Armonk, NY: M. E. Sharpe.

Van Wart, M. (2012). *Leadership in public organizations: An introduction.* New York, NY: Routledge.

Van Wart, M., & Kapucu, N. (2011). Crisis management competencies: The case of emergency managers in the U.S.A. *Public Management Review*, *13*(4), 489–511.

Varda, D. M., Forgette, R., Banks, D., & Contractor, N. (2009). Social network methodology in the study of disasters: Issues and insights prompted by Post-Katrina research. *Population Research Policy Review*, *28*(1), 11–29.

Waugh, W. L. (1994). Regionalizing emergency management: Counties as state and local government. *Public Administration Review*, *54*(3), 253–258.

Waugh, W. L. (2003). Terrorism, homeland security and the national emergency management network. *Public Organization Review*, *3*(4), 373–385.

Waugh, W. L. Jr., & Streib, G. (2006). Collaboration and leadership for effective emergency management. *Public Administration Review*, *66*(Suppl. 1), 131–140.

Appendix 10.1

The List of 38 Agencies for the 15 ESFs in the NRF

Department of Agriculture (USDA)
Department of Agriculture/Forest Service (USDA/FS)
Department of Commerce (DOC)
Department of Defense (DOD)
Department of Defense/Army Corps of Engineers (DOD/USACE)
Department of Education (ED)
Department of Education (DOE)
Department of Health and Human Services (HHS)
Department of Homeland Security (DHS)
Department of Homeland Security/Federal Emergency Management Agency (DHS/FEMA)
Department of Homeland Security/ National Communications System (DHS/NCS)
Department of Homeland Security/United States Coast Guard (DHS/ USCG)
Department of Housing and Urban Development (HUD)
Department of the Interior (DOI)
Department of Justice (DOJ)
Department of Labor (DOL)
Department of State (DOS)
Department of Transportation (DOT)
Department of the Treasury (TREAS)
Department of Veteran Affairs (VA)
Environmental Protection Agency (EPA)
Federal Communications Commission (FCC)
General Services Administration (GSA)
National Aeronautics and Space Administration (NASA)
Nuclear Regulatory Commission (NRC)
Office of Personnel Management (OPM)
Small Business Administration (SBA)
Social Security Agency (SSA)
Tennessee Valley Authority (TVA)
US Agency for International Development (USAID)

US Postal Service (USPS)
Advisory Council on Historic Preservation (ACHP)
American Red Cross (ARC)
Corporation for National and Community Service (CNCS)
Delta Regional Authority (DRA)
Heritage Emergency National Task Force (HENTF)
National Archives and Records Administration (NARA)
National Voluntary Organizations Active in Disaster (NVOAD)

11 Networks in Community and Economic Development

Community and economic development, similar to other complex societal challenges, require multi sector collaboration at local and regional levels. This chapter discusses how organizations, especially local governments, use networks to strengthen communities and develop economies. It emphasizes the necessity of collaboration in promoting economic and community development both locally and regionally. It introduces different types of collaborative networks for community and economic development, addressing how these collaborative networks influence local communities. In addition, it provides application examples of network analysis in community and economic development. The following questions are addressed in the chapter:

- Why is collaboration important in economic and community development?
- What types of economic and community networks are there? What structural characteristics do economic and community networks have?
- What factors influence the formation and development of community and economic development networks?
- How can social network analysis be used to study community and economic development networks?

Collaboration for Economic and Community Development

Economic and community development refers to a wide range of activities, ranging from land development, infrastructure construction, job creation, and business development (Agranoff & McGuire, 2003). Cross-sector collaboration is abundant in economic and community development. At the policy level, the rapid growth of cross-sector collaboration can be attributed to "the institutional context," meaning the decentralization of the federal government and increasing involvement of state and local government in economic and community development (Agranoff & McGuire, 1998, p. 150).

Since the late 1980s, the federal government has dramatically reduced its financial assistance to funding local development initiatives due to deregulation and downsizing. Instead, now it relies heavily on state and local government to promote regional and local economic development. State and local governments have taken a leadership role in creating a welcoming environment through enhancing economic development policies and providing supportive investment infrastructure. Over the past few decades, the number of regional partnerships has dramatically increased in the United States (Olberding, 2002, 2009). Under the pressure to compete for scarce resources and to attract and retain businesses, city governments not only interact with other local and state governments, but interact with chambers of commerce, business communities, and regional planning organizations (Agranoff & McGuire, 2003).

On a practical level, forming economic and community development networks can help overcome collective action dilemmas in collaboration (Feiock, Steinacker, & Park, 2009; Orr, 1999). Local economic development is highly competitive and sometimes fragmented (Gordon, 2007; Lee, 2011; Lee, Feiock, & Lee, 2012). Local governments compete with one another for resources such as land and business investment on a regular basis. In face of potential risks of losing resources to another city, city governments may demonstrate hesitation for intercity collaboration in economic development (Lee, 2011). Collective action dilemma occurs: Although cooperation can produce better outcomes, governments may not choose to do so without knowing the decision of the others and face risks of defective behaviors of other government agencies (Ostrom, 1990; Feiock, 2013). Forming networks may provide mechanisms for city governments to exchange information, reduce transaction costs, and build or strengthen partnerships (Hawkins, Hu, & Feiock, 2016). Government can choose to build formal networks through contracts or agreements or build informal policy networks through informal relationships between organizations.

While formal contracts, such as joint ventures, can impose agreed-upon processes and structures on government, formal contracts cannot rule out the possibility of defective behavior, thus often introducing high enforcement costs to monitor collaboration processes (Hawkins et al., 2016). Informal policy networks, though not legally binding, build on informal interactions among governments such as information exchange. Regular interactions may help organizations build trust and commitment for cultivating formal collaboration (Hawkins et al., 2016). For instance, government agencies may start with information exchange about funding opportunities and, later, the informal information exchange may lead to further collaboration.

The growth of social capital is one of the benefits of developing networks among government agencies and other non-state stakeholders in local economic development. Within economic and community networks, processes and venues are in place for organizations to build a variety types of relationships, which produce both bonding social capital (strengthening of existing relationships) and bridging social capital (bridging disconnected organizations). For instance, government may include economic development organizations (EDOs) in economic development networks to engage them in a wide range of services such as job creation and retention, business coaching, and workforce development (Compion et al., 2015). Within this network, the EDOs may establish new connections with government agencies (bridging capital) through a third-party or reinforce their collaboration ties with organizations they already know (bonding social capital).

Types and Structures of Economic and Community Development Networks

Like emergency and crisis management networks (Chapter 10) and human and social service networks (Chapter 12), economic and community development networks can take on different forms and engage a wide range of organizations in the network. In this section, we focus on two types of interorganizational networks in economic and community development: *Economic development policy networks* and EDO networks. Economic development policy networks include government agencies as the key actors in the network, but also include nonprofit, business, and regional institutions such as regional planning council and economic development commissions (Hawkins et al., 2016). EDO networks focus on the connections that EDOs build with other organizations and the role EDOs play in economic and community development. EDOs are led by nonprofits and private entities, as opposed to governments, and promote economic development through the provision of services, such as job training.

EDO Networks

A network where nonprofits and private organizations lead efforts in economic development.

Economic Development Policy Networks

Networks formed with government agencies (as the lead actors), nonprofits, and private entities to address policy issues in economic development.

Economic Development Policy Networks and EDO Networks

Local government has taken an active role in working with high-level government, other local governments, and a wide range of non-state stakeholders to promote community and economic development (Gordon, 2007). Government can establish formal economic development networks through contracts or agreements. Alternatively, government can develop informal policy networks through regular, informal, interactions with other organizations.

Formal Economic Development Policy Networks

Through signing legally binding documents, such as joint venture agreements and memorandum of understandings, government can build vertical and horizontal relationships to form formal economic development policy networks (Hawkins & Andrew, 2011). The vertical relationships refer to the interactions between local government with government agencies at the state and federal level. In fact, local government is in frequent contact with federal departments and agencies, such as HUD. Environmental Protection Agency, The Department of Transportation, and Commerce, Economic Development Administration, and Small Business Administration (SBA) for funding opportunities, regulation guidance, and other policy issues (Agranoff & McGuire, 1998). At the horizontal level, local governments interact with county government, other local governments in the region, Chambers of Commerce, local economic development corporations(organizations), regional institutions, and local utilities (Agranoff & McGuire, 1998; Hawkins & Andrew, 2011).

Informal Economic Development Policy Communication Networks

Many studies have paid attention to informal policy communication networks that build on informal interactions between local government and other organizations in the region (e.g., Hawkins et al., 2011; Lee, 2011; Lee, Lee, & Feiock, 2012; Lee et al., 2011). These informal networks do not have formal authority, but rely on government's embeddedness in social, economic, and political relationships (Lee et al., 2012). For instance, local governments may discuss, advise, or share information with other local governments concerning community and economic development (Hawkins et al., 2011; Lee et al., 2012). Researchers have conducted studies on informal economic development policy networks in the Orlando metropolitan areas (e.g., Hawkins et al., 2011; Lee, 2011; Lee et al., 2011, 2012). The informal economic development policy network includes 38 local and county governments and nongovernmental development organizations such as Metro Orlando Economic Development Commission and the East Central Florida Planning Council. They studied what factors influence the formation of collaboration ties among local governments. City governments tend to build informal networks with other city governments believed to be the most cooperative. In addition, similarities in community characteristics, such as median income and similarity in political institutions, may contribute to the formation of informal ties for community and economic development among city governments.

Economic Development Organization (EDO) Networks

Economic development organizations serve local communities by providing a wide range of services: job creation and retention, workforce development, business incubation, revitalization, infrastructure development, advocacy, and so on (Compion et al., 2015; Ofem, Arya, & Borgatti, 2018). Many of these EDOs are nonprofit organizations that are established to revitalize local communities and the local economy. An example of EDOs is Orlando Economic Partnership (www.orlandoedc.com/home.aspx), a nonprofit organization that help businesses start or expand their business through providing site selection assistance and financial assistance, building connections to key government and other partners in the region, and workforce development. Some EDOs, such as regional planning councils, provide important platforms for local governments and other non-state stakeholders to exchange information and discuss economic issues (Hawkins et al., 2016). The EDOs in a region often interact with one another to share information, referrals, or monetary resources, and work on joint projects, thereby forming collaborative networks (Compion et al., 2015). Compared with economic development policy networks, EDO networks have received little attention in the field of public administration and public policy.

Structure of Economic and Community Development Networks

The substructure of economic and community development networks has been examined to explain the formation of ties among local governments for economic development (e.g., Lee, 2011; Lee et al., 2011, 2012). The effects of reciprocity, transitivity, popularity (the number of indegree ties), and bridging (2-path) have highlighted the formation of the collaborative interorganizational development networks (Lee et al., 2012). Empirical studies have lent support to the positive effect of reciprocity and transitivity. Economic development-oriented organizations tend to form reciprocal ties. Transitive triad structure is also a noticeable structural effect. Although collaboration can bring in tremendous benefits, competition and fragmented authority system can produce risks to governments and other organizations (Lee et al., 2012). Therefore, when seeking new partners, organizations may rely on the organizations that have been scrutinized by organizations they know. The overall economic development network exhibits a closely clustered structure (Lee et al., 2012).

Researchers have further investigated how structural embeddedness—"the extent to which two organizations share multiple collaborators" and relative centrality—"the difference between one organization's centrality and another's" may influence EDOs' collaborative success in economic development (Ofem et al., 2018, p. 1116). In studying collaborative networks of 98 EDOs in rural Kentucky, Ofem and his colleagues argued that structural embeddedness can contribute to collaborative success for multiple reasons: A high number of shared ties allows the organization to achieve valuable information, to build high level of trust and cooperative norms, and to promote reciprocal behaviors. Relative centrality negatively influences collaborative success because relative centrality often implies resource imbalances and lead to differences in power, all of which can complicate the collaboration process and outcomes.

Few studies have examined the influence of whole network-level structures on network performance in the context of economic and community development. To address the transaction costs of collaboration, scholars proposed two network structures. First, a decentralized network structure that relies on weak ties to span boundaries and solve coordination issues. Second, a clustered network structure with reciprocal ties and dense connections that can reduce monitoring and enforcement costs, and further build trust and strong commitment among member organizations (Berardo & Scholz, 2010; Scholz & Feiock, 2010). Both types have benefits and costs: in a decentralized network, information flow is slow and trust among organizations can be low. In a clustered network, although it is easy to build trust, it is difficult to acquire new information and maintain close connections (Park & Park, 2009). In a high-risk cooperation situation such as attracting businesses, city governments may demonstrate more "bonding" behaviors and choose to create a clustered network to build trust and commitment (Berardo & Scholz, 2010). In a low-risk situation such as information seeking, city governments may exhibit more "bridging" behaviors and connect with unfamiliar partners through organizations they already know (Berardo & Scholz, 2010).

In the context of community and economic development, a hybrid of both structures can be observed in networks of community development (Park & Park, 2009). In their study of community development projects in South Korea, Park and Park found that there are three forms of network governance: "Government-leading network (entrepreneur network), participatory governed networks (clustered network), and public-private partnership network (hybrid network)" (2009, p. 90). Government-leading networks, similar to lead organization network discussed earlier in the book, have a decentralized and sparse structure, and local government serves as a network leader. Participatory governed networks, similar to self-governed, have a dense yet small network. Local government is a member of the network, while other local actors such as chamber of commerce take leadership roles. Public-private partnership is the hybrid mode. Government can still take lead roles, but other non-state stakeholders are heavily involved in community development projects. They found that although the government-leading network is popular in community projects in South Korea, it is the hybrid network structure that is more effective in obtaining funding from government.

Formation and Development of Economic and Community Development Networks

To better understand economic and community development networks, we discuss the factors that can influence the formation and development of community development networks. First, we need to differentiate the ties that local governments have in networks. Next, we will introduce the Institutional Collective Action (ICA) framework to lay the theoretical foundation for explaining the development of economic and community development networks.

Then, we discuss what factors contribute to the formation and development of these networks.

Local Governments' Networking Behaviors

Existing research has focused on local governments' ties with other governments (e.g., Lee et al., 2012). Yet, local governments' networking behaviors are not limited to horizontal and vertical governmental relations. Local governments build ties with four groups of organizations: private organizations, nonprofit development organizations, community or residential organizations, and government entities (Ha, Lee, & Feiock, 2016). Local governments often interact with businesses, as they are the main drivers of local economy. Local government relies on investment from businesses for job creation, and businesses receive policy support, funding, and guidance from local governments. In addition, local government often needs to resolve conflicts between businesses (e.g., real estate developers) and residential communities. Many nonprofit economic development organizations take on projects that focus on revitalization of communities, or the creation of favorable investment environment for small businesses. Local governments often provide funding and work with these EDOs to ensure the delivery of high-quality services. Another group of stakeholders are community or residential organizations such as neighborhood associations. Local government works with these organizations to mitigate potential conflicts concerning local development projects and gain their support (Ha et al., 2016). In addition to the three groups of non-state stakeholder groups, local governments often interact with other county and city governments, as well as higher-level governments, which has been covered already.

Other researchers differentiated internal networks from external networks when examining the impact of informal economic policy networks on economic development (Kim, Song, & Park, 2018). Depending on the boundary of the network, networks are categorized into internal networks and external networks. *Internal networks* focus on local governments' interactions with other stakeholders within its city boundary (such as city chamber of commerce, real estate or developers, and citizen advisory group) *External networks* explores local governments' interactions with organizations outside its city boundary (such as regional planning commission, council of government, and other local governments) (Kim et al., 2018). According to the 2014 national survey of municipality governments, internal networks have an inverse U-curve impact on local economic growth, while external networks have a positive impact on local economic growth (Kim et al., 2018). The findings of this research also call our attention to local governments' networking activities and their impact on local economies.

Institutional Collective Action Framework

Institutional collective action (ICA) frameworks have been introduced and applied in the field of economic development to understand the behaviors of local governments and to address collective action dilemmas (Feiock & Scholz, 2010; Feiock, 2013). Collective action dilemmas refer to the situations in which the behaviors of individual institutions lead to undesirable collective outcomes for all involved parties, although the involved institution would all benefit from certain action (Feiock, 2013; Ostrom, 1990). Collective action dilemmas occur in the context of economic development because one government's behavior can impact other governments in a fragmented system. For instance, economic development decisions in one city can have impacts on the environment and transportation that goes beyond that city's jurisdiction (Feiock, 2013). The ICA framework not only provides explanations about the behaviors of institutional actors such as city governments but also proposes mechanisms on how to solve the ICA dilemmas (Feiock, 2013).

ICA framework suggests that transaction costs, including negotiation, monitoring, and enforcement costs, constrain local governments' collaboration activities (Feiock, 2013). To mitigate transaction costs, ICA framework proposed four mechanisms: informal networks that build on social embeddedness of intertwined social, economic, and political relationships, contracts that are legally binding, delegate authorities such as special economic development districts, and imposed authority from high-level authority. In economic development, all four mechanisms are in place to address ICA dilemmas, but informal networks and contractual relationships have been more intensively studied in network research (e.g., Hawkins et al., 2016; Hawkins & Andrew, 2011).

Factors Contributing to Economic and Community Development Networks

Researchers have summarized the key contextual factors that can explain local governments' networking behaviors in community and economic development, including "financial/economic conditions, community business environment, and political/legal institutions." (Ha et al., 2016, p. 17) Furthermore, existing relationships and their structural characteristics between local governments and other organizations are important contributors (Lee et al., 2012). Table 11.1 further illustrates this point.

Economic Conditions and Business Environment

Stressful economic conditions such as the 2008 financial crisis often prompt local governments to participate in economic development networks to take advantage of network resources and buffer from external influence (Ha et al., 2016). The uncertainty of the business environment also motivates local governments to work with diverse stakeholder groups to create a favorable business environment (Ha et al., 2016).

Table 11.1 Factors Influencing Economic and Community Development Networks

Contextual Factors	Economic conditions	Economic stress, resource availability (Ha et al., 2016)
	Business environment	Tension between business development and environment protection (Ha et al., 2016)
	Political and legal institutions	Form of government (Ha et al., 2016)
Existing relationships	Homophily	Similarity in economic conditions, political institutions (e.g., form of government), community characteristics, and geographic proximity (Lee et al., 2012)
	Perceived competition and cooperation	Perceived cooperative relationship increases the likelihood of collaboration (Lee et al., 2012)
	Strengths of relationship	Frequency of interactions contributes to collaboration (Hawkins et al., 2016)
Structures of existing relationships	Reciprocity of relationships	Local government tends to build reciprocal relationships in resource exchange and information exchange (Lee et al., 2012)
	Transitivity of relationships	Choosing a partner which has been screened by another partner that local government has relationships with (Lee, 2011)

Political and Legal Institutions

The influence of political institutions on economic development networks has been intensively studied (e.g., Lee et al., 2012; Hawkins et al., 2016, 2017). For instance, the specific form of government is a key factor that influences local governments' networking activities. Researchers noted that both local governments with strong mayors and with council-managers are more likely to interact frequently with businesses, nonprofit EDOs, and other government entities to attract and retain businesses in order to "enhance their political power and prestige" (Ha et al., 2016; Kwon & Park, 2014). Furthermore, loose regulations can promote governments' networking with their stakeholders, whereas strict regulations can hinder governments' networking activities. In addition, cities' participation in different regional institutions may influence their formation of economic development networks (Kwon & Park, 2014; Hawkins et al., 2016). Some institutions, such as the East Central Florida Regional Planning Council, provide forums and meetings for local governments to discuss regional challenges, develop responses, and build consensus. This type of institution encourages information sharing and fosters coordination. Other institutions, such as the Metro-Orlando Economic Development Commission, focus on creating a competitive environment for attracting and retaining businesses (Hawkins et al., 2016). Participation in a cooperative regional institution can enhance the positive influence of informal relationships on formal relationships. Participation in a competitive regional institution may negatively influence the formation of formal ties among governments that have built informal ties into economic development (Hawkins et al., 2016).

Relationships

Local governments are embedded in social, political, and economic relationships with other organizations in the realm of economic and community development. Social capital that grows out of these relationships can benefit community by reducing transaction costs, improving information flow among economic actors, and improving the business environment (Engbers & Rubin, 2018; Woolcock, 1998). Therefore, it is important to create useful connections and expand these networks (Engbers & Rubin, 2018). Local governments with similar community characteristics (such demographics, median household income), and similarities in political institutions (in the same county, same form of government), and belief systems can increase the likelihood of building collaborative relationships between two local governments (Hawkins et al., 2016; Henry, Lubell, & McCoy, 2011; Lee et al., 2012). The strengths of relationships positively influence the formation of formal collaborative ties among local governments (Hawkins et al., 2016). Furthermore, the perceived effectiveness of relationship—competitive or cooperative—may also exert influence on local governments' inclination to collaborate on economic development activities. In addition to the relationship itself, the structural characteristics, such as reciprocity and transitivity, centralization, and density, can also influence collaborative arrangements among local governments (Lee et al., 2012), which is covered in detail in the following section.

Applications of Network Analysis in Community and Economic Development Networks

In this section, we first discuss how network analysis has been used to study EDO networks and economic development policy network. We review how key measures of network analysis have been used to describe network structure and organizations' position and roles in community and economic development networks. Furthermore, we illustrate how structural processes, such as reciprocity and transitivity, influence the formation of economic development networks. Then, we introduce a more specific type of economic development network—transportation planning networks—through the lens of a regional transportation partnership, MetroPlan Orlando (https://metroplanorlando.org/about-us/). We discuss the key actors in a metropolitan transportation planning network and analyze multiplex interactions among public, nonprofit, and private organizations.

Measures of network analysis have been used to describe the structural characteristics of economic development networks and identify influential actors in economic development. For instance, Compion and colleagues (2015) studied the EDO network in rural Kentucky that includes 98 EDOs and their interactions in information sharing, referrals, resources sharing, and joint projects. They found that a network density of .079 and suggested that the EDO network is disconnected, because only 7.9 percent of ties that could be potentially built among EDOs existed in that network. They also examined the connectedness in each of the four subnetworks: information sharing network, referral network, resource sharing network, and joint project network. They found that information sharing network is denser than the other three networks, and resource network is least connected. They also used eigenvalue centrality—a measure of influence—to identify the central actors in the EDO network. Researchers also use average degree to describe the number of links an organization has on average (e.g., Lee et al., 2012). Lee et al. (2012) studied the informal policy communication network in the Kissimmee-Orlando metropolitan area (including Lake, Orange, Osceola, and Seminole counties) that includes 38 local and county governments. They asked top economic development officials or city mangers whether their government interacted with other governments on economic development issues, in the form of discussion, advice, and information sharing. They found on average, of the 31 local governments that responded to the survey, each local government has approximately 6 links with other local governments to communicate about economic development issues.

Going beyond descriptive network analysis, researchers have used inferential network analysis such as Quadratic Assignment Procedure (QAP) analysis and Exponential Random Graph Model (ERGM) to understand the dynamics of tie formation among local governments (e.g., Hawkins et al., 2016; Lee et al., 2012). There is multiplexity effect in network formation: one type of relationships may influence the formation of another type of relationship (Lusher, Koskinen, & Robin, 2012). For instance, perceived cooperative relationship may encourage local governments to form ties (Lee et al., 2012). Informal policy communication network may increase the likelihood of building formal collaboration ties among local governments (Hawkins et al., 2016). Researchers also studied the influence of structural processes such as reciprocity, transitivity, popularity (the number of indegree ties), and bridging (2-path), on the formation of the collaborative interorganizational development networks (Lee et al., 2012). Table 11.2 explains these concepts and applications in community and economic development networks in detail.

Next, we discuss a transportation planning network through the lens of an organization—MetroPlan Orlando. MetroPlan Orlando was created in 1977 to carry out the transportation planning process in the central Florida area, covering Orange, Osceola, and Seminole counties (MetroPlan Orlando, 2018). MetroPlan Orlando receives its funding from federal grants, state grants, and local per capita assessments. Its website lists funding partners, including the following organizations listed in Table 11.3.

The MetroPlan Orlando Board is the governing body of the organization, which is responsible for the implementation of transportation planning in the three-county area. Board members are elected officials from three counties

Table 11.2 Structural Processes in Community and Economic Development Networks

Structural processes	Visualization	Examples in community and economic development
Reciprocity effect: In a directed network, a tie from A to B encourages B to form a tie with A (Lusher et al., 2012). Transitivity effect: one measure of network closure. A has a tie with B, B has a tie with C, then A has a tie with C (Lusher et al., 2012).		Government A reached out to government B for advice on economic development issues, government B is likely to turn to A for advice (Lee et al., 2012). Government A tends to build a tie to government C, because A already has a tie with B, and B has a tie with C. Governments creates this clustered structure to enhance commitments (Lee et al., 2012).
Non-closed 2-path effect: A can connect with C through B. B serves as a broker (Lusher et al., 2012).		Government A will connect with government C through a broker government B. Governments creates this bridging structure to seek efficient information exchange.
Popularity effect: It measures whether network ties concentrate on a few nodes. For undirected network, n-star measures the number of links a node has. In a directed network popularity measures the number of indegree ties and outdegree ties (Lusher et al., 2013).		Among the three governments A, B, and C, government E tends to form a tie with A, because A is popular with many ties that enable A to play important role in sharing information and coordinating action (Lee et al., 2012).
Multiplexity effect: one type of relationship may affect the formation of another type of relationship (Lusher et al., 2013).		Informal policy communication between government A and B may encourage these two governments to build formal ties in economic development (Hawkins et al., 2016).

Table 11.3 Funding Agencies for MetroPlan Orlando

Funding Organizations	Sector Type
City of Altamonte Springs	City government
City of Apopka	City government
Central Florida Express Authority	Independent agency of the state
US Department of Transportation	Federal government
Florida Department of Transportation	State government
Greater Orlando Aviation Authority	City government agency
City of Kissimmee	City government
LYNX	Bus corporation run by run by the Central Florida Regional Transportation Authority
Orange County Government	County government
City of Orlando	City government
Osceola County	County government
City of Sanford	City government
Orlando Sanford International Airport	City government agency
Seminole County	County government
Municipal Advisory Committee	Committee of city governments that are less populated

(Source: MetroPlan Orlando, 2018)

and large cities in the area and representatives from the region's transportation agencies (MetroPlan Orlando, 2018). In addition to the governing board, there are many committees that guide the operation of MetroPlan Orlando, as listed in Table 11.4. The diverse committees not only bring local, state, and federal agencies, but also include community members, business leaders, and community advocates in the transportation planning process, thereby forming a network of planning organizations, transportation authorities, governments, community organizations, and citizen groups. Members listed in the board and multiple committees are the key actors in the transportation planning network in Orlando metropolitan area. The organizations co-listed on the same board or committee creates an affiliation network, which includes the organizations and their affiliation with the board or committee. MetroPlan Orlando is a network administrative organization (NAO) in the transportation planning network that coordinates efforts from different groups of stakeholders. MetroPlan Orlando also organized forums and working groups for the involved stakeholders to share important information, discuss priorities, and work on specific transportation issues (MetroPlan Orlando, 2018). The interactions that occur in these forums working groups, and the relationships built through forums and working groups, are important for establishing transportation priorities in the region and build formal transportation partnerships.

Figure 11.1 uses hypothetical data to visualize the ego network of MetroPlan Orlando to illustrate the complex relations that involve working on the same transportation project(s), giving advice, and serving on the same advisory

Table 11.4 Committees in MetroPlan Orlando

Committees	Description
Community Advisory Committee (CAC)	Members include transportation advocates, community, and business representatives.
Municipal Advisory Committee (MAC)	Members include elected officials of cities that are less populated and do not serve on the governing board.
Technical Advisory Committee (TAC)	Members are engineers, plans, and other technical staff from local governments and transportation agencies.
Transportation Systems Management & Operations Advisory Committee (TSMOAC)	Members include technical experts from federal, state, regional, and local agencies and a community advocate.
Transportation Disadvantaged Local Coordinating Board (TDLCB)	Members include representatives from local governments and transportation providers to address the needs of the disadvantaged in the region.

Source: MetroPlan Orlando, 2018

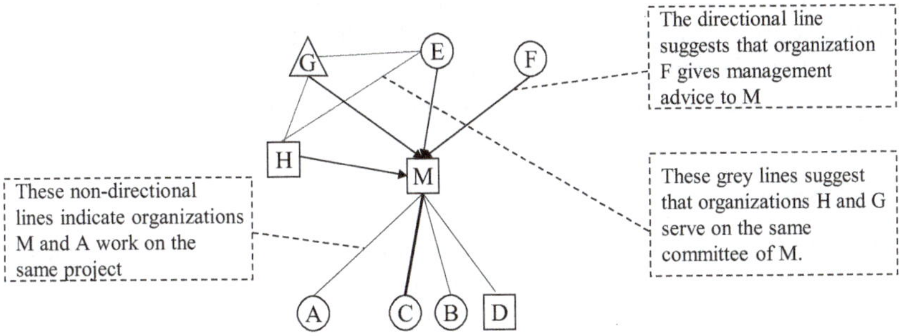

Figure 11.1 A Transportation Planning Network

committee. MetroPlan Orlando (M) works with multiple city and county governments, represented by A, B, and C, as well as private companies such as LYNX (represented by D) on local transportation projects. The width of the line between M and C is wider, indicating that M and C work on multiplex projects together. These relationships are nondirectional. MetroPlan Orland also has directional ties with government agencies, nonprofit and private organizations (represented by triangles and squares respectively). The directional lie can be advice tie through which organizations E, F, G. and H give management advice to M. Organization pairs H and G, H and G have ties because both organizations serve on the same committee of M, hence forming a relation. Additional survey data can be collected to further understand the interactions and relationships among organizations in the transportation planning network.

Conclusion

In this chapter, we discussed different types of community and economic development networks: policy networks led by local governments and EDO networks. Compared with EDO networks, community and economic development policy network has received more attention. Future research may focus more on how to integrate EDOs in the network of community and economic development networks.

ICA framework was introduced to illustrate why networks are needed to overcome challenges facing local governments in promoting economic development. Network embeddedness allows organizations to build connections, strengthen trust and commitments, and minimize transaction costs (Feiock, 2013). In addition to economic conditions, business environment, and political/legal institutions, relationships among governments and their relational structures influence how local governments build economic development networks.

In the application subsection, we discuss in detail how key measures of network analysis have been used to describe network structure and organization' position and roles in community and economic development networks. We further discuss how structural processes, such as reciprocity and transitivity, can influence economic development networks. We also include a specific type of transportation planning network and introduce how to identify the actors in the network, understand interactions diverse groups of organizations, and analyze the governance structure of the transportation planning network.

References

Agranoff, R., & McGuire, M. (1998). The intergovernmental context of local economic development. *State & Local Government Review, 30*(3), 150–164.

Agranoff, R., & McGuire, M. (2003). *Collaborative public management: New strategies for local governments*. Washington, DC: Georgetown University Press.

Berardo, R., & Scholz, J. T. (2010). Self-organizing policy networks: Risk, partner selection, and cooperation in estuaries. *American Journal of Political Science, 54*(3), 632–649.

Compion, B. S., Ofem, B., Ferrier, W., Borgatti, S., Cook-Craig, P., Jensen, J., & Nah, S. (2015). The collaboration networks for development organizations in Eastern Kentucky. *Journal of Appalachian Studies, 22*(1), 105–127.

Engbers, T. A., & Rubin, B. M. (2018). Theory to practice: Policy recommendations for fostering economic development through social capital. *Public Administration Review, 78*(4), 567–578.

Feiock, R. C. (2013). The institutional collective action framework. *Policy Studies Journal, 41*(3), 397–425.

Feiock, R. C., & Scholz, J. T. (2010). Self-organizing federalism: Collaborative mechanisms to mitigate institutional collective action dilemmas: An overview. In R. C. Feiock & J. T. Scholz (Eds.), *Self-organizing federalism: Collaborative mechanisms to mitigate institutional collective action* (pp. 3–32). Cambridge, UK: Cambridge University Press.

Feiock, R. C., Steinacker, A., & Park, H. J. (2009). Institutional collective action in economic development joint ventures. *Public Administration Review, 69*(2), 256–270.

Gordon, V. (2007). Partners or competitors? Perceptions of regional economic development cooperation in Illinois. *Economic Development Quarterly, 21*(1), 60–78.

Ha, H., Lee, I. W., & Feiock, R. C. (2016). Organizational network activities for local economic development. *Economic Development Quarterly, 30*(1), 15–31.

Hawkins, C. V. (2017). Political incentives and transaction costs of collaboration among US cities for economic development. *Local Government Studies, 43*(5), 752–775.

Hawkins, C. V., & Andrew, S. A. (2011). Understanding horizontal and vertical relations in the context of economic development joint venture agreements. *Urban Affairs Review, 47*(3), 385–412.

Hawkins, C. V., Hu, Q., & Feiock, R. C. (2016). Self-organizing governance of local economic development: Informal policy networks and regional institutions. *Journal of Urban Affairs, 38*(5), 643–660.

Henry, A. D., Lubell, M., & McCoy, M. (2011). Belief systems and social capital as drivers of policy network structure: The case of California regional planning. *Journal of Public Administration Research and Theory, 21*(3), 419–444.

Kim, S., Song, M., & Park, H. J. (2018). The network effect on the performance of economic development. *Public Performance & Management Review*. doi:10.1080/1 5309576.2018.1509010

Kwon, S-W., & Park, S-C. (2014). Metropolitan governance: How reginal organizations influence interlocal land use cooperation. *Journal of Urban Affairs, 36*(5), 925–940.

Lee, I. W., Feiock, R. C., & Lee, Y. (2011). Competitors and cooperators: A micro-level analysis of regional economic development networks. *Public Administration Review, 72*(2), 253–262.

Lee, Y. (2011). Economic development networks among local governments. *International Review of Public Administration, 16*(1), 113–134.

Lee, Y., Lee, I. W., & Feiock, R. C. (2012). Interorganizational collaboration networks in economic development policy: An exponential random graph model analysis. *Policy Studies Journal, 40*(3), 547–573.

Lusher, D., Koskinen, J., & Robins, G. (2012). *Exponential random graph models for social networks: Theory, methods, and applications*. New York, NY: Cambridge University Press.

MetroPlan Orlando. (2018). *Board and committees*. Retrieved from https://metroplanorlando.org/board-committees/

Ofem, B., Arya, B., & Borgatti, S. P. (2018). The drivers of collaborative success between rural economic development organizations. *Nonprofit and Voluntary Sector Quarterly, 47*(6), 1113–1134.

Olberding, J. C. (2002). Diving into the "third waves" of regional governance and economic development strategies: A study of regional partnerships for economic development in U.S. metropolitan areas. *Economic Development Quarterly, 16*(3), 251–272.

Olberding, J. C. (2009). Toward evaluating the effectiveness of regional partnerships for economic development in U.S. metropolitan areas. *International Journal of Public Administration, 32*, 393–414. doi:10.1080/01900690902799904

Orr, M. (1999). *Black social capital: The politics of school reform in Baltimore*. Lawrence, KS: University Press of Kansas.

Ostrom, E. (1990). *Governing the commons: The evolution of institutions for collective action*. New York, NY: Cambridge University Press.

Park, H. J., & Park, M. J. (2009). Types of network governance and network performance: Community development project. *International Review of Public Administration, 13*(Suppl. 1), 91–105.

Scholz, J. T., & Feiock, R. C. (2010). *Self-organizing federalism: Collaborative mechanisms to mitigate institutional collective action dilemmas*. New York, NY: Cambridge University Press.

Woolcock, M. (1998). Social capital and economic development: Toward a theoretical synthesis and policy framework. *Theory and Society, 27*(2), 151–208.

12 Networks in Human and Social Services

This chapter covers the application of network governance in human and social services. Human and social services networks have become one of the most studied topics in public management network research (Kapucu, Hu, & Khosa, 2014). Interorganizational networks are formed for solving issues such as health services (Bunger, 2013), homeless services (Mosley, 2014), and foster care (Steen & Duran, 2013). Delivering human and social services often demands collaboration among public, nonprofit, and private sector organizations, which provides a rich context for examining network performance, network structures, and network management and network governance. The chapter first addresses why interorganizational networks emerge and grow in the field of human and social services. Then, it discusses network structure, evolution, and governance in service delivery, followed by a discussion of network performance. This chapter also provides a number of network analysis applications to illustrate how network analysis can be used to strengthen community partnerships in human and social service delivery. In particular, this chapter addresses the following questions:

- Why do we need interorganizational networks in human and social services?
- In human and social services, what types of interorganizational networks are created? What structural characteristics do these networks exhibit? How are they are governed?
- How does one evaluate the performance of service delivery networks?
- How does one apply network analysis to understanding interorganizational networks in human and social services?

Why Do Interorganizational Networks Exist in Human and Social Services?

The rapid growth of interorganizational networks in social and human services can be attributed to the following reasons: First, the tension between increasing need and resource scarcity continues to unfold. Services need to expand to keep pace with the growing population in need of various social services. This creates an impetus for organizations, including government agencies, to innovate and coordinate efforts with others to meet growing service needs (Bunger, 2013; Bunger, Doogan, & Cao, 2014; Guo & Acar, 2005).

Second, a growing number of government contracts, or other funding mechanisms, encourage nonprofit organizations to work with government and other organizations to provide these services. Government is under institutional pressure to contain costs while providing high quality service. With the increasing contracting out and privatization of services, nonprofit and private organizations build contractual, or other types, of relationships with government agencies or other organizations. For instance, in the domain of mental health, the government has shifted its role from providing direct service to "managed care," which engages nonprofit organizations in serving the needs of people with mental illness (Provan, Isett, & Milward, 2004).

Third, the needs of clients tend to be diverse and involve multiple service areas, hence making it challenging for any single organization to address the issue. Homeless services are a good example. The homeless population often not only needs help with their immediate housing needs, but also need assistance with transportation, employment, and health services. This requires multiple organizations to coordinate efforts and deliver integrated services. From a theoretical perspective, inherent limitations in both public, private, and nonprofit sectors, or the coexistence of government failure, market failure, and voluntary failure make it necessary to build cross-sector collaboration and interorganizational networks (Salamon, 1987; Young, 2006).

Finally, interorganizational networks have advantages over hierarchical structures for service delivery. Networks not only provide channels for organizations to share information and resources, but also serve as crucial platforms for knowledge sharing, organizational and network learning (Chen & Graddy, 2010; Huang, 2014; Knight, 2002;). The development of connections and frequent communication among organizations in a network can cultivate the growth of social capital and trust for collaborations in substantive areas, such as case management or joint grant application (Guo & Acar, 2005). Furthermore, network members may build informal accountability systems that rely on interpersonal and interorganizational interactions to overcome dilemmas of collective action (Romzek, LeRoux, Johnston, Kempf, & Piatak, 2014).

Network Type, Structure, Evolution, and Network Governance in Service Delivery

This section of the chapter revisits the key concepts introduced in the opening chapters of the book in section I. It begins by discussing different types of networks based upon multiplex relations among organizations and then addresses the complex relationships between structure, evolution, and governance in service delivery networks.

Diverse Types of Service Delivery Networks

As covered in chapter three, depending on the ties among organizations, networks can be further categorized into information sharing networks, resource sharing networks (e.g., sharing volunteers, staff, and office space), and joint operation networks (e.g., client referral, advocacy, case management, volunteer recruitment, and service delivery). Another type of interorganizational network in service delivery that deserves attention is the competition network. Due to resource scarcity, organizations, especially nonprofit service providers may compete with one another for financial resources (e.g., government funding or private donations), volunteers, reputation, growth, and influence (Bunger, 2013; Sowa, 2009). Scholarship has focused on collaboration and coordination rather than look into competition among organizations in the context of service delivery (Bunger, 2013). Organizations with similar funding sources may perceive each other as competitors and frequent competition may lower organizations' inclination to collaborate (Arya & Lin, 2007; Bunger, 2013). Yet, trust may moderate the effect of competition on collaboration (Bunger, 2013). Building proper communication channels and early intervention may prevent interorganizational competition from escalating into widening conflicts. Studying competitive relationships among organizations can help managers seek a balance between competition and collaboration in service delivery networks (LeRoux, 2012).

Another way to categorize interorganizational networks in service delivery is to examine their formality. There are both mandatory networks and voluntary networks. Mandatory, or formal, networks are often built based upon contracts or other formal documents (Isett, Mergel, LeRoux, Mischen, & Rethemeyer, 2011; Gazley, 2008). For instance, the Tuscan mental health service network in Arizona was established, by contract, among the Regional Behavioral Health Authority, Community Partnership of Southern Arizona (CPSA), the State of Arizona Division of Behavioral Health Services (Milward & Provan, 2003), and local nonprofit service providers. This type of mandatory network tends to have formal decision-making processes and coordination mechanisms. The governing agency in the network tends to be the lead or coordinating agency. In the area of homeless service delivery, organizations may host community forums to meet, share and discuss concerns, policy changes, and develop concerted solutions, forming a voluntary network. This type of network does not have formal governance structure but functions on a self-governance mode. More research is needed to examine informal networks due to the practical need to share information and coordinate resources (Isett et al., 2011). In addition to the formal contractual relationships between government and nonprofit organizations, nonprofit organizations often build informal non-contractual partnerships with government agencies to deliver a variety of human and social services (Gazley, 2008; Young, 2006).

Structure, Evolution, and Governance of Service Delivery Networks

Organizations may leave or join the network and can build, develop, or break ties depending on their goals or the function of the network (Provan & Milward, 2001). Density and centralization are often used as measures to describe the structure of interorganizational networks and compare the network evolution in the domain of human and social services (e.g., Provan & Huang, 2012). Density measures the connectedness or cohesion of members and centralization assesses the extent to which that the network relies on a few dominant organizations. Research determining the most effective governance structure for human and social service delivery is limited. Yet, some empirical research suggests that certain network structures, such as a centralized network and the presence of a core agency may improve mental health services (Provan & Milward, 1995). However, a dense network without a core coordinating agency does not demonstrate high-performance in service delivery (Provan & Milward, 1995). Later an empirical study added network age (at least three years), stability, resource sufficiency, and network administrative organizations (NAOs) as necessary factors for network effectiveness (Raab, Mannak, & Cambré, 2015).

In addition to the overall measures of network structure (density and centralization), researchers have called attention to the substructures of networks to examine the dynamics of interorganizational relations and to develop a more nuanced understanding of network structures (Huang, 2014; Lemaire & Provan, 2018; Provan & Milward, 2001). Reciprocity, transitivity, and the Jaccard similarity coefficient are also used to describe and compare network structures (Bevc, Retrum, & Varda, 2015; Wasserman & Faust, 1994; Bunger et al., 2014). Researchers reported the number of reciprocal ties as a measure of tie strengths and the number of triads that are transitive as a measure of cohesion/closure. They also compared the changes in these substructures of networks (e.g., Bevc et al., 2015; Bunger et al., 2014). Jaccard similarity coefficient measures the changes of ties by reporting the proportion of reported same ties in different years (Wasserman & Faust, 1994). In addition, dynamics of subgroups have received growing attention. For instance, a common tie with a third party may influence the relationship between the pair of organizations (Huang, 2014; Lemaire & Provan, 2018). Between a pair of organizations, the strengths of their common tie with a network leader may enhance the relationship and strengthen the level of collaboration between the pair (Lemaire & Provan, 2018). Other research suggested that a common tie with a third party does not necessarily increase the likelihood of tie formation among two organizations (Huang, 2014). If the common tie between the two service provider organizations is with another service provider, the likelihood of sharing information may increase. However, when two service providers both have ties with a NAO, these two organizations may choose not to share information, as there is a chance that their ignorance might be exposed to the NAO by the other service provider organization (Huang, 2014).

Going beyond descriptive analysis, a growing number of studies have applied inferential network analysis to examine network formation and evolution (e.g., Bevc et al., 2015; Bunger et al., 2014; Park & Rethemeyer, 2014). When explaining the formation of ties and the changes of ties, researchers tend to use organizational attributes (e.g., age, size, sector affiliation), organizational similarities (homophily), and network substructures (e.g., reciprocity and transitivity) as explanatory factors. In a study of public health collaboratives, Bevc and her colleagues (2015) found homophily effects among law enforcement, nonprofits, and public health organizations. These groups tend to form ties with organizations of similar types. In a study of referral and staff expertise sharing networks in a regional network of children's mental health organizations, Bunger' research team (2014) found that organizations with a higher number of ties in referral and staff expertise tend to form or maintain ties. Trust may influence organizations' decisions to form or maintain referral ties but seems to have no significant influence on organizations' decisions to form or maintain staff expertise partnerships. In addition, agencies tend to have reciprocal ties in networks of staff expertise sharing, but not in the network of service referrals. In short, different set of factors influence the evolution of ties in the two networks (Bunger et al., 2014). Research on the evolution of service delivery networks is ongoing and has produced partial answers to the formation and development of service delivery networks.

Performance and Management of Interorganizational Networks in Human and Social Services

Chapter 9 discussed the complexity of evaluating network performance and addressed how to evaluate network effectiveness at organizational, network, and community levels (Provan & Milward, 2001). Here we first highlight a few strategies for measuring the performance of interorganizational networks in human and social services and then stress the importance of conflict management and managerial networking for managing service delivery networks.

Evaluating Performance of Service Networks

It is important to bring in voices from multiple groups of stakeholders to come up with appropriate measures of network performance (Provan & Milward, 2001; Willis et al., 2015). Although it is difficult, researchers need to work with network leaders, members, clients, and funders to reach consensus on what the key outcome measures should be for different levels of evaluation. At the organizational level, researchers have evaluated the impact of network relations on legitimacy, resource access, service quality, goal achievement, and organizational learning (e.g., Chen & Graddy, 2010). Due to the nature of the human and social services, a client's evaluation of service quality is crucial.

In the study of mental health service networks, Provan and Milward noted the importance of measuring clients' well-being as one dimension of network outcomes, although different constituencies—"clients, families, service professionals, state-level policymakers, funders, agency staff and administrators, and taxpayers"—may hold different perspectives (1995, p. 8). A more commonly used approach is to ask clients to assess the improvement of service quality and provision based on their service experience.

At the network level, a common goal that is formally set for a network can be used as a performance measure. Aggregate service costs and social capital are often used as community-level measures (e.g., Varda, 2011). Varda studied of the impact of a national program (AmeriCorps National Civilian Community Corps, NCCC)—a community service program that assigns volunteers to work with government or nonprofit organizations to address community issues. Varda (2011) used the number of weak ties (ties with strength lower than average tie strength) and constraint scores (with low scores suggesting structural holes) to measure the changes in social capital before and after the program was implemented. She found that communities that are highly connected and cohesive tend to have higher level of social capital after the implementation of the program.

As networks evolve, it is good practice to develop measures for intermediate and long-term outcomes and link these measures with different stages of network development (Willis et al., 2015). It takes time to observe the long-term outcomes for most of social services, hence it is useful to track intermediate changes before long-term outcomes can be evaluated (Willis et al., 2015). A longitudinal study is often required to conduct a comprehensive review of network performance in the field of human and social services. For instance, researchers might be able to evaluate whether the immediate housing needs (such as shelters or temporary housing) of the homeless population have be met by the local service providers. It takes more time to track whether the clients have successfully found jobs and retained economic security.

Compared with a few commonly used network measures, such as network density and centralization, researchers may use some understudied variables in future performance evaluation of networks. Researchers may examine carefully the content of ties and further study what negative ties mean for network function and performance (Edinger & Edinger, 2016). Most research has focused on evaluating the impact of positive ties, such as information sharing and resource sharing, on organizational and network performance. Yet, organizations may also develop negative ties that can be detrimental to performance. In addition to focusing on dyadic relationships, substructures such as cliques may reveal interesting insights into network performance.

Network Management in Service Delivery Networks

Rather than discussing network management in general, we stress two important tasks for network management in service delivery networks:

conflict management and boundary spanning through managerial networking. Goal conflict is one of the major concerns of managers in an interorganizational network (O'Leary & Vij, 2012; Piatak, Romzek, LeRoux, & Johnston, 2017), as organizations may join the service delivery network with divergent backgrounds and unique organizational goals. This is especially true in the field of human and social services, as network members face diverse stakeholder demands, various funder expectations, and complex clients' needs. Therefore, conflict management is crucial for network management and leadership. Network managers and leaders need to work with member organizations to establish common goals, enhance commitments, and manage conflicts (Piatak et al., 2017). Through a case study of children service delivery networks in Kansas, Maryland, and Michigan, Piatak and her colleagues (2017) found that a lead organization that participates in direct service delivery with other service organizations can better address goal conflicts through building "shared norms" (e.g., trust and reciprocity) and "facilitative behavior" (e.g., information sharing, open communication, and relationship building).

Another important activity for network managers in service delivery networks is boundary spanning through managerial networking (Johansen & LeRoux, 2012; O'Toole, Meier, & Nicholson-Crotty, 2005). Meier and O'Toole's study showed a clear linkage between managerial networking and their organizational performance, because managerial networking can help exploit resources in the external environment and buffer external economic or political impacts (2001). A survey of 314 nonprofit organizations in 16 US states showed that nonprofit managers' networking with government agencies and officials can positively influence advocacy effectiveness in "raising public awareness of the organization's cause and influencing local government's priorities or agenda." Networking with other nonprofits, businesses, and faith-based organizations can improve organizational effectiveness "with regard to making strategic decisions, increasing organizational funding, meeting funders' performance expectations, and responding timely to client complaints" (Johansen & LeRoux, 2012, p. 358). In short, managerial networking is useful for service delivery networks to overcome resource constraints, tap into unused resources, and manage potential conflicts.

Applications of Social Network Analysis

In this section, we first introduce a wide array of questions about service delivery networks that can be addressed through network analysis. We start with setting network boundaries and data collection. Then we discuss how to use network analysis to identify the central actors and examine the multiplex relationships between nonprofit organizations. Then, we analyze the substructures of the network. Through this example, you may find how multiplex network relations among organizations can be studied from a network approach.

Network Analysis as Asset Mapping for Strengthening Community

Network analysis has been used to better allocate resources, strengthen community partnership, enhance service quality, and improve service integration in the context of human and social services. Provan and his colleagues (2005) summarized eight important questions that can be addressed through network analysis to better utilize community assets and resources and strengthen relationships among organizations. We adapt their questions and propose a series of questions that can, and should, be asked in the context of human and social service delivery. We begin by asking about interorganizational relations and their patterns and structures, and then discuss the impact of relations and network structure on service delivery or individual member organizations.

First, which organizations play a central role in delivering human and social services? Through analyzing the relational data, we can identify organizations with high centrality scores. Centrality measures can be used to measure "the control of resources and information" (Provan, Veazie, Staten, & Teufel-Shone, 2005, p. 603). Effective resource allocation is crucial for building and sustaining service delivery networks. Network analysis can provide more information about the role(s) an organization plays in a network. Furthermore, network analysis can inform decisions regarding the allocation of resources by comparing network centrality findings with community leaders' perceptions about critical actors in the network (Provan et al., 2005). The central actors differ in various types of interorganizational networks. Actors that are central in information sharing do not necessarily serve as key actors in networks for resource sharing, case management, volunteer management, grant writing, and joint housing services. When the network involves diverse groups of participants, or is relatively large, it is not uncommon that a network participant may not know the central actors or may lack access to the central actors in the network. When there are discrepancies between the network centrality results and the perceived critical actors, organizational leaders may implement strategies to build information channels, foster new links, and tap into underused resources (Provan et al., 2005). Mapping the key actors can help identify leadership roles and utilize potential resources in the network (Provan et al., 2005).

Second, what are the relationships among organizations in the network of human and social services? Are they strong or weak? Are they formal or informal ties? Compared with informal relationships, formal ties through contracts or memorandums of understanding tend to be more stable and sustainable. Organizations tend to have strong ties with each other if the ties involve multiple types of relations or interactions such as information sharing, resource sharing, and joint action (Provan et al., 2005).

Third, what characteristics does the service network exhibit? Are there closely connected subgroups? Are there structural holes that need to be bridged? Network density and centralization are often used to evaluate the connectedness (cohesion) of networks and the extent to which the network ties center around a few key organizations. Understanding network centralization can help community leaders evaluate the dispersion of information and resources in different networks. Networks with structural holes may benefit from having brokers or intermediaries that can bridge disconnected subgroups in a network (Provan & Huang, 2012).

Fourth, how does the service network evolve over time? Researchers can examine whether there is formation of new ties, demise of ties, and increased/decreased strengths of ties (Provan & Huang, 2012). Understanding the changes in relations in networks is an understudied yet important topic in service networks.

Lastly, do relations and substructures in networks improve the performance of organizations and network in service delivery? Researchers can examine whether organizations with specific roles in a service network have better access to resources (assets) or information and what can be done to improve service quality and promote organizational and network learning (Chen & Graddy, 2010).

A Regional Homeless Service Delivery Network: An Example

In this section, we use a regional homeless service network as an example to discuss a few important elements of network research, including establishing a network boundary, developing measures of ties, and analyzing the structural patterns of interorganizational relationships. Homeless issues present an important policy domain and require collaboration among organizations across sectors. This case represents complexity of collaboration as well as provides a case to help us better understand application of conceptual and methodological application of network research.

Data for the case came from an empirical research conducted by Qian Hu in 2013. We selected the three counties in a southern state—looking at three counties A, B, and C—as the study site for two reasons First, this state has the third highest number of homeless population in the nation (Council on Homelessness, 2011). The increasing demand for homeless services drives organizations to interact with other service organizations. Second, these three counties were designated as one major service area for the Continuum of Care Supportive Housing Program funded by HUD. The collaborative structure of Continuum of Care (CoC) is implemented at state and local levels to coordinate services and meet diverse needs of homeless population (Wong, Park, & Nemon, 2006). The system of homeless service delivery has evolved from heavy reliance on charitable donations to the current collaborative system that is supported by multiple sources, including government funding and private donations (Mosley, 2014). This provides a social setting for studying interorganizational relationships. Lastly, there is one CoC system that involves public agencies, nonprofits and other stakeholders in this region. This allows us to narrow our focus and study the existing interorganizational networks.

Boundary Setting

To define the boundary of the homeless service networks, we further narrowed down the focus to the interorganizational networks providing housing services to the homeless population in the three counties. To identify nonprofit organizations that serve the housing needs of the homeless population, we first searched an online homeless shelter directory (www. homelessshelterdirectory.org/) that lists homeless shelters, transitional housing organizations, and many types of other homeless service organizations. Then, we conducted an internet search of the nonprofits' and their partners' websites in providing housing services. In order to be included, nonprofit organizations need to have helped the homeless population through one of their key programs. We also sent this list to two executive directors of highly respected nonprofit homeless service delivery organizations to cross-check the list. In addition, we included open-ended questions asking the organizational representatives to add to the list if their partners were not included in the list. The collaborative homeless delivery network data were collected through surveying the executive directors of nonprofit organizations and government agencies. We surveyed 16 organizations in County A, nine organizations in County B, and nine organizations in County C, including 28 nonprofit organizations and six government agencies. We received responses from 27 organizations, a response rate of 79.4 percent.

Measures

We used the roster method to collect data on four types of relationships among housing service providers: collaboration; information sharing (about service needs or funding opportunities); competition for government financial resources (contracts, grants, funding, etc.); and competition for private donations (individual and philanthropic donation). Respondents (the executive directors) were asked to identify the organizations that have the four listed relationships and indicate the frequency of their interactions. The respondents were asked to identify organizations with which they collaborated in four areas including case management, volunteer recruitment, grant writing, and joint housing service and the frequency of collaboration on a 0–4 scale (0 = no collaboration, 4 = very frequent collaboration). We created a matrix by adding each of the cells in the matrices of the collaboration content and averaging the values. The cell ranges from 0–4. The matrix of collaboration provides information about the existence of interorganizational collaboration and strength of collaboration. The interorganizational competition was categorized into two types: competition for government financial resources and competition for private resources. These two variables measure the extent to which organizations compete for financial resources in the network. We created a matrix with cell values ranging from 0 (never) to 4 (very frequently). Higher scores suggest greater competition exists between organizations.

Understanding the Multiplexity of Interorganizational Relationships

The survey captured the multiplex relationships between organizations within the homeless service delivery network, as presented in Figures 12.1a–c. The width of the line is proportionate to its tie strength ranging from 1–4. Organizations collaborated in substantial areas such as case management, volunteer recruitment, grant writing, and joint housing service. Besides the collaborative relationship, organizations compete for public and private financial resources.

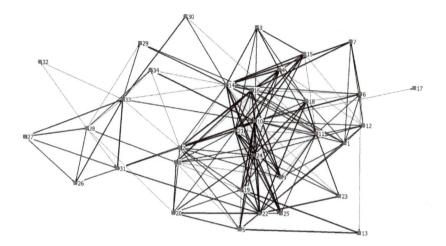

Figure 12.1a Information Sharing

Note: The numbers represent different organizations.

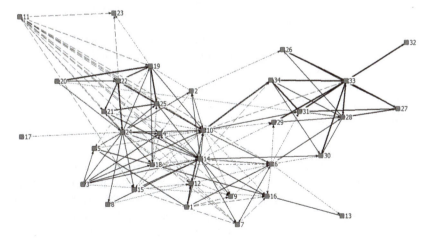

Figure 12.1b Collaboration in Case Management, Volunteer Recruitment, Grant Writing, and Joint Housing Services

Note: Dash line—case management, dotted line—volunteer management, dash and dot line—grant writing, and dash, dot, and dot line—housing service, solid line—multiple relations

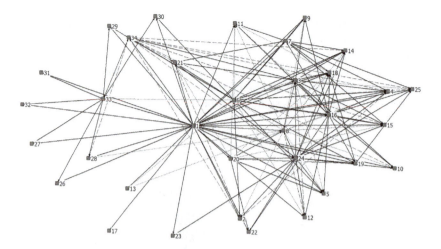

Figure 12.1c Competition for Government Financial Resources and Private Donations

Note: Dash line—competition for government financial resources, dotted line—competition for private donations, solid line—competition for both government financial resources and private donations

Structures of the Interorganizational Networks

Among the various types of interorganizational networks, information sharing has the highest density. As shown in Table 12.2, the densities of the collaboration networks are below .1. In the four areas of collaboration, grant writing network has the lowest density score, .027, followed by volunteer management with a density score of .29. In other words, service providers seldom form collaboration ties with other organizations to write grant proposals or recruit volunteers. Relatively more collaboration ties were built to collaborate in managing cases and serving the housing needs of homeless population. The competition network for private donation is denser than the competition network for government financial resources.

Different from network density, network centralization measures whether the network ties are concentrated in few actors (Scott, 2013). The network concentration values in this study are relatively low, none of which is close to 1. No actor completely dominates in the diverse types of networks. This finding is also consistent with the visualizations of the networks in Figures 12.1a–d. The core-periphery correlation measures the extent to which a network is close to the core-periphery structure, in which core nodes are connected to other core nodes and peripheral nodes are not connected to other peripheral nodes (Borgatti, Everett, & Johnson, 2013). None of the various interorganizational networks has a typical core-periphery structure. Information sharing has the highest core-periphery correlation, .528, with seven organizations in the core.

Table 12.1 Network Structure

	Network Density	Network Indegree Centralization	Network Outdegree Centralization	Core-Periphery Correlation	# Core Members
Information sharing Collaboration	.167	.134	.327	.528	7
Case management	.084	.08	.233	.324	8
Volunteer recruitment	.029	.048	.08	.393	2
Grant writing	.027	.102	.167	.413	3
Joint housing service Competition	.097	.185	.386	.504	1
Government financial resources	.119	.085	.455	.510	4
Private donations	.130	.11	.448	.526	5

Table 12.2 Central Actors in the Information Sharing Network

		Degree (Indegree)	Betweenness	Perceived Central Organizations
Information Sharing	1st	HSN	HSN	HSN
	2nd	CHCF	OURM	CH
	3rd	CHH	HOPE	OCDHS
Resource Sharing	1st	ROMCF	SCCS	HSN
	2nd	CBCCFS	CHH	CHCF
	3rd	RH HHOC OCDHS	HHSGA	NA

This study used indegree centrality and betweenness centrality to assess the central roles organizations play in the homeless housing service delivery network. The results are presented in Table 12.2. This study also used indegree centrality to measure the number of connections a service provider receives in the network. The organizations that have high indegree centralizations are named lead organizations, as other organizations reach out to them for information or resource sharing. Furthermore, the study used the betweenness centrality to measure the extent to which a service provider is involved in the connections between all other pairs of organizations (Hanneman & Riddle, 2011). A high betweenness centrality may suggest that an organization serves as a mediator or information broker (Hanneman & Riddle, 2011).

As seen in Table 12.2, lead organizations are not necessarily the mediators or information brokers. The network analysis identified HSN (a government funded nonprofit organization) as a central organization with its high indegree centrality and betweenness centrality in the information sharing network. This is also consistent with the organizational leaders' perception. Yet, when it comes to the second or third central organizations in information sharing, the network analysis results differed from the organizational leaders' perception. It was not surprising that the discrepancies existed between the network survey results and organizational leaders' knowledge. What organizational leaders need to do is to utilize the results to inform their decisions on allocating resources and to build new connections or partnerships. This type of network analysis can be informative for funding agencies to identify the influential actors in the service network and invest in strengthening the communication channels and resource conduits.

Conclusion

In this chapter, we discussed various types of networks in human and social services, highlighted the multiplex types of relationships among organizations, and called attention to interorganizational competition in addition to traditional focus on collaboration. We introduced network measures that are used to study the formation and evolution of service delivery networks. Existing empirical study, though limited to the field of mental health services, suggests that a centralized network with a core agency is effective for service delivery. More studies, especially longitudinal and explanatory studies, are needed in the future to examine the complex relationship among network structure, management, and performance in service delivery networks. We stressed the importance of conflict management and managerial networking to improve the performance of service delivery networks. The use of network analysis as an asset mapping strategy were also presented for managers and leaders to build and sustain effective network governance for human and social services.

References

Arya, B., & Lin, Z. (2007). Understanding collaboration outcomes from an extended resource-based view perspective: The roles of organizational characteristics, partner attributes, and network structures. *Journal of Management, 33*(5), 697–723.

Bevc, C. A., Retrum, J. H., & Varda, D. (2015). New perspectives on the "silo effects": Initial comparisons of network structures across public health collaboratives. *American Journal of Public Health, 105*(Suppl. 2), S230–S235.

Borgatti, S. P., Everett, M. G., & Johnson, J. C. (2013). *Analyzing social networks*. Los Angeles, CA: Sage Publications.

Bunger, A. C. (2013). Administrative coordination in nonprofit human service delivery networks: The role of competition and trust. *Nonprofit and Voluntary Sector Quarterly, 42*(6), 1155–1175.

Bunger, A. C., Doogan, N. J., & Cao, Y. (2014). Building service delivery networks: Partnership evolution among children's behavioral health agencies in response to new funding. *Journal of Social Work Research, 5*(4), 513–538.

Chen, B., & Graddy, E. A. (2010). The effectiveness of nonprofit lead-organization networks for social service delivery. *Nonprofit Management & Leadership, 20*(4), 405–422.

Council on Homelessness. (2011). 2011 report. Retrieved fromhttps://www.myflfami-lies.com/serviceprograms/homelessness/docs/2011CouncilReport.pdf

Edinger, S. K., & Edinger, M. (2016). Unpacking team performance: The role of positive and negative network ties. *Academy of Management Proceedings* (1). doi:10.5465/ambpp.2016.16321abstract

Gazley, B. (2008). Beyond the contract: The scope and nature of informal government-nonprofit partnerships. *Public Administration Review, 68*(1), 141–152.

Guo, C., & Acar, M. (2005). Understanding collaboration among nonprofit organiza-tions: Combining resource dependency, institutional, and network perspectives. *Nonprofit & Voluntary Sector Quarterly, 34*(3), 340–361.

Hanneman, R. A., & Riddle, M. (2005). *Introduction to social network methods*. Riv-erside, CA: University of California. Retrieved July 2, 2014, from http://faculty.ucr.edu/~hanneman/

Hanneman, R. A., & Riddle, M. (2011). A brief introduction to social network data. In J. Scott & P. J. Carrington (Eds.), *The Sage handbook of social network analysis* (pp. 331–339). Thousand Oaks, CA: Sage Publications.

Huang, K. (2014). Knowledge sharing in a third-party-governed health and human ser-vices network. *Public Administration Review, 74*(5), 587–598.

Isett, K. R., Mergel, I. A., LeRoux, K., Mischen, P. A., & Rethemeyer, R. K. (2011). Net-works in public administration scholarship: Understanding where we are and where we need to go. *Journal of Public Administration Research and Theory, 21*(Special issue), i157–i173.

Johansen, M., & LeRoux, K. (2012). Managerial networking in nonprofit organiza-tions: The impact of networking on organizational and advocacy effectiveness. *Public Administration Review, 73*(2), 355–363.

Kapucu, N., Hu, Q., & Khosa, S. (2014). The state of network research in public adminis-tration. *Administration & Society, 49*(8), 1087–1120. doi:10.1177/0095399714555752

Knight, L. (2002). Network learning: Exploring learning by interorganizational net-works. *Human Relations, 55*(4), 427.

Lemaire, R., & Provan, K. G. (2018). Managing collaborative effort: How Simme-lian ties advance public sector networks. *American Review of Public Administration, 48*(5), 379–394.

LeRoux, K. (2012). *Balancing competition and collaboration within a home-less service provider network: Brookfield County's continuum of care*. Retrieved November 12, 2015, from www.maxwell.syr.edu/uploadedFiles/parcc/eparcc/simu-lations/2012.2%20LaRoux%20Simulation.pdf

Meier, K. J., & O'Toole, L. J. (2001). Managerial strategies and behavior in networks: A model with evidence from U.S. public education. *Journal of Public Administration Research and Theory, 11*(3), 271–294.

Milward, B., & Provan, K. G. (2003). Managing the hollow state collaboration and contracting. *Public Management Review, 5*(1), 1–18.

Mosley, J. E. (2014). Collaboration, public-private intermediary organizations, and the transformation of advocacy in the field of homeless services. *The American Review of Public Administration, 44*(3), 291–308.

O'Leary, R., & Vij, N. (2012). Collaborative public management: Where have we been and where are we going? *American Review of Public Administration, 42*(5), 507–522.

O'Toole, L. J., Meier, K. J., & Nicholson-Crotty, S. (2005). Managing upward, down-ward, and outward: Networks, hierarchical relationships, and performance. *Public Management Review, 7*(1), 45–68.

Park, H. H., & Rethemeyer, R. K. (2014). The politics of connections: Assessing the determinants of social structure in policy networks. *Journal of Public Administration Theory and Research, 24*(2), 349–379.

Piatak, J., Romzek, B., LeRoux, K., & Johnston, J. (2017). Managing goal conflict in public service delivery networks: Does accountability move up and down, or side to side? *Public Performance & Management Review.* doi:10.1080/15309576.2017.1400993

Provan, K. G., & Huang, K. (2012). Resource tangibility and the evolution of a publicly funded health and human services network. *Public Administration Review, 72,* 366–375.

Provan, K. G., Isett, K. R., & Milward, H. B. (2004). Cooperation and compromise: A network response to conflicting institutional pressures in community mental health. *Nonprofit and Voluntary Sector Quarterly, 33*(3), 489–514.

Provan, K. G., & Milward, H. B. (1995). A preliminary theory of interorganizational network effectiveness: A comparative study of four community mental health systems. *Administrative Science Quarterly, 40*(1), 1–33.

Provan, K. G., & Milward, H. B. (2001). Do networks really work? A framework for evaluating public-sector organizational networks. *Public Administration Review, 61*(4), 414.

Provan, K. G., Veazie, M. A., Staten, L. K., & Teufel-Shone, N. I. (2005). The use of network analysis to strengthen community partnerships. *Public Administration Review, 65*(5), 603–613.

Raab, J., Mannak, R. S., & Cambré, B. (2015). Combining structure, governance, and context: A configurational approach to network effectiveness. *Journal of Public Administration Research and Theory, 25*(2), 479–511.

Romzek, B., LeRoux, K., Johnston, J., Kempf, R. J., & Piatak, J. C. (2014). Informal accountability in multisector service delivery collaborations. *Journal of Public Administration Research and Theory, 24*(4), 813–842.

Salamon, L. M. (1987). Of market failure, voluntary failure, and third-party government: Toward a theory of government-nonprofit relations in the modern welfare state. *Nonprofit and Voluntary Sector Quarterly, 16*(1–2), 29–49.

Scott, J. (2013). *Social network analysis* (3rd ed.). Los Angeles, CA: Sage Publications.

Sowa, J. E. (2009). The collaboration decision in nonprofit organizations: Views from the front line. *Nonprofit and Voluntary Sector Quarterly, 38*(6), 1003–1025.

Steen, J. A., & Duran, L. (2013). The impact of foster care privatization on multiple placements. *Children and Youth Services Review, 35*(9), 1503–1509.

Varda, D. M. (2011). A network perspective on state-society synergy to increase community level social capital. *Nonprofit and Voluntary Sector Quarterly, 40*(5), 896–923.

Wasserman, S., & Faust, K. (1994). *Social network analysis: Methods and applications.* New York, NY: Cambridge University Press.

Willis, C., Kernoghan, A., Riley, B., Popp, J., Best, A., & Milward, H. B. (2015). Outcomes of interorganizational networks in Canada for chronic disease prevention: Insights from a concept mapping study. *Preventing Chronic Disease, 12.* doi:10.5888/pcd12.150297

Wong, Y. I., Park, J. M., & Nemon, H. (2006). Homeless service delivery in the context of continuum of care. *Administration in Social Work, 30*(1), 67–94.

Young, D. R. (2006). Complementary, supplementary, or adversarial? A theoretical and historical examination of nonprofit-government relations in the United States. In E. T. Boris & C. E. Steuerle (Eds.), *Nonprofits and government: Collaboration and conflict* (pp. 31–67). Washington, DC: The Urban Institute Press.

13 Networks in Virtual Environments

Virtual environments provide a platform for government agencies to partner with non-governmental agencies and individual citizens. Emerging technologies, especially information and communication technology (ICT), offer significant potential for fostering the development of virtual networks. Members in virtual networks are usually geographically, functionally, and organizationally dispersed. Any collaboration and communication that occur through the use of ICT are more likely to be temporally displaced or asynchronous. To date, however, relatively little research exists to help practitioners and scholars understand and manage networks in virtual environments.

This chapter discusses key concepts related to network governance in virtual environments, and analyzes the key attributes, theories, and evaluation methods of virtual networks. In addition to addressing this important network topic, the chapter highlights how virtual networks can complement in-person networks. It also discusses network analysis applications in understanding the virtual networks. This chapter examines the following research questions:

- How are virtual networks defined?
- What are the roles of trust and social capital for network development and functioning in virtual environments?
- How can performance issues be addressed for virtual networks?
- What are some challenges for governance and leadership in virtual networks?
- How can network analysis be applied in virtual environments?

Interorganizational Networks in Virtual Environments

It is hard to imagine our life without the internet or engagement in virtual environments. Internet technologies break geographical boundaries as well as organizational boundaries. It helps search, monitor, connect, and exchange ideas. The growing popularity of *virtual networks* and social networking applications are global trends. Billions of people are active users of social media outlets such as Facebook; YouTube; WhatsApp; WeChat, and Instagram.

Virtual Networks

Networks formed and administered using information communication technologies for addressing social and policy problems.

New technologies allow for new ways of creating social capital, building relationships, and networking. The potential of the internet and social media platforms to mobilize and coordinate community initiatives are essential to network development and sustainability. On the other hand, internet usage has been linked to a decline in civic involvement, lessening the ability of citizens to influence their government, causing the degradation of community life and in social isolation. A counterargument to this statement is that the use of internet did not reduce face-to-face and over-the-phone contact, but rather supplemented those interactions (Kavanaugh & Patterson, 2001; Nie, 2001; Putnam, 2000; Wellman, Haase, Witte, & Hampton, 2001). Similar to interest in studying social capital and networks, the development of social networks and networking in virtual environments also received interest. Traditionally, social capital has been viewed as a side effect of direct contact and participation in community organizations. Yet, with the development of the internet, the ways that people interact have transformed and we are now witnessing a shift from the community and personal contact participation to virtual social contact (Fischer, 1997; Resnick, 2002; Sarker, Ahuja, Sarker, & Kirkeby, 2011; Wellman et al., 2001).

Resnick (2002) posited that there is a new way of developing social capital, "sociotechnical capital" which is the dynamic combination of social interactions that arise when people use new technologies to communicate, regularly interact, and build relationships. From this perspective, sociotechnical capital enhances the traditional ways people interact and may present an entirely new way of collaborating and solving community issues. There is a positive correlation between increases in social capital and better collective and individual outcomes in health, education, and economic development (Resnick, 2002). The use of sociotechnical capital with human-computer interaction can improve the design of network systems that support community initiatives in virtual systems.

In addition to social networking, new technologies can be used to facilitate telecommuting, which became quite popular for government and private organizations (Breu & Hemingway, 2004; Kasper-Fuehrer & Ashkanasy, 2001; Kavanaugh & Patterson, 2001). New technologies can also be used for transparency and faster E-government service delivery. Citizens can monitor public officials' activities and leverage their influence on policymaking in democratic systems via online petitions (Meijer, 2011). In the case of an emergency, critical personnel and resources can be mobilized faster using virtual networks and ICT (Hu & Kapucu, 2014; Roberts, 2011). Educational materials can also be distributed easily. Education and training programs can be facilitated in virtual environments (Aviv, Erlich, & Ravid, 2008). Some of the examples mentioned in this paragraph can be examples of cost and transaction cost reduction through the use of virtual networks.

Similar to virtual communities, we see shifting trends in organizational practice with routine use of technology and ICT (Adalat, Niazi, & Vasilakos, 2018). Many organizations have remote workers, and employees are required to communicate via an internal communication system. One useful aspect for ICT usage is that it provides easier means by which to capture data. For example, the use of such @mentions can create a directional network within the organization in virtual environments, which has implications for leadership and network performance.

Virtual networks change not only the location in which tasks are performed but also the definition of organizing and networks. The function of networks relies on horizontal structures. A virtual environment makes the network arrangements even flatter, potentially bringing up additional questions of control. Virtual environments provide a cyberspace for network members to operate anywhere and anytime away from their managers/supervisors and from one another.

Virtual environments can provide a shared space for the members of a successful operation of interorganizational networks. The ICT designs should be interoperable and help all members of the network to communicate and function seamlessly and transparently. ICT tools in in virtual environments help collective effort be achieved, stored, reviewed, and modified by all the members in the network irrespective of location (using DropBox, Google Drive, or OneDrive). In this shared space, ideas can be discussed, synthesized, and finalized in a timely manner. ICT provide platform for collaborative effort in virtual environment. However, its success depends on trust, relationship building, and human elements. Managers and leaders need greater levels of trust in network representatives from other organizations to work virtually together, as they cannot be seen and monitored regular basis (Kasper-Fuehrer & Ashkanasy, 2001; Krackhardt & Kilduff, 1999). This can become a special challenge for virtual networks that do not rely on informal personal contact to establish trust.

Virtual environments provide more opportunities for interorganizational networks with technologically savvy organizations. Where and when people work, and how they communicate, is increasingly seamless due to electronic communications media such as email, text, and teleconferencing. Virtual environments can reduce employees' expenses such as travel and rent, increase productivity, improve service delivery, and coordination, if used correctly. Despite multiple benefits, virtual environments bring substantial challenges for management, organization, governance, and leadership. In the following section, we will briefly compare and contrast networks in face-to-face environments and in virtual environments.

Networks in Face-to-Face and Virtual Environments

Virtual networks, similar to face-to-face networks, connect organizations across sectors, functions, and geography to address a common problem or materialize a benefit (Aviv et al., 2008; Fountain, 2001; Shen & Cage, 2015). Each network member's own culture, identity, goals, culture, structure, and systems might not easily mesh with other members in virtual environments, introducing additional challenges for technical compatibility or interoperability. The dynamic nature of networks in virtual environments, as well as the number of organizational boundaries crossed, increases uncertainty and complexity. Members of a network in virtual environments might not have similar technology or work culture and communication methods in common. Networks in virtual environments need to develop their own culture of working together, openness to collaboration, and using compatible technology. Functioning collaboration and decisiveness are key in dealing with complexity and uncertainty in dynamic environments (Ahuja & Carley, 1999; Kasper-Fuehrer & Ashkanasy, 2003; Nohria & Berkley, 1994; Shen & Cage, 2015).

The internet gives an opportunity for members of a virtual community to interact and communicate without needing to be in the same place. Removing distance as a boundary has both drawbacks and positives. Among the scholarly community, there is a debate regarding if a virtual community can function without interpersonal interaction in real life and colocation. Even though organizations in virtual environments have their own culture, language, and norms, they can collectively utilize virtual communities (Adalat et al., 2018; Gruzd, Wellman, & Takhteyev, 2011; Kasper-Fuehrer & Ashkanasy, 2003).

Table 13.1 provides some similarities and differences between networks in virtual and face-to-face environments in terms of communication and interaction, temporal nature, structure, culture, policies, needs of the actors in the network. Some of the ideas here can be applied to individual actors as members of virtual communities, as well as individual actors that represent organizations. Common language and in-person communication are key in face-to-face networks. Instant messaging and other electronic communication means replace in person communication in virtual networks. Although both virtual and face-to-face networks can have influential actors, virtual networks tend to decentralize hierarchical structures.

Despite the negative and positive effects of virtual networks we have discussed, some scholars remain neutral toward the virtual networks (Kraut et al., 2002). Instead of considering the benefits or drawbacks in social capital, some observed that the internet is a supplement of the existing patterns of offline networks (Quan-Haase & Wellman, 2004). The internet does not appear to have radically transformed civic involvement in voluntary organizations and politics (Quan-Haase & Wellman, 2004). People who engage social issues tend to use the internet as much as those who do not. However, the virtual network is associated with significantly larger number of weak ties in the community, less significant for mid-strength ties, and not significant in increasing the number

Table 13.1 Networks in Face-to-Face and Virtual Environments

Characteristics	Face-to-Face Environment	Virtual environment
Communication & interaction	Common language and in-person interactions are key communication a co-location	The use of labeling the events or topics in form of hashtag (#), @mentions, comments and reposting posts, instant messaging
Temporal nature	Common values, norms, and culture in a shared space Membership of the face-to-face network is sustained over time	Difficult to sustain membership. Membership is temporary to solve an issue or to raise awareness around a policy, advocacy, or a social problem
Structure	Network can be centralized around core members or informal and decentralized	Decentralized structure There might be some influential actors such as political leaders with impact and substantial followers
Identity Culture, policies	Feeling of a belonging to the community or a network and have a distinct identify, organizational culture and policies	Lack of common sense of belonging and identity to 'imagined community' Virtual environment as a platform for functional collaboration
Influence	Each member of a network in face-to-face environments can influence other members in the network	Thought leaders or influential lead actors in the network can influence behavior and opinions of the others
Addressing actors' need	Actors in face-to-face environments can provide support to the other actors	Actors in networks in virtual environments are 'information neighbors.' Virtual connection to other actors and information sharing in virtual platform

Source: Ahuja & Carley, 1999; Nohria & Berkley, 1994; Shen & Cage, 2015; Wellman et al., 2001.

of strong ties via bonding social capital (Hampton, 2003). Participants in the virtual networks are not rational information processors (Meijer, 2011) and thus, the public sector should make efforts to design their virtual networks to encourage regular engagement for effectiveness.

Virtual networks are way of organizing that challenges some assumptions of traditional network arrangements and structures. These relatively new forms and network arrangements will have significant implications for organizational and network behavior in addition to human capital management, as they challenge well-defined organizational boundaries and job descriptions by adding additional technology use, capacity, and openness toward a flexible environment.

Examples of Networks in Virtual Environments

Virtual environments provide platforms for interorganizational collaboration and intra-organizational coordination. Here we provide one brief example on how virtual environments can be used in supporting emergency management coordination. Emergency Operations Centers (EOCs) form the basic framework for coordinating information and resources during a disaster response and early recovery. A Virtual Emergency Operations Center (VEOC), such as a WebEOC, is an EOC that exists fully or partially in cyberspace and utilizes web-enabled software. A VEOC "permits effective direction and control of resources, automates processes and methodologies, assigns and tracks tasks, and efficiently communicates real-time information" (Davis, 2002, p. 46). There are a variety of tools that are being applied by VEOC organizations such as conference calls, online databases, wireless mobile networks, intranet chat for support groups, and e-mailing.

Virtual coordination of emergency operations is gaining popularity. Web EOCs use different web-based platforms for efficiently coordinated response operations among geographically dispersed organizations. VEOCs provide add-on functions of flexible communication and knowledge sharing to aid traditional emergency operation centers and incident management teams. The benefits of VEOCs include tracking response activities and resources according to previously existing plans, helping triage problems in deployment and response, automating checklists and incident tracking in addition to providing regular updates from vendors. However, there are few drawbacks, such the lack of opportunity to get everyone on the table in person; face-to-face communication benefits, risk of server breakdowns, and the potential bridge of security of sensitive data (Davis, 2002).

At a different level, Virtual Operations Support Teams (VOSTs) support the use of new communication technologies and social media in response to crises. VOSTS are managed and operated by the Virtual Operations Support Group, which is a global community of interest. The group was established in New York in 2012. The nonprofit organization has a global advisory council with regional centers in Americas, Europe, and Oceania (Katims, 2013). VOSTs provide mutual aid assistance during the response to man-made or natural incidents. VOST services are provided in cyberspace and coordinated by a virtual office website (www.vosg.us). VOST volunteer teams are emergency managers and volunteers that coordinate information for relief as the emergency mangers on site will be overwhelmed by the data and available information. VOST also assists facilitating volumes of information generated in social media during disasters. FEMA uses VOST and develops guidelines for virtual teams for better operational communication (FEMA, 2018). FEMA considers memorandum of understandings (MOUs) to better coordinate digital information sharing in social media, especially in response to catastrophic disasters.

Input from citizens in tracking disasters, through social media, should not be overlooked in managing emergencies. This network would be especially critical for countries or localities that lack a well-established emergency management system. Park and Johnson (2018) emphasized the role of communication technology for citizen participation in supporting formal emergency and crisis management efforts in response to the 2015 Nepal Earthquake. In the US and other countries, there is an established emergency and crisis management system. Sometimes these systems cannot respond quickly. Citizens and other emergent groups can organize disaster relief services face-to-face or virtually to mobilize additional relief efforts. The data collected by citizens can be shared and utilized by the formal disaster response organizations and government agencies. Park and Johnson (2018) called this a 'digital volunteer network'. Citizens used Facebook to communicate and coordinate their immediate needs during Hurricane Harvey in Houston, Texas, in 2017. The New York Times (2017) produced a story that included real time data on this citizen coordination effort at a neighborhood level. The primary use of Facebook was to coordinate neighborhood level damage and individual assistance to neighbors before the government resources arrived.

Social media is increasingly used to share information during emergency and mass convergence events. Hughes and Palen (2009) conducted a study to analyze how Twitter is being used differently during emergency and mass convergence events compared to general daily use. Analyzing two natural disasters, Hurricane Ike and Hurricane Gustav, and mass convergence events, the US Democratic National Convention and US Republican National Convention, all of which took place within a month between August 21, 2008, and September 14, 2008 (Hughes & Palen, 2009). The highest number of tweets took place on the day of the conventions and on the days when the hurricanes made landfall. Per the study, out of the four events, the highest number of tweets was during Hurricane Ike because of its impact, size, and level of media coverage compared to three other cases in the study (Hughes & Palen, 2009). In addition, during these events twitter users included more URLs compared to general usage. This suggests that users were functioning as information brokers for others, including government agencies, and helping provide safety-related resources for major events. Interestingly, results demonstrated that most of the new users during high-profile events later become active users of Twitter and other social media. In the future, we expect more utilization of social media for sharing information among organizations and the public-at-large in disaster communications.

Studying Virtual Networks

Virtual networks can be considered a major innovation. The internet provides additional channels for public service provision, provides access to citizens' experiences and knowledge, and provides additional social outlets (Meijer, 2011). Through virtual networks, citizens receive efficient services through e-government services, and they are connected with public officials. The citizens have the platform to call attention to issues affecting them locally as well as nationally (Roberts, 2011). In addition to being a major platform for efficient information sharing, the internet is a useful tool for cultivating weak ties among virtual networks. The weak ties are capable of "bridging" clusters of stronger ties and of providing access to information and resources not available through closest circles of network members (Hampton, 2003; Siegel, 2009). Actors might be better connected with colleagues using virtual platforms (Meijer, 2011) and are able to share information faster and therefore able to build partnerships quicker and easier.

With the greater prevalence of virtual networks, we observed p a growing interest in the relational approach to study organizations. This approach emphasizes networks as intraorganizational and interorganizational ties, as opposed to the traditional mode of hierarchical organizing (Hu, Khosa, & Kapucu, 2016; Klijn & Koppenjan, 2016; Popp, MacKean, Casebeer, Milward, & Lindstrom, 2014). Network perspectives highlight that actors are embedded in a system of relations (Granovetter, 1985; Uzzi, 1997), rather than focusing on the attributes of members of a network. For example, this perspective addresses how network structural variables such as the density, strength, and multiplexity yield different outcomes and network learning. This can be especially critical for the design and coordination of virtual interorganizational networks. It is also necessary to examine how virtual relations generate opportunities and challenges for collective action. Hence, managing the balance between technology and relationship becomes critical for the success of networks in virtual environments.

Social capital, with implications for both personal and organizational networks in face-to-face and virtual environments, is viewed as a resource that people gain through interaction within their networks (Lin, 2002; Shen & Cage, 2015). There are three forms of social capital: network capital, which is usually for individual social relations with friends, neighbors, relatives. Participatory capital, which is used for people to bond, create joint accomplishments, and aggregate and articulate their demands and desires in politics and voluntary organizations. Finally, community commitment, which is a strong attitude toward communal mobilization of people's social capital more willingly and effectively (Wellman et al., 2001). Social capital, regardless of its form, plays a critical role for organizational and network success. Stronger connections in virtual environments provide better opportunities, knowledge, and resources (Galaskiewicz, Bielefeld, & Dowell, 2006; Krebs & Holley, 2004).

Community and organizations are not just bricks-and-mortar, but are interpersonal ties that provide sociability, support, information, a sense of belonging, and social identity (Ardichvili, 2008; Breu & Hemingway, 2004; Quan-Haase & Wellman, 2004). The growth of social capital within virtual networks can remove barriers to communication for community members and organizational hierarchy, as well as provide a platform for flexible communication. Virtual networks can also help decentralize the allocation of responsibilities and resources for actors in a network (Breu & Hemingway, 2004). Public administrators need to determine whether virtual environments encourage participatory capital, community commitment, and increased organizational and network performance or discourage these.

Trust plays an important role in the success of any network structure (Breu & Hemingway, 2004; Sarker et al., 2011; Shen & Cage, 2015). Despite the flexibility of virtual platforms, trust may be compromised through virtual collaborations, because some of the key elements to building trust that come from face-to-face interactions are lost through virtual interactions (Breu & Hemingway, 2004). Virtualization might increase the complexity of boundaries, which could be an obstacle for interpersonal trust and personal networks. In the virtual network, those actors in central positions will have a higher level of communication and influencing power with a higher level of trust (Sarker et al., 2011). Virtual environments, on the other hand, promote boundary spanning activities. Virtual environments allow work units to span, buffer and limit the boundaries to accomplish their goals (Breu & Hemingway, 2004; Kasper-Fuehrer & Ashkanasy, 2001). Virtual environments bring opportunities for boundary spanners, but the actors with this capacity need to understand this environment in addition to traditional roles and leadership capacities.

Performance in Virtual Networks

Defining, facilitating, and encouraging performance are critical challenges for organizational and interorganizational arrangements (Cascio, 1999). Network arrangements need to have clear expectations for each organizational member or representative who lead member organizations to work for the success of the overall network. Network arrangements need to provide resources, or the expectation of resources, to achieve higher performance results for the individual organizations, as well as the collective effort of the entire network. Network, or collective, effectiveness is dependent on an individual's capacity, as well as additional support from the members of a network (Engel, Woolley, Jing, Chabris, & Malone, 2014). Careful selection of member organizations, as well as preparation of members, is critical for success of the network. The network administrative organization (NAO), or lead agency, need to provide a clear orientation for the network as well as timely feedback as needed.

Virtual environments present substantial questions and challenges for network performance. How do virtual environments change the perception of network performance? How do we evaluate the performance of network members in virtual environments? How do virtual environments impact the structure of the network and eventually its performance? These and many other questions around network performance in virtual environments are unanswered. These are challenging, especially for interorganizational arrangements, as the representatives of network member organizations are already engaged with other organizations with clear goals, objectives, and position descriptions. Networks add additional challenges to the performance issue. Lack of in-person of supervisors and network organizational representatives and team members in the virtual environments provides additional challenges for performance.

The structure of a network and behaviors of the process, which are immediate enablers of collaboration, need to be carefully considered as they are the conditions that most directly impact the collaborative process and outcomes. Included in the structure category are characteristics of the task (such as task interdependence, task significance, and task identity) and the conditions (such as shared space) that make up the immediate environment within which the tasks are performed. The cognitive and interpersonal behaviors and skills that make collaborations possible, such as lateral skills which can be defined as the ability to work with and learn from other individuals with different functional backgrounds, perspectives, and agendas (Cohen & Mankin, 1999).

The organizational policies, programs, culture, structures, and systems that support collaboration play important role for performance in virtual networks. Cohen and Mankin (1999) highlighted the importance of dealing with uncertainty and complexity and how to successfully develop effective ways of working arrangements in virtual networks. Developing a shared understanding of goals is crucial for effective collaboration in virtual networks. Virtual networks themselves require new structures to be created. Creating a shared space, using information technologies, becomes even more important when people are not located close to each other.

As a virtual network does not have a fixed structure or hierarchy, relationships in virtual environments are more open and in flux (Ganley & Lampe, 2009). Since there is not much information provided on how the network functions, and not all participants have fixed roles and responsibilities, and roles are more driven by informal agreement than authority, possibly resulting in less transparency (Ganley & Lampe, 2009; Shen & Cage, 2015). Virtual environments might not be optimum for all kinds of networks. The following are characteristics of individual actors that can function in networks virtual environments: self-motivated, comfortable with the function of a job, effective communicator, flexible with the use of technology, knowledgeable about the network and the functions expected from the organization, self-sufficient, capable with technology, and result oriented (more so for the collective goal of the network) (Cascio, 1999).

Networks in virtual environments require different managerial and leadership techniques than traditional networks to achieve high performance. It is critical that organizations help managers and members of the network obtain necessary competencies. Members of the network, for example, need to learn how to use and facilitate meetings using Skype or other teleconferencing systems. Some elements of leadership and management in virtual networks are provided in the following section.

Leadership and Management in Virtual Networks

Technological developments provide faster and better communication tools that can improve public services. Yet, governance and management are still the most critical challenge for virtual networks, as well as face-to-face networks. Virtual organizations and networks are growing, as is their study. However, while these virtual arrangements may prove to be somewhat convenient, they face barriers involving governance and leadership issues (Grabowski & Roberts, 1999). Technology's role in networks can provide a means for structuring teamwork, enhancing the available information to the team, and providing a communication system. There are three dimensions of virtual organizations, which include traditional, hybrid, and pure virtual. Most organizational and network arrangements, and virtual teams, are likely to fall into the hybrid category (Griffith, Sawyer, & Neale, 2003).

Leadership in virtual networks can be defined as the behaviors of public managers that aim to organize and facilitate productive interaction among participants in a network and to solve shared problems or meet needs effectively (McGuire & Silvia, 2009; Huxham & Vangen, 2000). Leadership is seen as a mixture of skills, knowledge, and abilities to facilitate work of an organization (Eglene, Dawes, & Schneider, 2007). In virtual environments, a leader can be defined as a person who has the influence to encourage communication, interaction, social networking, and frame discussion (Adalat et al., 2018; Huffaker, 2010).

Not all managers, as well as newcomers, will be comfortable working in virtual environments (Ahuja & Galvin, 2003). Result oriented managers, managers with high trust in their employees and network representatives, managers with effective communication skills, and managers that are effective in delegating tasks and following up remotely can be successful in the virtual environments (Mowshowitz, 1997). An initial screening of network members to determine which among them require training would be useful before final task assignment is made.

Reliability is valuable in these virtual arrangements because of the risk involved in these settings. The main difference between virtual organizations and traditional ones include the fact that virtual organizations are networked, typically electronically, and transcend conventional organizational barriers that can be limiting. Virtual networks inherit many of the same risks that traditional network organizations possess, some of which include trusting in technology, system error, human error, and issues around organizational culture. Because networks are temporary in nature, it is extremely challenging to develop shared goals, shared culture, and shared commitments "as the presence of simultaneous interdependence and autonomy creates an inherent tension" among members of the network (Grabowski & Roberts, 1999, p. 705).

It is important to structure networks appropriately to ensure that tasks are disseminated in a way that can be coordinated toward the common network goal. Developing strong organizational cultures in virtual networks is difficult because they are often comprised of several conflicting or different cultures. Thus, developing a single culture of reliability can prove challenging. Network leaders and mangers should pay close attention to developing trust in virtual networks as it requires continual communication among members to build relationships that provide the foundation for trust. Without trust, commitment to the goals of the organization can waiver, as members can perceive the alliance as weak, fractured by misunderstanding or trust. Developing trust is a complex task, as it is difficult to trust people who are not as committed as you to a goal (Grabowski & Roberts, 1999).

The role of a leader in virtual networks is significant to the point where it might be one of the decisive factors of a network's success (McGuire & Silvia, 2009). To make a network function effectively, a leader has to fulfill the following core functions: activation (start a network), framing (frame the network structure, provide roles to network participants, shape norms and values, form a common identity, culture, and shared goals), mobilizing (find support and resources inside and outside of the network in accomplishing the common goal), and synthesizing (formation of trust and creation of a favorable and collegial environment to promote productive network) (McGuire & Silvia, 2009).

To fulfill the activation function in virtual environments, a leader might start a discussion on an important policy/political/economic/social issue. A leader's reputation and followers are crucial to reduce uncertainty when new online partnership begins. Framing in virtual environments can be seen as framing and moderating a discussion. The messages should be clear and formed in the language familiar to followers and users. At this stage, it is important to show knowledge of the community, history, culture, unique attributes and values, or to demonstrate familiarity with other virtual networks and its members. A leader in the virtual environment can mobilize people with the help of posts and shares. The number of posts, re-posts, and comments play an important role in mobilizing followers, as well as other members of the network. Additionally, a leader has to be able to provide connection, information, and coordination between other members of a network in case of crisis. Because users can follow and unfollow a leader in the virtual environment, the main task is to build trust and create a collegial environment with interesting content and regular activity. A leader needs to have regular information exchange to avoid becoming isolated in virtual networks in both formal and informal settings.

Application of Network Analysis in Virtual Networks

Chapter 2 provided a brief application of social network analysis in network governance. Social network analysis can be applied in virtual environments to capture relational data. Social network analysis is an appropriate tool and perspective in studying relational data, patterns, and structures of a virtual network. In Facebook, liking or sharing can be considered an interaction and relational. In a similar fashion, replying to a tweet or re-tweeting it is also an indication of an interaction among the users in virtual environments (Jung & Park, 2014).

These virtual interactions can provide rich content, depending on the context or event, with which to explore the impact of communication and connections as relational data. Similar to face-to-face networks, social network analysis can be used to examine interaction patterns among actors, identify and highlight key actors, identify subgroups or cliques, and evaluate the properties of network structure (Borgatti, 2002; Borgatti, Everett, & Johnson, 2017). Similar to social capital and informal networks research, studying Twitter, for example, can provide useful information in understating the use of technology in building a community or in building relationships or sustaining existing ones (Gruzd et al., 2011). Huffaker (2010) used social network analysis of more than 632,000 messages from more than 33,000 participants in Google Groups to analyze the behavior of online leaders, the language they use to start a discussion, and influence others. He found that high centrality, frequency of communication, and credibility were critical for effectiveness of leadership in virtual environments.

As we highlighted in different part of the book, networks are utilized, as well as studied substantially, in emergency and crisis management. Virtual networks are also utilized heavily in the field. Application of social network analysis is becoming more common in studying networks in face-to-face environments as well as in virtual ones. Chatfield, Scholl, and Brajawidagda (2013) studied citizens' share of emergency information generated in response to tsunamis in Indonesia as early warning system, as well as real time data sharing. Citizens' re-tweets of the Indonesian government's early warnings were considered as coproduction and re-sharing to a larger audience during 2012 earthquake. The early warning tweet reached more than four million citizens in less than 15 minutes, according to the authors. As dynamic environments of disasters require timely sharing of critical information, without virtual networks and opportunity to share or re-share the emergency information, it would be impossible to reach out to that many people in a short period of time. The researchers used the social network analysis techniques to analyze the information share and spread of information in the network using Twitter. The Indonesian Agency for Meteorology, Climatology and Geophysics (Badan Meteorologi, Klimatologi, dan Geofisika—BMKG) and its tweet were used as a case in analyzing information sharing. Citizens and other agencies were considered actors in the network and information sharing and exchange with others was considered as links in this particular case. Chatfield, Reddick, and Brajawidagda (2015) studied an important concept in networks and network governance: trust. They use Twitter data to investigate the impact of government surveillance policy and practice on reciprocal trust and international security cooperation between Indonesia and Australia. The study primarily focuses on the role of social media use and its impact on trust and security agreements between the two countries using social network analysis to investigate pattern of reciprocal communication on trust. Indonesian citizens start a protest and policy advocacy against Australia using a hashtag on twitter #ganyangaustralia ("Crush Australia") (p. 119). As the social network analysis results demonstrated, the Indonesian government halted the bi-lateral agreement as a result of the virtual protest.

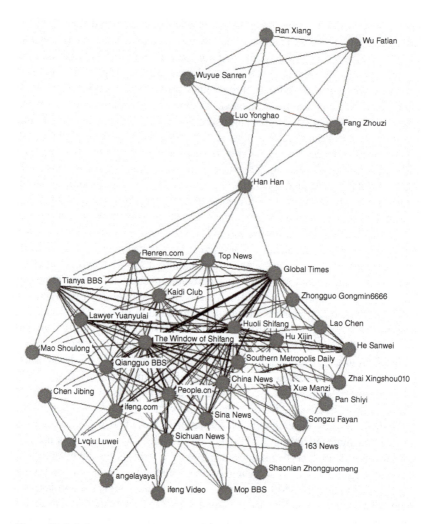

Figure 13.1 Subgroup Relations in Risk Communication Network in Virtual Environments

   Shi, Kapucu, Zhu, Guo, and Haupt (2017) studied risk communication and critical actors in social media with potentially negative influence, which shared harsh criticism (potentially leading to protests) of government agencies over social media. The study used social network analysis and relational data, with focus on traditional measures such as density, centralization, structure holes, and subgroups. The study also provides visualization of network data in social media using UCINET and NetDraw software programs. The study highlighted that central actors in the network controlled most of the information and critical resources and demonstrated most threat diffusion. This study found limited interaction between core actors in the network and government agencies and substantial discrepancy in their risk perception.

As an example of social network analysis in virtual environments, Shi et al. (2017) operationalized subgroups as cohesive structures within the network. Having minimum 3 members in each group, there are 274 subgroups identified in the network. Overlapping subgroups were also identified, which is very common in both face-to-face and virtual networks. The study identifies 53 subgroups with 6 members in each clique. Connections of nodes or ties in the network mean the nodes belong to the same subgroup in the entire network. The more connections a subgroup has, the thicker the lines are in the visual representation. *People.cn*, *Huoli Shifang*, the *Window of Shifang*, and *Global Times* had most connections. Visual representation, as demonstrated in Figure 13.1, can be useful in identifying central actors as well as actors in the periphery.

Conclusion

The internet and new technologies offer a wealth of opportunities and resources, which can increase the productivity of virtual networks. There is a growing concern among researchers in public administration that technology is leading to a decrease in organizational citizenship behavior and reduced organizational performance. This concern continues to grow with the advancement of new technologies and social networking platforms. These concerns can be replaced by opportunities if public administrators can embrace ICT and virtual networks as tools for re-engaging citizens and increasing public service performance. Research shows that these tools are can enhance people's involvement in social networking and social capital building. Their increased social capital and trust, in turn, leads them to develop a sense of community commitment both at organizational and network levels. Yet their new community may be defined more by their online social network, more so than the traditional community boundaries of neighborhood. This involvement in their community eventually leads some people to become civically engaged online and may even lead to physical civic engagement. With its potential, the internet and its multiple uses will continue to be a central topic in network governance and leadership in virtual networks in the future.

Networks in virtual environments, in addition to complementary nature to face-to-face networks, have certain advantages over traditional network arrangements. If properly arranged and encircled with appropriate infrastructure, such networks provide vast benefits of speed, flexibility, and easy and fast access to knowledge and information. Networks and the impact of virtual environments on networks will provide a rich research agenda and healthy research questions to explore in the future.

References

Adalat, M., Niazi, M. A., & Vasilakos, A. V. (2018). Variations in power of opinion leaders in online communication networks. *Royal Society Open Science*, 5(10). doi:10.1098/rsos.180642

Ahuja, M. K., & Carley, K. M. (1999). Network structure in virtual organizations. *Organization Science, 10*(6), 741–757.

Ahuja, M. K., & Galvin, J. E. (2003). Socialization in virtual groups. *Journal of Management, 29*(2), 161–185.

Ardichvili, A. (2008). Learning and knowledge sharing in virtual communities of practice: Motivators, barriers, and enablers. *Advances in Developing Human Resources, 10*(4), 541–554.

Aviv, R., Erlich, Z., & Ravid, G. (2008). Analysis of reciprocity and transitivity in online collaboration networks. *Connections, 28*(1), 27–39.

Borgatti, S. P. (2002). *NetDraw: Graph visualization software.* Harvard, MA: Analytic Technologies.

Borgatti, S. P., Everett, M. G., & Johnson, J. C. (2017). *Analyzing social networks.* Los Angeles, CA: Sage Publications.

Breu, K., & Hemingway, C. J. (2004). Making organisations virtual: The hidden cost of distributed teams. *Journal of Information Technology, 19*(3), 191–202.

Cascio, W. F. (1999). Virtual workplace: Implications for organizational behavior. In C. L. Cooper & D. M. Rousseau (Eds.), *Trends in organizational behavior: The virtual organization.* New York, NY: Wiley.

Chatfield, A. T., Reddick, C. G., & Brajawidagda, U. (2015). Government surveillance disclosures, bilateral trust and Indonesia-Australia cross-border security cooperation: Social network analysis of Twitter data. *Government Information Quarterly, 32*(2), 118–128.

Chatfield, A. T., Scholl, H. J., & Brajawidagda, U. (2013). Tsunami early warnings via Twitter in government: Net-savvy citizens' co-production of time-critical public information services. *Government Information Quarterly, 30*(4), 377–386.

Cohen, S. G., & Mankin, D. (1999). Collaboration in the virtual organization. In C. L. Cooper & D. M. Rousseau (Eds.), *Trend in organizational behavior: The virtual organization* (pp. 105–120). Chichester: John Wiley & Sons Ltd.

Davis, S. C. (2002). Virtual emergency operations centers. *Risk Management,* 46–52.

Eglene, O., Dawes, S. S., & Schneider, C. A. (2007). Authority and leadership patterns in public sector knowledge networks. *The American Review of Public Administration, 37*(1), 91–113.

Engel, D., Woolley, A. W., Jing, L. X., Chabris, C. F., & Malone, T. W. (2014). Reading the mind in the eyes or reading between the lines? Theory of mind predicts collective intelligence equally well online and face-to-face. *PLoS One, 9*(12), e115212.

FEMA. (2018). *Virtual operations support team administrator.* Retrieved from www.fema.gov/media-library-data/1541075761399-4e4b70542f63fccc962 da2281fac648c/NIMS509_VirtualOperationSupportTeamAdministrator_10042018_CLEAN.PDF

Fischer, C. S. (1997). Technology and community: Historical complexities. *Sociological Inquiry, 67*(1), 113–118.

Fountain, J. E. (2001). *Building the virtual state: Information technology and institutional change.* Washington, DC: Brookings Intuition Press.

Galaskiewicz, J., Bielefeld, W., & Dowell, M. (2006). Networks and organizational growth: A study of community-based nonprofits. *Administrative Science Quarterly, 51*(3), 337–380.

Ganley, D., & Lampe, C. (2009). The ties that bind: Social network principles in online communities. *Decision Support Systems, 47*(3), 266–274.

Grabowski, M., & Roberts, K. H. (1999). Risk mitigation in virtual organizations. *Organization Science, 10*(6), 704–721.

Granovetter, M. (1985). Economic action and social structure: The problem of embeddedness. *American Journal of Sociology, 91*(3), 481–510.

Griffith, T. L., Sawyer, J. E., & Neale, M. A. (2003). Virtualness and knowledge: Managing the love triangle of organizations, individuals, and information technology. *MIS Quarterly, 27*(2), 265–287.

Gruzd, A., Wellman, B., & Takhteyev, Y. (2011). Imagining Twitter as an imagined community. *American Behavioral Scientist, 55*(10), 1294–1318.

Hampton, K. N. (2003). Grieving for a lost network: Collective action in a wired suburb special issue: ICTs and community networking. *The Information Society, 19*(5), 417–428.

Hu, Q., & Kapucu, N. (2014). Information communication technology (ICT) utilization for effective emergency management networks. *Public Management Review, 18*(3), 323–348.

Hu, Q., Khosa, S., & Kapucu, N. (2016). The intellectual structure of empirical network research in public administration. *Journal of Public Administration Research and Theory, 26*(4), 593–612.

Huffaker, D. (2010). Dimensions of leadership and social influence in online communities. *Human Communication Research, 36*(4), 593–617.

Hughes, A. L., & Palen, L. (2009). Twitter adoption and use in mass convergence and emergency events. *International Journal of Emergency Management, 6*(3–4), 248–260.

Huxham, C., & Vangen, S. (2000). Leadership in the shaping and implementation of collaboration agendas: How things happen in a (not quite) joined-up world. *Academy of Management Journal, 43*(6), 1159–1166.

Jung, K., & Park, H. W. (2014). Citizens' social media use and homeland security information policy: Some evidences from Twitter users during the 2013 North Korea nuclear test. *Government Information Quarterly, 31*(4), 563–573.

Kasper-Fuehrer, E. C., & Ashkanasy, N. M. (2001). Communicating trustworthiness and building trust in interorganizational virtual organizations. *Journal of Management, 27*(3), 235–254.

Kasper-Fuehrer, E. C., & Ashkanasy, N. M. (2003). The interorganizational virtual organization: Defining a Weberian ideal. *International Studies of Management & Organization, 33*(4), 34–64.

Katims, L. (2013). *Virtual operations support Teams harness social media.* Retrieved December 7, 2018, from www.govtech.com/em/disaster/Virtual-Operations-Support-Teams-Social-Media.html

Kavanaugh, A. L., & Patterson, S. J. (2001). The impact of community computer networks on social capital and community involvement. *American Behavioral Scientist, 45*(3), 496–509.

Klijn, E. H., & Koppenjan, J. (2016). *Governance networks in the public sector.* New York, NY: Routledge.

Krackhardt, D., & Kilduff, M. (1999). Whether close or far: Social distance effects on perceived balance in friendship networks. *Journal of Personality and Social Psychology, 76*(5), 770–782.

Kraut, R., Kiesler, S., Boneva, B., Cummings, J. N., Helgeson, V., & Crawford, A. M. (2002). Internet paradox revisited. *Journal of Social Issues, 58*(1), 49–74.

Krebs, V., & Holley, J. (2004). Building sustainable communities through social network development. *The Nonprofit Quarterly* (Spring), 46–53.

Lin, N. (2002). *Social capital: A theory of social structure and action* (Vol. 19). Cambridge: Cambridge University Press.

McGuire, M., & Silvia, C. (2009). Does leadership in networks matter? Examining the effect of leadership behaviors on managers' perceptions of network effectiveness. *Public Performance & Management Review, 33*(1), 34–62.

Meijer, A. J. (2011). Networked coproduction of public services in virtual communities: From a government-centric to a community approach to public service support. *Public Administration Review, 71*(4), 598–607.

Mowshowitz, A. (1997). On the theory of virtual organization. *Systems Research and Behavioral Science, 14*(6), 373–384.

New York Times. (2017). *Thousands cried for help as Houston flooded.* Retrieved November 19, 2018, from www.nytimes.com/interactive/2017/08/30/us/houston-flood-rescue-cries-for-help.html

Nie, N. H. (2001). Sociability, interpersonal relations, and the internet: Reconciling conflicting findings. *American Behavioral Scientist, 45*(3), 420–435.

Nohria, N., & Berkley, J. D. (1994). The virtual organization: Bureaucracy, technology, and the implosion of control. In C. Heckscher & A. Donellon (Eds.), *The post-bureaucratic organization: New perspectives on organizational change* (pp. 108–128). Thousand Oaks, CA: Sage Publications.

Park, C. H., & Johnson, E. (2018). Determinants of collaboration between digital volunteer networks and formal response organizations in catastrophic disasters. *International Journal of Organization Theory and Behavior, 22*(2), 155–173.

Popp, J., MacKean, G., Casebeer, A., Milward, H. B., & Lindstrom, R. (2014). *Interorganizational networks: A review of the literature to inform practice.* Washington, DC: IBM Center for the Business of Government.

Putnam, R. D. (2000). *Bowling alone: The collapse and revival of American community.* New York, NY: Simon and Schusters Paperbacks.

Quan-Haase, A., & Wellman, B. (2004). How does the internet affect social capital. *Social Capital and Information Technology, 113*, 135–113.

Resnick, P. (2002). Beyond bowling together: SocioTechnical capital. In J. M. Carroll (Ed.), *HCI in the new millennium* (pp. 247–272). New York, NY: Addison-Wesley.

Roberts, N. C. (2011). Beyond smokestacks and silos: Open-Source, web-enabled coordination in organizations and networks. *Public Administration Review, 71*(5), 677–693.

Sarker, S., Ahuja, M., Sarker, S., & Kirkeby, S. (2011). The role of communication and trust in global virtual teams: A social network perspective. *Journal of Management Information Systems, 28*(1), 273–310.

Shen, C., & Cage, C. (2015). Exodus to the real world? Assessing the impact of offline meetups on community participation and social capital. *New Media & Society, 17*(3), 394–414.

Shi, J., Kapucu, N., Zhu, Z., Guo, X., & Haupt, B. (2017). Assessing risk communication in social media for crisis prevention: A social network analysis of microblog. *Journal of Homeland Security and Emergency Management.* doi:10.1515/jhsem-2016-0058

Siegel, D. A. (2009). Social networks and collective action. *American Journal of Political Science, 53*(1), 122–138.

Uzzi, B. (1997). Social structure and competition in interfirm networks: The paradox of embeddedness. *Administrative Science Quarterly, 42*(2), 35–67.

Wellman, B., Haase, A. Q., Witte, J., & Hampton, K. (2001). Does the internet increase, decrease, or supplement social capital? Social networks, participation, and community commitment. *American Behavioral Scientist, 45*(3), 436–455.

14 Global Perspectives on Networks

This chapter draws attention to networks in a global context. Even though networks are used around the world, the analysis of global networks is in its early stages relative to the utilization of networks in addressing domestic policy domains and social problems. These networks are conceptualized and studied in different ways around the globe. This chapter offers perspectives of global network research and provides examples of global networks, with an emphasis on interorganizational coordination across national territories and on a global scale. This chapter also provides a network analysis application of the UN SDGs to illustrate how network analysis can be used to study complex global networks within an important policy domain. The chapter addresses the following questions:

- How can we define and characterize global networks?
- What are some of the examples of global networks?
- How are networks and partnerships applied in global context?
- Can network analysis tools and methods be applied in analyzing global networks?
- How network governance principles can be applied in dealing networks and partnerships at a global scale?

Global Networks

The emergence of new public management was a central part of public sector reforms in the 1980s and 1990s, in which international organizations such as the World Bank and International Monetary Fund (IMF) played a role in promoting (Kapucu, 2010; Kopell, 2010; Koza & Lewin, 1999; McNutt & Pal, 2011). In this regard, governance referred to governing with and through networks. The administrative reforms around the globe illuminated the importance of public management and governance in economic and societal performance. *Global networks* refer to two or more international or global organizations collaboratively addressing complex policy issues at a global scale.

Public policy agendas are not set within national boundaries anymore. Many major policy issues, such as impact of climate change and anti-terrorism efforts, require regional and international collaboration (Kapucu, 2012). Governance networks in Europe, for example, "attempt to improve coordination between relatively dependent actors for the purpose of solving societal problems" (Klijn, 2008, p. 505). Successful governance networks address a

---

Global Networks

Institutional arrangements with resources and capabilities to address policy problems at global scale.

---

properly functioning public administration, the improvement of performance and accountability, intergovernmental relations, and network governance, which involves networks of state and non-state actors (Klijn, 2008).

In earlier chapters of the book, we provided network governance concepts and applications primarily from the United States. This chapter extends those network concepts and perspectives to a global level. Global networks can be developed in addressing issues at regional, continental, international, and global significance. Similar to networks previously mentioned in the book, global networks can also address policy domains such as healthcare, economic development, security, environment, and disasters. Global networks involve global, international, regional, and local actors (Feiock, Moon, & Park, 2008; Reinicke et al., 2000; Marcussen & Torfing, 2007). Actors can be states, international organizations, and civil society actors as well as organized groups. Sometimes the global networks might engage local organizations as partners in host countries.

Global networks complement public policy institutions through certain activities, such as creating agendas, gathering and disseminating knowledge, and creating new markets and deepening existing ones (Reinicke et al., 2000). Global networks address important global policy concerns that cannot be addressed by local or national actors. We will focus on sustainability as a major policy issue with detailed background and a network analysis as United Nations and its sub-units as major global actors.

A global network, for example, formed around environmental concerns specific to the case of the ozone layer's degradation that began in 1977 (Reinicke et al., 2000). The network, facilitated by the United Nations, linked individuals and organizations from different countries, sectors, and civil society groups. They proved themselves effective in combining diverse groups to discuss common problems that required collaborations and resources (intellectual, financial, and physical). Certainly, CFC emission (chlorofluorocarbons) was of global concern and required the action from many countries, particularly those that produced the largest quantities of these chemicals. Civil-society organizations were part of the network that provided scientific evidence to address this important issue. Global network arrangements "embrace the very forces of globalization that have confounded and complicated traditional governance structures, challenging the operational capacity and democratic responsiveness of governments" (Reinicke et al., 2000, p. xxi).

Factors Influencing Success of Global Networks

Global networks are formed to bridge the governance gaps left behind by economic and political liberalization and technological innovation (Reinke & Deng, 2000). Global networks are also formed to address policy problems at global significance. These networks differ in purpose and scope compared to the networks we discussed earlier in the book.

Even though global networks are different in scope and scale, some of the network characteristics we discussed before can lead to stability and sustainability for global networks. These include prior relationships and trust, legitimacy, capacity, formal legal agreements, specific member characteristics in line with the needs of the network, and the existence of a well-organized structure promoted by a network administrative organization that ensures administrative control of the network (Considine & Lewis, 2012; Koza & Lewin, 1999; Lee & Kim, 2011; Van Raaij, 2006). However, in a global environment, there are various possible pitfalls for this type of network, including the prospect that individual actors might lose their interest in the issue at hand.

Effective facilitation of global networks needs to strike a balance between the actors that have differing perspectives and objectives, the level of participation, and the linkages between processes and outcomes of networks. Although actors disagree on certain matters which lead them to believe that they might not get along, there might be some similarities in views regarding certain policy issues that can be highlighted by lead actors in the network. It is also important to encourage connections between the actors in order to aid in building trust and common understanding across the network (Hubacek et al., 2006).

Regardless of how a sudden development pushes organizations and other actors to engage globally, trust and legitimacy building are critical for global networks, as we discussed earlier in the book as a critical issue in network governance. Network managers and/or key players may be selected to progress the network, depending on how trusted they are by fellow actors. As network governance effectiveness require processes to be clearly linked to network outcome, actors in the network must simultaneously balance consultation with goal delivery or "getting the process right while getting the product out the door" (Reinicke et al., 2000, p. xvi). Adequate funding is also an issue in global networks, and should be addressed in the beginning stages because, undeniably, all networks absorb financial and other resources, especially globe-spanning ones. Sustaining global networks are also as critical in formation and development phases. Adding members to the network can strengthen a network and also provide additional resources to the global network. Important parties should always be involved in global networks to ensure that the network is well-resourced. In the previous ozone example, the United Nations could not tackle this problem alone as other parties were critical to effectively addressing the problem of the CFC emission.

Measuring the success of the global networks is not easy. Success will vary across networks and policy domains. Success may be measured by the achievement of a goal (its outcomes), a continued collaboration across organizations (its longevity), or in forming ties with new organizations (its growth). There are benefits to forming networks with many ties, especially at a global scale, where more contributors are needed by default (Siegel, 2011). This strategy of multiple actors could be utilized in a number of examples of global networks. The Global Water Partnership is one (Bodin & Prell, 2011; Brousseau, Dedeurwaerdere, & Siebenhuner, 2012; Reinicke et al., 2000). International organizations, local businesses, and NGOs were brought together to create innovative and participatory forms of governance in water management. Global network can bring additional opportunity to apply holistic perspectives on network analysis in public policy and management (Jho, 2007; Kapucu & Demiroz, 2011; Koza & Lewin, 1999; Scott & Ulibarri, 2019). Effectiveness of global networks might have challenges similar to local or national scale networks discussed earlier in the book. Challenges because of resource needs, legitimacy building at the global level, and transaction cost facilitating multiple actors at a global level might bring additional challenges to global networks.

In order to form global networks, visionary leaders (whether individuals or institutions) are needed to promote the creation of these networks. In order to ensure sustainability, these networks must include appropriate members, engage stakeholders from different sectors, create a shared vision collaboratively, be willing to share power, develop leadership, ensure legitimacy, and have appropriate resources (Reinke & Deng, 2000; De Rynk & Voets, 2006; Tang & Tang, 2014). The diversity of actors makes it possible for them to use different expertise and approaches to bear on policy problems and give a voice to otherwise unheard or unengaged institutions.

The study of networks and relational approaches involve the role that the structure of interactions plays in understanding individual behavior and ultimately aggregate network behavior. The study of networks has assisted in further understanding of several political topics. First, civic culture plays a role in enabling democracy and delivering favorable democratic performance. Second, the participation in a social movement is a frequently risky action that depends fundamentally on the behavior of others. Third, the development of party systems and the potential for civil strife can be predicted by the presence of societal cleavages. Fourth, networks of individuals can describe the connections and interactions between members of legislative bodies, such as the relationships behind the introduction and passing of legislation in the US Congress (Siegel, 2011). Even though global networks primarily address globally significant issues, effective implementation of the strategies cannot be accomplished without fully engaging local groups and actors.

Differences in understanding and appreciation of networks and networking might play important role in effective participation and success in global networks. Public managers might interact with the external environment depending on their perceived understanding, or context of the network or policy environment, before they go as far to participate and/or create their own network. Similar to success in political networks, public managers and their networking skills can play an important role in member participation and therefore, the effectiveness of network governance. Public managers in the US and the UK were studied utilizing large data sets of local government managers. Frequent interactions with those holding political positions suggested an openness to allowing changes to occur relating to preferences and policies (O'Toole, Walker, Meier, & Boyne, 2007). While there were similarities between the public managers in the two countries, there were still substantial differences as well. Some of the differences occurred because of different functional needs and the political realities or policy settings, such as unitary and federal systems (O'Toole et al., 2007). Overall, it appears that the public managers in the US and UK face similar challenges when it comes to effective collaboration and network governance. However, trying to collaborate on an international level presents a whole new depth of barriers in relation to the respective political frameworks and the understanding of global actors and their cultures.

Flexibility and adaptability are key to success for networks in a global environment. Rai (2007) examined the sustainability and growth of a decades-old food delivery network, dabbawallas (lunchbox), in India. The endurance of this network as a custom is significant as "many traditions are being overturned as a result of globalization" (Rai, 2007, p. 1). This food delivery network consists of a complex network of individuals and systems that, together, provide a reliable way for customers to receive home-made food at work. Instead of stagnating, this network has shown flexibility by utilizing new technologies, such as the internet and cell phones, to enhance its service (Rai, 2007). Beyond flexibility, the longevity and proven reliability of this system creates a strong sense of legitimacy and trust that plays a part in its survival and growth. Furthermore, there is high interdependency amongst the different components of this network, from customers who rely on the system, to the dabbawallas cooks, and railway system. Rai (2007) noted that the lunches are delivered even in the most difficult or circumstances and "the precision and efficiency of the dabbawallas has been likened to the internet" (p. 1). Thus, all of these factors, along with societal customs and needs, will likely continue to promote the growth of this network system.

Technological innovations create new ways of measuring and researching global networks, similar to virtual networks we discussed in chapter thirteen. McNutt and Pal (2011) explored virtual policy networks (VPNs) and the promise of analyzing networks by utilizing the internet. In this case, they were able to map and explore policy networks through the web, making general findings on the prominence of policy networks worldwide. They note that utilizing traditional methods such as inductive research, along with web network analysis, can provide a much clearer picture of global policy networks (McNutt & Pal, 2011).

From a broader international perspective, that "profound and continuing change in our global environment—social, political, and economic—today demands commensurate changes in our institutions of global governance, not the least in the institution that lies at the core of the international system, the United Nations" (Reinicke et al., 2000, p. vii). Thus, the UN finds itself acknowledging that they can no longer simply deal with governments. It is imperative for them to also partner with a variety of public, private, nonprofit, nongovernmental entities to achieve their goals. The role of the UN must adapt to new realities depending on specific contexts and needs. This means that the UN could be a network administrator, implementer, facilitator, coordinator, financier, or convener depending on what is needed at that point in time. Furthermore, it could serve as a neutral and safe platform for a variety of global networks, or alternatively, as the driving agency—setting the standards for various global issues.

Examples of Global Networks

From industry players to nations and global actors collaborating to address global problems, horizontal collaborations are the ways in which organizations at all levels are dealing with the increasingly dynamic global environment. Global alliance networks, for example, are "multiparty alliances, in which multilateral transactions among the network members are facilitated by the network" (Kosa & Lewin, 1999, p. 639). Koza and Lewin (1999) examined how mid-tier accounting firms' inability to individually compete with large global firms led to the formation of an international alliance network, Nexia International. As an example of business strategy, "Nexia international was created to provide new incremental revenue opportunities, as well as expanded global reach beyond what any of the member firms could achieve on their own" (Koza & Lewin, 1999, p. 645). Thus, Nexia International has to continually find new ways to promote member identification within the network and ensure control and compliance, making it a continually evolving network.

In addition to business alliances, we can provide several examples of global networks with specific emphasis on policy and social issues, which is our focus in the book. The Organization for Economic Cooperation and Development (OECD) (2007) highlighted the importance of measuring societal progress worldwide in order to promote evidence-based decision-making that addresses global challenges. To this end, various global organizations such as the European Commission, the OECD, the Organization of the Islamic Conference, the United Nations Development Programme, and the World Bank made a commitment to join together toward "measuring and fostering the progress of societies in all their dimensions and to supporting initiatives at the country level" (OECD, 2007, p. 1). We can highlight the UN Millennium Development Goals as an example of best practice toward creating uniform indicators of international progress. They invite other potential partners to join in this effort to promote measurement of societal progress. The eight Millennium Development

Goals are now replaced by seventeen UN Sustainable Development Goals, which we will discuss in detail later. Different from business strategy, global networks require different set of network arrangements and characteristics to be successful and sustainable.

Several international organizations play a lead or network administrative organization (NAO) role at the global scale. Major examples of applications of international organizations and global networks are the OECD, UN, UN Office of the Coordination of Humanitarian Affairs (OCHA), and World Health Organization (WHO). Similar to applications Chapters 10–13, these global actors play critical role in health, economic development and environment (sustainability), and humanitarian relief and disaster assistance.

The Organization for Economic Cooperation and Development (OECD) is a global public policy network that has turned "modernizing government" into a key part of its activities for its member and nonmember government partnerships (McNutt & Pal, 2011). The objective of the OECD is to promote policies that aim to improve the economic and social well-being of people around the world (OECD, n.d.) In the Istanbul Declaration of 2007, the OECD, the European Commission, The Organisation of Islamic Cooperation (OIC), the UN and its Development Program, and the World Bank stated their commitment to measuring and fostering the progress of societies in all dimensions in order to reach their ultimate goal of improving policy making, democracy, and the well-being of citizens (OECD, 2007).

The International Space Station (ISS) exemplified the ways in which a multinational project is initiated, sustained, altered, and completed (Lambright & Pizzarella, 2008). Unlike much of the public administration research that focuses on domestic social service delivery, the study of the ISS involves a technological project in an international environment, although it began as transnational US project with foreign assistance. One key factor that explains its successful multinational collaboration is strong international relations among fifteen participating nations, in addition to technology, organization, domestic relations, and leadership. Other types of policy issues that involve science and technology are climate change, global energy, disease, natural disaster, and terrorism.

The UN is an international organization that involves the governmental, nongovernmental, private, and civil society sectors. The major goals of UN for the global community are maintaining worldwide peace and security, developing relations among nations, and fostering cooperation between nations in order to solve economic, social, cultural, or humanitarian international problems. Its three-track approach, "from vision to reality," is comprised of the following steps: strengthen and consolidate existing networks by focusing on learning processes, build implementation networks to revitalize important conventions, and launch new networks (Reinicke et al., 2000, pp. 80–81). The many roles of the UN in global public policy networks include convener, platform for negotiations, social entrepreneurs, norm entrepreneurs, multilevel network manager, capacity builders, and financier for operational programs (Reinicke et al., 2000, p. 83). In order to make the UN fit for global networks, it must use mechanisms for issue prioritization and coordination to ensure that its activities do not duplicate the work of other multilateral organizations (Reinicke et al., 2000, p. 88).

The UN Office of the Coordination of Humanitarian Affairs (OCHA), along other UN agencies and organizations, plays a major role in the United Nations International Strategy for Disaster Reduction (UNISDR). The UN system, as a global platform, aims to decrease risk of disasters, through technology, knowledge sharing, capacity building, economic development tools, and global partnerships. A global platform is referred to intentional institutional arrangements with resources and capabilities for facilitating the formation, development, and implementation of collaborative networks at global scale. The UNISDR is a useful international vehicle for leaders and officials to share their experiences, commit to action, and further guide the UN international strategy for disaster reduction system in building disaster resilience communities worldwide. The platform encourages the role of regional and sub-regional organizations in coordinating implementation of disaster plans in addition to the involvement of global actors. Standards and indicators for measuring the effectiveness of disaster risk reduction should be developed by UNISDR system. UNISDR encourages cross-sector cooperation that makes best use of available information and technology to identify and prepare for emerging risks associated with technological hazards and pandemics. The depletion of ecosystems and increasing urban risk, coupled with the role of local governments and partnerships to transform policies and knowledge into concrete actions, make the role of UNISDR and its collaboration with local and national actors. Previous experiences, such as 2011 earthquake in Japan and 1999 earthquake in Turkey, illustrate that well-planned and coordinated recovery realizes better outcomes, and supports sustainability and disaster resilience as promoted by UNISDR (Kapucu & Liou, 2014).

In addition to global networks addressing issues around health, economic and environmental sustainability, and disasters, there are examples of global advocacy. Most of the advocacy networks are formed around human rights and environmental issues. For example, the International Campaign to Ban Landmines, a transnational advocacy network, puts pressure on the international community to deal with the issue of landmines, utilizing media and international personalities to advance their cause. While such transnational advocacy networks aim to "pressure states and international organizations to address specific policy issues" (Reinke & Deng, 2000, p. 25) other networks, such as Roll Back Malaria (RBM) aim to coordinate efforts and spread knowledge to better address an important health issue (Reinke & Deng, 2000). These are just two of the many types of global advocacy networks that seek to bridge gaps and meet needs at a global scale.

Leadership, partnership, and coordinated support from the international community are essential for the success of global networks. In the following section, we provide a specific example of United Nations SDGs with a brief network analysis of the UN agencies and the global level organizations involved in implementing said goals.

United Nations Sustainable Development Goals

The UN has several initiatives and goals, yet one of the primary goals of the organization is to improve individual's well-being. One way to ensure the improvement of individual's well-being is through sustainable development, which includes the promotion of prosperity and economic opportunities, increased social well-being, and environmental protection. In this section, we analyze the 17 SDGs laid out by the recent UN initiative. The question remains however, if the UN sustainable development goals are critical for the global community, how can the global community find ways to successfully implement them (Bacchus, 2018)?

The United Nations compiled a list of goals to achieve sustainable development. The goals, based on the success of Millennium Development Goals, also combine the three core dimensions of sustainability: economic, environmental, and social (Bacchus, 2018). The list was compiled via a Resolution at a General Assembly Meeting and was adopted in 2015 (UN, n.d.). The SDGs also include 169 targets to measure implementations of them. In this chapter, we primarily focus on the 17 goals with a specific focus on the partnership goal of 17. SDG goal 17 is our special emphasis, because of its focus on strengthening global partnerships for sustainable development. We will provide some network analysis examples of the SPGs, and organizations responsible for implementing them, toward the end of the chapter (Table 14.1).

Partnerships for Sustainable Development

Partnership networks are critical for the successful implementation of the SGD initiative in the global platform. The platform is open to all interested stakeholders, including government agencies at all levels, nongovernmental organizations, the private sector, and scientific and academic communities to share knowledge and resources. Stakeholder partnerships and engagement are critical for bringing economic, technology, knowledge, and human resources in building capacity and achieving SDGs and targets.

SDG 17, partnership for the goals, targets capacity building by enhancing "international support for implementing effective and targeted capacity-building in developing countries to support national plans to implement all the sustainable development goals, including through North-South, South-South and triangular cooperation" (UN, n.d.). The SPG partnership goal requires "the global partnership for sustainable development, complemented by multi-stakeholder partnerships that mobilize and share knowledge, expertise, technology and financial resources, to support the achievement of the sustainable development goals in all countries, in particular developing countries" (UN, n.d.). This critical partnership role can be addressed within the network

Table 14.1 United Nations Sustainable Development Goals (SDGs)

#	SDG Title	SDG Goals
1	No Poverty	Reduce the proportion of men, women, and children of all ages living in poverty.
2	Zero Hunger	End hunger and ensure access by all people, to safe, nutritious, and sufficient food all year round.
3	Good Health and Well-Being	Reduce the number of health-related issues and deaths caused by diseases, substance abuse, traffic accidents, pollution, and other factors.
4	Quality Education	Meet education minimum targets for children and adults; additional funding for education facilities; increase number of educators.
5	Gender Equality	End all forms of discrimination and violence against women.
6	Clean Water and Sanitation	Achieve universal access to safe and affordable drinking water and sanitation.
7	Affordable and Clean Energy	Ensure universal access to affordable, reliable, and modern energy services.
8	Decent Work and Economic Growth	Promote inclusive and sustainable economic growth, employment, and decent work for all.
9	Industry, Innovation, and Infrastructure	Build resilient infrastructure, promote sustainable industrialization, and foster innovation.
10	Reduced Inequalities	Policies should be universal in principle, paying attention to the needs of disadvantaged and marginalized populations.
11	Sustainable Cities and Communities	Make cities inclusive, safe, resilient, and sustainable.
12	Responsible Production and Consumption	Promoting resource and energy efficiency, sustainable infrastructure, and providing access to basic services, green and decent jobs and a better quality of life for all.
13	Climate Action	Take urgent action to combat climate change and its impacts.
14	Life Below Water	Conserve and sustainably use the oceans, seas, and marine resources.
15	Life on Land	Sustainably manage forests, combat desertification, halt and reverse land degradation, and halt biodiversity loss.
16	Peace, Justice, and Strong Institutions	More efficient and transparent regulations put in place; comprehensive, realistic government budgets to combat corruption.
17	Partnerships for the Goals	Sustainable development agenda requires partnerships between governments, the private sector and civil society; Needed at the global, regional, national and local levels.

Source: UN Sustainable Development Goals (n.d.)

governance framework, as it requires multi-jurisdictional and cross sectoral, public, private, and nonprofit engagement. Within a very short period of SDG adaption, more than 1,800 partnerships were identified. The Action Network on Sustainable Transport, the Higher Education Sustainability Initiative, and Every Woman Every Child are some of the examples (Bacchus, 2018, p. 159).

Even though the sustainable development goals are critical, and the partnership for success is imperative, these SDG's are not legally binding. It requires cooperation and collaboration amongst the states and entities within each. As noted, successful development requires partnerships between governments, the private sector, and civil society (UN, n.d.). The UN has begun collaborations with different industries already, which we list here and further discuss in terms of current arrangements in what follows:

SDG Media Zone—consists of live interviews, panel discussions, and other digital content. To be used as coverage during UN meetings. It was created as an initiative of the Office of the President of the UN General Assembly. *Media (SDG Media Compact)*—consists of more than 100 media and entertainment outlets. The compact requires companies to use their resources and leverage to advance the cause(s).

Mobile Industry—nearly 800 mobile device companies and Project Everyone, in tandem with the UN, created an app called "SDGs in Action." The app is a one stop shop to learn about the SDGs and contains an event creation and action section (social media aspect).

Advertising Industry—six of the world's largest communication companies each focused on a SDG for advocacy. Other agencies include social media presence.

Creative Community—includes Sony Pictures and Mattel. Using campaigns aimed at young children and television programming for UN SGDs implementation.

Spotlight Initiative—EU and UN program that specifically focuses on many forms of violence against women and girls.

The SDG was located within the 2030 Agenda (per UN Resolution 70/1.), which established the 17 pillars. In addition to this, a section further along in the Resolution is dedicated to Goal 17 implementation. The only core agencies listed under this section that were the UN and the World Trade Organization (WTO). All member states are also included. However, within the Resolution it mentions the funding mechanism to achieve these goals (which are usually one of the main obstacles) and references another Resolution. This leads to the Third International Conference on Financing for Development (per Resolution 69/313). Bringing the UN and WTO to a joint action is especially critical for addressing economic development and environmental sustainability discussions together.

Within the sustainability documents, financial institutions are identified that assist with infrastructures initiatives and SDGs implementation. The banks are

Asian Infrastructure Investment Bank, the Global Infrastructure Hub, the New Development Bank, the Asia Pacific Project Preparation Facility, the World Bank Group's Global Infrastructure Facility and the Africa50 Infrastructure Fund, as well as the increase in the capital of the Inter-American Investment Corporation. These are important actors in the network.

Additional partners for SDG implementation identified in Res. 69/313 include Organization for Economic Cooperation and Development (OECD) for the Group of 20 on base erosion and profit shifting. Also, to help combat illicit money flows, the International Monetary Fund (IMF) and the World Bank will assist both source and destination countries via risk mitigation mechanisms, such as the Multilateral Investment Guarantee Agency, while managing currency risk. The Green Climate Fund, the largest dedicated climate fund, was mentioned, as was the International Capital Market Association, both of which reduce the vulnerability of developing states to holdout creditors. The Basel Committee on Banking Supervision and other main international regulatory standard-setting bodies continue efforts to increase the voice of developing countries in the norm-setting process. As far as technology, the Climate Technology Centre and Network, the capacity-building wing of the World Intellectual Property Organization (WIPO), and the UNIDO National Cleaner Production Centres networks are also mentioned. As well as International Telecommunication Union.

The complexity of networks in addressing SDGs and jurisdictional overlaps require substantial effort for effective coordination and careful analysis of networks and network governance. In the following section, we provide some preliminary network perspectives on partnerships and interorganizational arrangements. This preliminary analysis primarily focuses on SPG and core organizations at global level. Detailed future research can add local, regional, and national level organizations to the network.

Network Analysis Application: Sustainable Development Goals and Global Actors

Networks and their characteristics are being studied across the globe to understand how organizational goals and network goals are achieved in different agency and policy settings. This section addresses using network analysis in understanding the SDGs goals and partnerships of global organizations. Data for this section was collected as an initial part of Belmont Forum Collaborative Research Food-Water-Energy Nexus: Enabling adaptive integration of technology to enhance community resilience (NSF Award #1830036). Kapucu is an investigator in this project.

Each agency and organization as part of SDG network was identified in the core UN SDG documents available online such as the UN system, UN Office of Partnerships, UN General Assembly Resolutions, and UN Water for this demonstration example in the chapter. The UN SDG website has a separate page for each goal. Each SDG page lists agencies, departments, partnerships, and programs that are responsible for that specific SDG. The UN program or department websites also explain what their focus is and which SDGs they specifically target. Primary agencies listed in accomplishing the SPG goals and core targets are identified. We kept the agencies and organizations at global level. Adding local, state, and regional organizations are beyond this demonstration example. Interorganizational ties are directional in this data set.

Network Visualization

Network analysis in this chapter was conducted using UCINET 6 and its NetDraw function (Borgatti, 2002; Borgatti, Everett, & Freeman, 2002). Figure 14.1 visually demonstrates core UN agencies at the global level and their interactions with other agencies in addressing SPGs implementation. Visualization of the UN agencies provides a diagnostic opportunity to observe organizational relationships. UNEP, UNDP, and UNISDR are connected in the network, for example.

Centrality

Centralization refers to the extent to which a network revolves around a single node or the node's centrality in a network is structural attributes of nodes in a network (position). The centrality measure of network position reflects the importance, influence, prominence of an actor in a network (Borgatti, Everett, & Johnson, 2017; Wasserman & Faust, 1994). In this directional Interorganizational network, indegree centrality measures the number of ties an

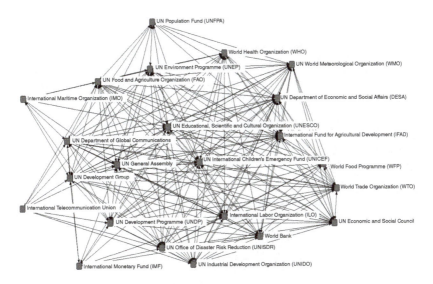

Figure 14.1 UN SDG Organization-to-Organization Network

organization receives and outdegree centrality measures the number of ties an organization sends to others (Borgatti et al., 2017). Organizations with high indegree centralities can have direct influence on many others; organizations with high outdegree centralities can be influenced directly by many other organizations in the network. In Table 14.2, we list key organizations based on degree and betweenness centrality measures. UN General Assembly,

Table 14.2 Key Organizations Based on Degree and Betweenness Centrality Measures

Indegree Centrality	Outdegree Centrality	Betweenness
UN General Assembly (22)	UN General Assembly (22)	UN General Assembly (12.927)
UN Department of Global Communications (22)	UN Department of Global Communications (22)	UN Department of Global Communications (12.927)
UN Development Group (22)	UN Development Group (22)	UN Development Group (12.927)
UN Environment Programme (UNEP) (21)	UN Environment Programme (UNEP) (21)	UN Development Programme (UNDP) (9.677)
UN Development Programme (UNDP) (21)	UN Development Programme (UNDP) (21)	UN Environment Programme (UNEP) (9.505)
UN Educational, Scientific and Cultural Organization (UNESCO) (21)	UN Educational, Scientific and Cultural Organization (UNESCO) (21)	UN Food and Agriculture Organization (FAO) (8.976)
UN Food and Agriculture (21)	UN Food and Agriculture (20)	UN Office of Disaster Risk Reduction (UNISDR) (7.944)
UN International Children's Emergency Fund (UNICEF) (20)	UN International Children's Emergency Fund (UNICEF) (20)	UN International Children's Emergency Fund (UNICEF) (5.515)
UN Office of Disaster Risk Reduction (UNISDR) (20)	UN Office of Disaster Risk Reduction (UNISDR) (20)	UN Industrial Development Organization (UNIDO) (4.781)
UN Department of Economic and Social Affairs (DESA) (19)	UN Department of Economic and Social Affairs (DESA) (19)	International Labor Organization (ILO) (2.625)
International Fund for Agricultural Development (IFAD) (19)	World Health Organization (WHO) (19)	
UN World Meteorological Organization (WMO) (19)	UN Industrial Development Organization (UNIDO) (19)	
World Bank (19)	World Bank (19)	
International Labor Organization (ILO) (19)	International Labor Organization (ILO) (19)	

Department of Global Communications, and UN Development Group have received 22 ties from other organizations and sent 22 ties to others. These organizations are most central actors in successful implementation of SDGs.

Betweenness

Betweenness, loosely, is the number of geodesic paths that pass through a node or an actor in a network. The number of times that any node need a given node to reach any other node by the shortest path or geodesic distance. If two non-adjacent actors j and k want to interact and actor i is on the path between j and k, then i may have some control over the interactions between j and k. Betweenness measures this control of i over other pairs of actors. The i may act as a bridge, an intermediary, broker, gate keeper, or a liaison actor. In its absence network communication gets substantial damage due to disruption of links between smaller groups or networks (Borgatti et al., 2017; Wasserman & Faust, 1994). Betweenness measures, in this demonstration, highlight the following organizations as critical for network success in implementing UN SDGs: UN General Assembly; UN Department of Global Communications, UN Development Group; UN Development Programme; UN Environment Programme (UNEP) and UN Food and Agriculture Organization (FAO). These organizations are in a better position to serve as brokers, intermediary, or liaisons in the network.

Clique Analysis

In addition to visualization and degree and the betweenness centrality measures we discussed, clique or subgroup analysis might be important for the networks responsible implementing SDGs. Networks are built from combining of dyads and triads into larger, but still closely connected sub-structures called cliques. A clique is simply a sub-set of actors who are more closely tied to each other than they are to actors who are not part of the group. Clique measures in also a useful tool in identifying closely linked groups of individuals or organizations in a network as a subgroup. Many of the approaches to understanding the structure of a network emphasize how dense connections are compounded and extended to develop larger cliques or subgroupings. This view of networks focuses attention on how connection of large networks structures can be built up out of small and tight components (Borgatti et al., 2017; Wasserman & Faust, 1994).

Network analysis with UCINET provides the following five cliques in implementing SDG goals of United Nations. UN General Assembly and UN Environment Programme (UNEP) plays critical role among the members of cliques in the network. In these cohesive subgroup actors interact or work together more frequently than actors are not part of these subgroups. Serving in a same group in addressing certain SDG goals might be one of the core reasons for this frequent interaction. Cliques identified in the following list using UCINET analysis can also be inspected visually in organization-to-organization network in Figure 14.1.

1. UN General Assembly UN Environment Programme (UNEP); UN World Food Programme (WFP); UN Department of Economic and Social Affairs (DESA); UN Development Programme (UNDP); UN Department of Global Communications; UN Economic and Social Council; UN Educational, Scientific and Cultural Organization (UNESCO); UN Food and Agriculture Organization (FAO); UN International Children's Emergency Fund (UNICEF); International Fund for Agricultural Development (IFAD); UN Office of Disaster Risk Reduction (UNISDR); UN World Meteorological Organization (WMO); UN Development Group; World Health Organization (WHO); World Trade Organization (WTO); UN Industrial Development Organization (UNIDO); World Bank International Labor Organization (ILO)

2. UN General Assembly UN Environment Programme (UNEP); UN Development Programme (UNDP); UN Department of Global Communications; UN Educational, Scientific and Cultural Organization (UNESCO); UN Food and Agriculture Organization (FAO); UN Development Group International Maritime Organization (IMO)

3. UN General Assembly; UN Environment Programme (UNEP); UN Development Programme (UNDP); UN Department of Global Communications; UN Food and Agriculture Organization (FAO); UN Office of Disaster Risk Reduction (UNISDR); UN Development Group; UN Industrial Development Organization (UNIDO); International Telecommunication Union

4. UN General Assembly; UN Development Programme (UNDP); UN Department of Global Communications; UN Educational, Scientific and Cultural Organization (UNESCO); UN International Children's Emergency Fund (UNICEF); UN Office of Disaster Risk Reduction (UNISDR); UN Development Group; International Monetary Fund (IMF); World Bank International Labor Organization (ILO)

5. UN General Assembly; UN Environment Programme (UNEP); UN Department of Economic and Social Affairs (DESA); UN Department of Global Communications; UN Educational, Scientific and Cultural Organization (UNESCO); UN Food and Agriculture Organization (FAO); UN International Children's Emergency Fund (UNICEF); International Fund for Agricultural Development (IFAD); UN World Meteorological Organization (WMO); UN Development Group World Health Organization (WHO); UN Population Fund (UNFPA)

Affiliation Networks

Affiliation networks are included here to provide organizational groupings in response to SDGs. Affiliation networks are two mode networks that allow us to study the dual perspectives of the actors and the core functions or events

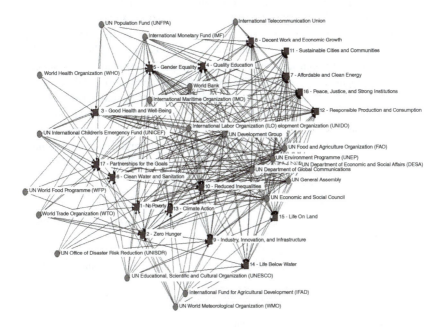

Figure 14.2 UN SDG Affiliation Network

(unlike one mode networks which focus on only one of them at a time). Affiliation networks look at collections or subsets of actors or subsets rather than ties between pairs of actors in a given network. Connections among members of one of the modes as based on linkages established through the second mode (Borgatti et al., 2017; Wasserman & Faust, 1994). In this example, SDGs provide affiliation for each global agency and UN sub agencies to address each goal for successful implementation. An affiliation network perspective allows the network to be examined from the perspective of an individual agency and an individual SDG because the actor's engagement or affiliations and the SPGs are included in the dataset (Figure 14.2).

We can get some insights from affiliation network visualization. Actors close together such as IMF, International Telecommunication Union, International Maritime Organization, International Labor Organization (ILO), and UN Development Groups are all listed for SDG 7, Affordable and Clean Energy. They are closely connected because they serve in implementing the same goal.

Conclusion

Global networks have not been studied from network perspective using network analysis methods and tools. We hope that this chapter will provide some ideas for further research on this domain in a global context. The impacts of network governance strategies for global networks, the conditions under which they are necessary, and which strategies prove to be most effective can be areas of investigation in the future. Another area can investigate the way that decisions are reached, the democratic nature of these decision processes, and how networks relate to more traditional institutions of democratic representation on a global scale. Networks in global communities require understanding how other cultures and communities work and value a relationship as part of the collaboration process. Throughout the book, we highlighted the importance of interorganizational collaboration and coordination; the role of trust, vision, and leadership; and shared cultures and mental models. These and other important elements of network governance plays facilitative role in dealing with global networks as well.

References

Bacchus, J. (2018). *The willing world: Shaping and sharing a sustainable global prosperity* Cambridge, UK: Cambridge University Press.

Bodin, Ö., & Prell, C. (Ed.). (2011). *Social networks and natural resource management: Uncovering the social fabric of environmental governance.* Cambridge, UK: Cambridge University Press.

Borgatti, S. P. (2002). *NetDraw: Graph visualization software.* Harvard, MA: Analytic Technologies.

Borgatti, S. P., Everett, M. G., & Freeman, L. C. (2002). *UCINET 6 for windows: Software for social network analysis.* Harvard, MA: Analytic Technologies.

Borgatti, S. P., Everett, M. G., & Johnson, J. C. (2017). *Analyzing social networks* (4th ed.). Los Angeles, CA: Sage Publications.

Brousseau, E., Dedeurwaerdere, T., & Siebenhuner, B. (Eds.). (2012). *Reflexive governance for global public goods.* Cambridge, MA: MIT Press.

Considine, M., & Lewis, J. M. (2012). Networks and interactivity: Ten years of street-level governance in the United Kingdom, the Netherlands, and Australia. *Public Management Review, 14*(1), 1–22.

De Rynk, F., & Voets, J. (2006). Democracy in area-based policy networks: The case of Ghent. *The American Review of Public Administration, 36*(1), 58–78.

Feiock, R. C., Moon, J. M., & Park, H. J. (2008). Is the world "flat" or "spiky"? Rethinking the governance implications of globalization for economic development. *Public Administration Review, 68*(1), 24–35.

Hubacek, K., Prell, C., Reed, M., Boys, D., Bonn, A., & Dean, C. (2006). Using stakeholder and social network analysis to support participatory processes. *The International Journal of Biodiversity Science and Management, 2,* 249–252.

Jho, W. (2007). Liberalization as a development strategy: Network governance in the Korean mobile telecom market. *Governance: An International Journal of Policy, Administration, and Institutions, 20*(4), 633–654.

Kapucu, N. (2010). *Governance reforms: Comparative perspectives.* Ankara, Turkey: International Strategic Research Organization (ISRO) Publications.

Kapucu, N. (2012). *The network governance in response to acts of terrorism: Comparative analyses.* New York, NY: Routledge.

Kapucu, N., & Demiroz, F. (2011). Measuring performance for collaborative public management using network analysis methods and tools. *Public Performance and Management Review, 34*(4), 551–581.

Kapucu, N., & Liou, K. T. (2014). *Disaster & development: Examining global issues and cases.* New York, NY: Springer.

Klijn, E-H. (2008). Governance and governance networks in Europe: An assessment of ten years of research on the theme. *Public Management Review, 10*(4), 505–525.

Kopell, G. S. J. (2010). *World rule: Accountability, legitimacy, and the design of global governance.* Chicago, IL: The University of Chicago Press.

Koza, M. P., & Lewin, A. Y. (1999). The coevolution of network alliances: A longitudinal analysis of an international professional service network. *Organization Science, 10*(5), 638–653.

Lambright, W. H., & Pizzarella, C. (2008). The space station and multinational collaboration: A merger of domestic and foreign policy. In L. B. Bingham & R. O'Leary (Eds.), *Big ideas in collaborative public management.* New York, NY: M. E. Sharpe.

Lee, J., & Kim, S. (2011). Exploring the role of social networks in affective organizational commitment: Network centrality, strength of weak ties, and structural holes. *American Review of Public Administration, 41*(2), 205–223.

Marcussen, M., & Torfing, J. (2007). *Democratic network governance in Europe.* New York, NY: Palgrave Macmillan.

McNutt, K., & Pal, L. A. (2011). "Modernizing government": Mapping global public policy networks. *Governance: An International Journal of Policy, Administration, and Institutions, 24*(3), 439–467.

OECD. (2007). *Istanbul declaration.* Retrieved December 17, 2018, from www.oecd.org/site/worldforum/49130123.pdf

OECD. (n.d.) *About the OECD.* Retrieved April 2, 2014, from www.oecd.org/about/

O'Toole, L. J. Jr., Walker, R. M., Meier, K. J., & Boyne, G. A. (2007). Networking in comparative context: Public managers in the USA and the UK. *Public Management Review, 9*(3), 401–420.

Rai, S. (2007, May 29). In India, Grandma cooks, they deliver. *New York Times.*

Reinicke, W. H., & Deng, F. M. (2000). *Critical choices: The United Nations, networks, and the future of global governance.* Toronto, Canada: International Development Research Council.

Reinicke, W. H., Deng, F. M., Witte, J. M., Benner, T, Whitaker, B., & Gershman, J. (2000). *Critical choices: The United Nations, networks, and the future of global governance.* Ottawa, ON: The International Development Research Centre.

Scott, T. A., & Ulibarri, N. (2019). Taking network analysis seriously: Methodological improvements for governance network scholarship. *Perspectives on Public Management and Governance.* doi:10.1093/ppmgov/gvy011

Siegel, D. A. (2011). Social networks in comparative perspective. *Political Science and Politics, 44*(1), 51–54.

Tang, C., & Tang, S. (2014). Managing incentive dynamics for collaborative governance in land and ecological conservation. *Public Administration Review, 74*(2), 220–231.

UN. (n.d.). *United nations: Sustainable Development Goals (SDGs).* Retrieved January 4, 2019, from www.un.org/sustainabledevelopment/sustainable-development-goals/

UNISDR. (2011). *Global platform for disaster risk reduction and world reconstruction conference.* Geneva, Switzerland: UNISDR.

Van Raaij, D. (2006). Norms network members use: An alternative perspective for indicating network success or failure. *International Public Management Journal, 9*(3), 249–270.

Wasserman, S., & Faust, K. L. (1994). *Social network analysis: Methods and applications.* New York, NY: Cambridge University Press.

Appendix 14.1
List of Organizations for United Nations SDGs

UN General Assembly
UN Environment Programme (UNEP)
UN World Food Programme (WFP)
UN Department of Economic and Social Affairs (DESA)
UN Development Programme (UNDP)
UN Department of Global Communications
UN Economic and Social Council
UN Educational, Scientific and Cultural Organization (UNESCO)
UN Food and Agriculture Organization (FAO)
UN International Children's Emergency Fund (UNICEF)
UN International Fund for Agricultural Development (IFAD)
UN Office of Disaster Risk Reduction (UNISDR)
UN World Meteorological Organization (WMO)
UN Office of Partnership
World Health Organization (WHO)
UN Population Fund (UNFPA)
World Trade Organization (WTO)
UN Industrial Development Organization (UNIDO)
International Monetary Fund (IMF)
World Bank
Organization for Economic Cooperation and Development (OECD)
International Energy Agency (IEA)
International Labor Organization (ILO)
International Maritime Organization (IMO)
International Telecommunication Union

15 Conclusion
Network Governance
Scholarship and Practice

In this chapter, we begin by summarizing the key highlights of the previous chapters, followed by a reflection on the scholarship of network governance. We review the conceptual, theoretical, and methodological issues in advancing network governance research. We also reiterate the practical implications of network governance research and discuss both opportunities and challenges facing this research field.

Key Highlights from the Book

In the book, we highlighted network related issues and concepts within an interorganizational setting, discussed network governance concepts and applications, and provided examples of network governance applications in different policy and administrative domains. The first section of the book provided an overview of interorganizational networks and network governance. Chapter 1 defined the concepts of networks and network governance and introduced key theories and frameworks that inform network governance scholarship and practice. Chapter 2 discussed benefits and challenges of interorganizational networks and provided a synopsis of network analysis as an analytical tool. Chapter 3 addressed the types of networks, informal and formal networks, network structures as it relates to network types, functions, and effectiveness of interorganizational networks. Chapter 4 covered the evolution of networks, the driving factors for network formation and development, network resilience and sustainability, and management and policy implications.

The second section of the book discussed key elements of network governance: network leadership and management, knowledge management and information exchange, power and decision-making, legitimacy and accountability, and network performance and evaluation. Chapter 5 addressed the complexity of network management and leadership, the unique network leadership activities, relationships between network management, leadership, and governance structures with practical implications and future research suggestions. Chapter 6 detailed knowledge management and information exchange in networks, the process of information seeking and data gathering in networks, barriers to knowledge sharing in networks, and the use of current information and communication technologies to facilitate knowledge sharing in interorganizational networks.

Chapter 7 analyzed power relations and decision-making in complex network settings, the relationships among power structure, leadership, decision-making mechanisms, and network structures for effective interorganizational arrangements. Chapter 8 addressed legitimacy and accountability issues in advancing participatory network governance, the characteristics and nature of network accountability systems, and formal and informal accountability. Finally, Chapter 9 covered network performance and network analysis tools and approaches to evaluate network performance at organizational, network, and community levels, and governance structures' impact on network performance and measurement challenges in evaluating network performance.

The third section of the book provided examples of network governance in diverse contexts of emergency and crisis management, community and economic development, human and social services, virtual environments, and global networks. Chapter 10 highlighted the importance of networks and coordination in emergency and crisis management, interorganizational networks in response to disasters, collaborative emergency management, and provided examples of network analysis applications in emergency and crisis management. Chapter 11 discussed local governments' use of networks to strengthen communities and economic development. It emphasizes the necessity of collaboration in promoting regional economic development. It also addressed types of collaborative networks for community and economic development and provided application examples of network analysis in community and economic development.

Chapter 12 covered the application of network governance in human and social services with emphasis on performance, structures, and community capacity, and illustrated network analysis to strengthen community partnerships in human and social service delivery. Chapter 13 defined key concepts of networks in virtual environments, virtual networks as complementary face-to-face networks, network analysis applications in understanding virtual networks. Chapter 14 brought our attention to networks in a global context with emphasis on global policies and actors and provided a network analysis application using UN sustainable development goals and global responsible agencies as example.

Scholarship of Network Governance

Since Larry O'Toole (1997) called for systematic and methodological research on networks in public administration, network research has made substantial progress. However, "the work is far from complete" (O'Toole, 2015, p. 368). Network scholars continue to face challenges such as definitional ambiguity, inconsistent network terminology, and methodological concerns. Scholars in the field called attention to the following research areas: a clear description of network governance in public administration, integration of quantitative methods with qualitative ones, failed networks, and large-N studies for potential network meta-analysis, and understanding the role of context in network governance, network structure and network effectiveness (Hu, Khosa, & Kapucu, 2016; Isett, Mergel, LeRoux, Mischen, & Rethemeyer, 2011; Kapucu, Hu, & Khosa, 2014). In this conclusion chapter, we do not intend to address all the challenges but discuss what this book has addressed and what deserves more research attention in the future from our perspectives. Figure 15.1 summarizes the key concepts of network governance covered in this book. We use this figure as the baseline to reflect on the key research highlights of the book and then move on to discuss what remains unanswered.

Theoretical and Conceptual Issues

Contexts Matter

Network governance scholarship addressed management, leadership, performance, and other topics on network arrangements. In the book, we examined five domains for network governance applications: emergency and crisis management; community economic development; human and social services; networks in virtual environments, and global networks. Networks in public administration and policy are diverse and operate according to contextual factors and varied institutional forms that are specific to the issue and problem communities and societies face. Network scholars can group similar contextual studies and compare them to generate some universal propositions and theories in guiding network governance. We need more comparative research on network governance structures in different domains and contexts. For example, what are the structural characteristics of networks in emergency and crisis management compared to networks in community and economic development? Can we summarize generalizable governance structures applicable to different policy and administrative domains? In the future, we should pay more attention to the impact of policy domain on governance structures and governance processes in accomplishing the shared network goals. In addition, factors central to network performance and effectiveness such as cohesion, trust, and social capital are contextual. Future scholarship should consider cross-national and cross-cultural factors, as global networks and international networks are becoming more popular in the public administration and policy.

Intertwined Relationships Between Network and Network Governance

As shown in Figure 15.1, the relationship between networks and network governance is bidirectional. On one hand, properties and relational patterns of networks influences how networks are managed, how power is distributed, and decision is made within networks, how knowledge management and information

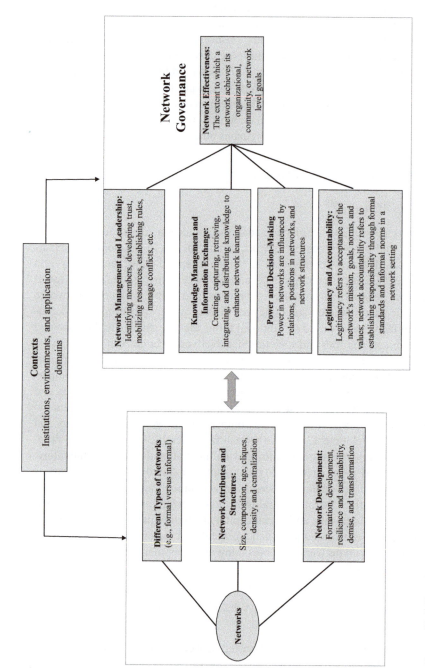

Figure 15.1 Key Concepts of Network Governance

exchange functions, how networks build legitimacy and establish accountability systems, and how networks perform. As Chapter 9 suggested, contextual factors such as resource availability, properties, and structural characteristics of networks such as size, composition of networks, formalization, and integration, as well as network management activities, influence how a network performs. On the other hand, network governance will shape network structures and network evolution. For instance, network management and power sharing are important for network to sustain its functionality. Without conflict management and proper power balances, a network can collapse before accomplishing its goals. Therefore, moving forward, we need a more nuanced and empirical analysis of the intertwined relationship between networks and network governance. Different network structures and properties (e.g., centralized versus decentralized, formal versus informal, temporary versus long term) impacts the use of management strategies (e.g., hierarchical versus vertical, majority rule versus participatory, strategic versus bureaucratic) and ultimately, their sustainability and functionality of networks (Varda, Miller, & Shoup, 2012).

Multilevel and Multiplex Networks

Networks are very complex, multilevel, and multiplex entities. Existing scholarship either focuses on individual organization's position in networks or the overall structural characteristics of the network. Recent years have seen growing interest in the substructures of networks (e.g., cliques and stakeholder clusters) and the dynamic relationships among actors, such as reciprocity and transitivity. In chapter ten on emergency and crisis management networks, and chapter fourteen on global networks, we highlighted the importance of understanding multilevel networks and substructures of networks. More research is needed to understand how network relations and structures on one level influences and interacts with the counterparts on another level. Organizations in networks can build and develop multiplex relationships. Existing network scholarship also focuses primarily on formal networks. Informal networks add complexity to networks and make scholarship challenging. As we addressed in the book, more research is needed on the role of informal networks in network governance and interorganizational networks. Interpersonal relationships can provide additional insights on the dynamic interactions between individuals and organizations, and between individuals and communities. In addition, most of the network governance scholarship, including this book, focused on whole networks. We need to conduct more research on ego networks focusing more on individual nodes in a network.

Network Management and Leadership and Network Effectiveness

A behavioral approach dominates existing studies on network management and leadership, which focuses on what activities or roles that differentiate network management and leadership from the counterparts in a traditional organizational setting. In this book, we introduced a relationship perspective about network leadership and linked network position with leadership roles and discuss the different manifestations of leadership in formal and informal networks. Future research needs to dig into the emergence and complex dimensions of leadership in networks. Another concept that needs better conceptualization is network effectiveness. Evaluation of network performance has substantial challenges as we addressed in the book. The multilevel nature of networks demands that network performance needs to be evaluated at individual organizational level, network level, and community level (Provan & Milward, 2001). Current literature focuses more on the organizational level. More studies are needed to develop and empirically test performance measures at network and community levels.

Methodological Issues

Validity of Data Collection

Network governances focus on relations among organizations. The network data collected by surveying organizational representatives aims to capture interactions between the focal organization and others in the network. A crucial critique arises: how representative can the individuals be for their organizations? The question is even more prominent when we study community networks that involve more diverse actors in the network and focus on community-level impact. More studies should use mixed methods and include multiple groups of respondents in order to cross-validate data accuracy.

Setting up a boundary is important for network studies because it impacts sampling strategies used in network scholarship. If a network boundary is clearly identified, such as the emergency and crisis management networks in chapter ten, no sampling is needed for data collection. We used documentary analysis to identify the key actors for network analysis. If setting a boundary for a network is not feasible, snowball sampling method can be used with a survey without a roster for example. Data mining techniques for social networking sites such as Facebook or other big data sources, as we briefly highlighted in virtual networks chapter, can provide additional opportunities for network scholarship.

Interdisciplinary Study and Mixed Method

Network scholarship in public administration benefits from other disciplines such as sociology, management, political science, and organization studies. Interdisciplinary perspective, dialogues, and cross-fertilization can benefit network scholarship in public administration and policy. Interdisciplinary approaches can help balance both generalizability and contextual specificity of networks. In addition to interdisciplinary focus on networks, mixed-method designs will help increase reliability and validity of network scholarship and research (Rasmussen, Malloy, & Agarwal, 2003). Surveys can be complemented by documentary analysis as well as qualitative open-ended interviews to better capture contextual-rich information and disseminate the results to both academic and practitioner communities. Furthermore, there is need to develop more engaged scholarship by tackling issues and challenges that practitioners face in managing and operating in networks. Engaged scholarship aims to bridge the gap between theory and practice through collaborative inquiry that guides practical knowledge.

Methods and Network Analysis Applications

Different methods and analytic techniques are used in network scholarship. Network analysis, with its focus on relations among network actors, patterns, and structures of relations can be a powerful framework and analytic techniques in studying networks. Network analysis can be utilized in understanding, designing, developing, and sustaining networks. Network analysis can provide practical value and insight in understanding community partnerships and further examination of them for effective public service delivery within collective arrangements (Provan & Lemaire, 2012; Provan, Veazie, Staten, & Teufel-Shone, 2005). Chapter 2 provided a brief introduction to network analysis as an analytical tool while discussing benefits and challenges within inter-organizational network setting. We demonstrated in the applications chapters some network analysis examples using UCINET program (Borgatti, Everett, & Freeman, 2002). Our examples were primarily descriptive and served as simple illustrations to students and beginning researchers. We tried to highlight some practical implications without substantial hypothesis testing or advanced level network analysis tools.

As introduced in the application chapters, an increasing number of scholars have conducted advanced network analysis to addressing complex explanatory and more theory-driven questions. Network scholars used advanced network analysis tools and techniques, such as Quadratic Assignment (QAP) and Exponential Random Graph Modeling (ERGM), and Stochastic Actor-oriented Models (SAOM) to examine network formation, complex relationships between network structures, multilevel networks, and network evolution and change (Kapucu et al., 2014; Parkhe, Wasserman, & Ralston, 2006; Isett et al., 2011).

Ethical Issues in Network Scholarship

Addressing ethical concerns in research is critical. The relational nature of network analysis might generate additional privacy and ethical concerns (Borgatti & Molina, 2005). However, there are certain methods that can reduce the threats to confidentiality which are further justified by the potential gains of network analysis (Kadushin, 2005). Network analysis help network managers and leaders to visualize and examine the relationship that can facilitate or hinder knowledge sharing and innovation and network effectiveness (Parker, Cross, & Walsh, 2001). The results from network analysis can shed valuable insight to improve information communication within organizations and networks. The threats to confidentiality or potential damage of network research can be addressed by carefully designing and careful application of IRB rules of confidentiality in data security and confidentiality (Parker et al., 2001). While there are some solutions suggested for some more exploratory forms of network analysis, they might not apply to all network analysis inquiries and severely limits the scope of these types of scholarship.

Conclusion

Networks are appealing for their advantages over a hierarchical structure. Networks provide a horizontal platform for engaging various stakeholder groups in public service delivery. Networks foster the growth of social capital and promote creativity and organizational learning through formal or more frequent and informal communication. However, a network approach is not a panacea and it can be costly and ineffective. One managerial paradox of operating in a network is the need to balance autonomy and interdependency. The inclusion of diverse organizations in a network leads to difficulties in negotiating and reaching a desired common solution. Thus, the success of a network is dependent on both autonomy and interdependencies between organizations.

Network scholarship and network analysis have tremendous implications and benefits in our networked world today for educating and training present and future public administrators. This book presented network research and network analysis tools that can be used by public administrators and managers to build and map their relational assets, understand the embeddedness of their organizations, to diagnose management issues, and use as policy tools to overcome barriers to collective action.

References

Borgatti, S. P., Everett, M. G., & Freeman, L. C. (2002). *UCINET 6 for windows: Software for social network analysis*. Harvard, MA: Analytic Technologies.

Borgatti, S. P., & Molina, J. L. (2005). Toward ethical guidelines for network research in organizations. *Social Networks*, 27(1), 107–117.

Hu, Q., Khosa, S., & Kapucu, N. (2016). The intellectual structure of empirical network research in public administration. *Journal of Public Administration Research and Theory*, 26(4), 593–612.

Isett, K., Mergel, I., LeRoux, K., Mischen, P., & Rethemeyer, K. (2011). Networks in public administration scholarship: Understanding where we are and where we need to go. *Journal of Public Administration Research and Theory*, 21, i157–i173.

Kadushin, C. (2005). Who benefits from network analysis: Ethics of social network research. *Social Networks*, 27(1), 139–153.

Kapucu, N., Hu, Q., & Khosa, S. (2014). The state of network research in public administration. *Administration & Society*, 49(8), 1087–1120.

O'Toole, L. J. (1997). Treating networks seriously: Practical and research-based agendas in public administration. *Public Administration Review*, *57*(1), 45–52.

O'Toole, L. J. (2015). Networks and networking: The public administrative agendas. *Public Administration Review*, *75*(2), 361–371.

Parker, A., Cross, R., & Walsh, D. (2001). Improving collaboration with social network analysis: Leveraging knowledge in the informal organization. *Knowledge Management Review*, *4*(2), 24–28.

Parkhe, A., Wasserman, S., & Ralston, D. A. (2006). New frontiers in network theory development. *Academy of Management Review*, *31*(3), 560–568.

Provan, K. G., & Lemaire, R. H. (2012). Core concepts and key ideas for understanding public sector organizational networks: Using research to inform scholarship and practice. *Public Administration Review*, *72*(5), 638–648.

Provan, K. G., & Milward, H. B. (2001). Do networks really work? A framework for evaluating public sector organizational networks. *Public Administration Review*, *61*(4), 414–423.

Provan, K. G., Veazie, M. A. Staten, L. K., & Teufel-Shone, N. I. (2005). The use of network analysis to strengthen community partnerships. *Public Administration Review*, *65*(5), 603–613.

Rasmussen, K., Malloy, D., & Agarwal, J. (2003). The ethical climate of government and non-profit organizations: Implications for public-private partnerships. *Public Management Review*, *5*(1), 83–98.

Varda, D. M., Miller, S. E., & Shoup, J. A. (2012). A systematic review of the collaboration and network research in public affairs literature: Implication to public health practice and research. *American Journal of Public Health*, *102*(3), 564–571.

Index